Best Wishes.

UNDER THE HILLS OF BREMRIDGE

Dorinda Jaynes.

Also by Dorinda Jeynes:

Back Along, Up Bremridge
— A Diary of Times Remembered

UNDER THE HILLS
of
BREMRIDGE

Dorinda Jeynes

UNITED WRITERS
Cornwall

UNITED WRITERS PUBLICATIONS LTD
Ailsa, Castle Gate, Penzance, Cornwall.

British Library Cataloguing in Publication Data:
A catalogue record for this book is
available from the British Library.

ISBN 1 85200 088 0

Printed in Great Britain by
United Writers Publications Ltd
Cornwall.

To all my good friends.

Preface

My book *BACK ALONG, UP BREMRIDGE – A Diary of Times Remembered* contains an entry on Tuesday, 7th October, which has a reference to the family of Bremridge.

Because the book was reviewed in the magazine *This England* it was read by a member of the Bremridge family and he contacted me through the publishers.

For several years we enjoyed communication and exchange of information about his family and I received details from many years ago. One fact – that young John Bremridge had died on a 4th November, aged 22 – the same day and month having much significance in my own circle – led me to investigate further.

There is also a mention of Thomas Bremridge Melhuish in a church in a Devon village, and the notice of a farm sale advertised years ago where the owner's name was – yes – Bremridge. Speaking from memory I believe the location was near Sidmouth, Devon.

Thomas Julius Bremridge is referred to in White's History of Devon as being a very important lawyer in Exeter, and there is a Richard Bremridge and his wife who appear to have retired to Exmouth. Could he be the Richard Bremridge whose photo I have which was found in a second-hand bookshop in New Zealand? If so, he was M.P. for Barnstaple 1863.

As well as the interest of following the fortunes of the family whose name was given to the farm where I was born and grew up, there is another reason why *UNDER THE HILLS OF BREMRIDGE* has been written.

i

To own a property and know that it is being run down and ruined in every way possible is not a pleasant experience and there was nothing I felt I could do about it, only wait for someone to die! In due course it did happen – and then, what?

Therefore this book deals with the period in between, with the fortunes of the family in war-time and after, and the solution which presented itself, much to the astonishment of so many people who knew me.

It also acknowledges the help which I received from my friends who have been so generous in every way. Without their help life would have been much more difficult. I am indeed fortunate to have such friends and writing an account of it all is one way for me to say 'Thank you'!

Contents

Introduction

It could be easy to say that some things are 'just coincidence' when they happen on the same dates, but I think there is a little more involved than that. Perhaps certain trends, whether for good or evil, are influenced by the time of year and since 1605 the early few days of November have been remembered, often with bonfires, fireworks and displays.

There must have been such fierce loathing and discontent in England in the time of James I – after all he was the child of Mary Queen of Scots and Lord Darnley, both of whom suffered untimely and unnatural deaths – that the Gunpowder Plot to blow up the Houses of Parliament and all therein very nearly came to be fact.

Such a plot would have needed some time to prepare, even to bring it as near success as history records, so the feelings of hatred and evil must have been very strong.

If the spirit of Christmas can be one of love and hope and charity, and last, at least, for days, why should not a destructive or unfortunate element be felt at the time, again, of such other anniversaries?

The 4th November has featured several times in my own family, connected with serious illness. It was also the date of the death of young John Bremridge.

On the lighter side, however, William of Orange was born on that day, in 1650, and on the 4th November 1677 he married his cousin, the Princess Mary, elder daughter of Anne Hyde and the Duke of York who became King James II, but not for long, because this same William was invited to replace him, hence the landing in Devon.

My first interest in the Bremridge/Melhuish family began, though I did not know it, in Poughill Church with the name of the Reverend Thomas Bremridge Melhuish on a wall plaque. It continued when there was a visit from members of the Bremridge family to Bremridge by means of a big black horse in a gig – already described on page 210 in my book *Back Along, Up Bremridge*.

As already mentioned in the Preface, this book was reviewed in the magazine *This England* and the review read by a member of the Bremridge family who lived in London. He contacted me and we enjoyed an exchange of correspondence. I still have the pleasure of writing to his widow.

Mr Bremridge sent me a copy of his 'Family Table' showing dates of births, marriages and deaths since 1685. The John Bremridge who died on 4/11/1769 was only 22. Since there are no official records of accidents in which he was involved it would seem to be the result of illness. His sister, two years younger, was Anna Maria and she married into the Melhuish family from Poughill when she was 26. She was, in fact, the Grandmother of the Reverend Gentlemen who had the living up there.

When we lived at Bremridge the yew trees on the lawn fascinated me. They were old and very tall. There had been four but the one right in front of the kitchen window had been 'taken out' so many years ago that the long trunk resting underneath the window had no bark and looked quite smooth, very old. It was near the three trees that my sister Lavinia and I made our tent out of all sorts of oddments – an army blanket, a couple of umbrellas, an ulster from the pegs in the front hall and the little wooden clothes horse used for the airing of clothes by the kitchen fire – often after all the grown-ups had gone to bed, when it was safe. In the afternoon we would lie in our tent and look up under the branches stretching up tight against their thick trunks. It was peaceful and quiet with only the twittering of a few birds making any sounds at all – the men were all out in the fields, the calves and other animals all having their afternoon naps.

Lying there in our tent and looking up at the tall giants I had a feeling of what I can only describe as 'history'. I knew those trees had lived through much that I did not understand. They had been loved, or hated, for both sensations must have lurked in the farmhouse over the years – joyful or sorrowful occasions, births and illness and deaths, children and grandparents, all came and went.

I experienced much the same sense of the past at one other place on the farm. It was not really on our land but it had belonged to the Bremridges or Melhuishes at some time and was the gateway – one of several – which always had to be opened on the journey to and from Crediton, Upton Hellions way.

Equally, this was about the quickest way to Sandford and it could be that whoever was riding had a bit of a tangle with the gate. Many years ago one of the Bremridges who had duties in, or to, Sandford Church, combined with other riders to construct a stable for their horses, so probably the gentleman as he grew older had more of a job to get to the church on time and grew impatient with the gate.

1

Bremridge, Sandford and Other Places

The Bremridge Farm I knew is in the Parish of Sandford, near Crediton, Devon. I know that there is another property by the same name, near Barnstaple, and that it seems to have been in the occupation of the Bremridge family. I have received a postcard bearing the photo of a gentleman of 'good middle age' which was found in a second-hand bookshop in New Zealand and underneath is written in a firm hand in dark ink which does not appear to have faded 'R. Bremridge, M.P. 1863'. This is obviously a studio photo and taken, I should imagine, when photography was 'a new thing' and something which the gentry thought appropriate to their station.

From the photo it is difficult to tell the gentleman's age. He has dark hair but a short white beard; a face which I would describe as 'long'; he is wearing a long 'frock coat', probably black, over a waistcoat and checked trousers, is holding a stick in his right hand as if he is about to walk off. I would say he has quite strong features and is something like the impression I received from the Pharmaceutical Society of Elias Bremridge, whose father was the last member of the family of that name to be born on Bremridge Farm, Sandford. It was Elias that did much to establish the Society. So much, in fact, that 'Bremridge, London' was, and still is, included in their address for cables to the firm!

It seems the original Bremridges came to this country with William the Conqueror and were settled in the farm in Sandford from that time. It could have been known then as 'Bramble Ridge'!

The farmhouse was much like others throughout Devon – a house with a large lawn in front divided by a pebbled path, elbow shaped where it turned from the wrought iron gate. There was a stone wall dividing the court from the lawn high enough to keep the animals out but low enough for people walking near it to be seen.

The problem of keeping the grass in trim was probably solved all through the years by the keeping of a couple of sheep feeding off it for a few days. There were no lawn mowers years ago, nor when we lived there, for I can remember cutting the lower part of the lawn with sheep shears and going round and round until I had finished!

It was also a very safe area in which to rear a few baby chicks, or ducklings, goslings or turkeys when they needed special attention.

Although parts of the farm are very hilly, where the house had been built was almost on a plateau and sheltered by the many elms in the lane, apple trees in the orchard so old and large they gave protection and privacy, and all the fields had hedges worthy of the name.

Who was who in the Bremridge Family so long ago! Most of this information was supplied by Mr Eric Bremridge but more was available from other sources:

John Bremridge of Bremridge (b.1685, d.1769), married Mary Reed of Priors Town, Sandford (m.1713, d.1766). They had four children:

> John (d.1784)
> William who married Elizabeth Reed from Chawley
> Richard
> Samuel

The first son, John, also had a son called John who died at age 22 on 4/11/1769. Anna Maria, his daughter, married Richard Melhuish of Poughill at Sandford 30/11/1755. They had:

> John Bremridge b.13/11/1776
> Thomas b.18/6/1778
> Richard b.13/10/1779
> Mary b.29/ 7/1783

William and Elizabeth Reed of Chawley had a son, William who, in due course, married and was the father of Elias, born 1810. Elias married and had a son, Richard, born 1841. Richard was the father of Richard Harding Bremridge. There were three children, Eric Harding, a little girl always known as 'Do-Do' and a son, David, who went to Canada.

Anna Maria's second son, Thomas, married and it was the name of his son, Thomas Bremridge Melhuish, which I saw in Poughill Church so long ago when he was Vicar and Rector there.

Of the first Richard I know nothing but I believe Samuel became Vicar of Winkleigh, Devon.

Although Mr Eric Bremridge maintained that there was only one family of the name of Bremridge I think there must now be several more branches to the family. For instance, one of the Bremridges married twice and 'was the father of a large family' away from the South of England.

Then, too, there was the photo of the M.P. which was picked up in a second-hand bookshop in New Zealand, the country which was — and I suppose still is — home to Miss Anne Bremridge, although she is in England at times.

Mrs Agnes Bremridge, the widow of Mr Eric Bremridge, sent me a cutting from the *Daily Telegraph* some time in June 1994. This has an Obituary Notice for Sir John Bremridge who died aged 68. He was Financial Secretary of the Hong Kong Government during a period of extreme turbulence in the territory's currency, property and stock markets.

Quite a comprehensive account of his life is given and he was appointed an OBE in 1976 and knighted in 1983. He married in 1956 Jacqueline Everard and they had two sons and two daughters. Sir John himself was born in South Africa on July 12th 1925 but educated in Cheltenham. During the war he served with the Rifle Brigade in the Middle East and elsewhere.

I know there are still some Bremridges in Devon — maybe some even descended from Thomas Julius Bremridge who seems to have been a very important person with duties and obligations in Exeter about 1870. He was a Church Charity Trustee, Registrar of Archdeacons, Public Notary and one of the Governors of Sir John Maynards Foundation High School for Girls.

Sandford

Sandford Parish is divided into three distinct areas — Sandford Village itself with its substantial church, Post Office, the Rose and Crown, the Lamb and the school, and the two outlying areas of New Buildings and East Village, sometimes referred to as

'East Sandford'.

East Village only had one shop – selling a few oddments mainly of toffees, sherbets, liquorish ropes or twists, cigarettes and tobacco and matches. The papers could be collected from 'Shop' on a Friday afternoon. There was one other commodity which always proclaimed its presence – paraffin; this had to be fetched in a can from another part of the house down the red tiled passage.

There was a post box referred to locally as a 'posting box' down at the crossroads opposite the village pump. It was from this pump that a big lad from the school had the job of collecting a large jug of water every morning, this was always used cold as there was nothing on which to heat it – I've never seen as much as a saucepan of water placed carefully on top of the slow combustion stove in the middle of the one large room of the school which had been built on similar lines to the one at New Buildings.

Several farms, with their workers' cottages, fronted the road back to Sandford and Crediton. Doddridge in East Village, then Priorton, North Creedy and Rocks Court, the smallholding of Land where the Lees used to live before the Mattins took over, and so on. Throughout the parish steep hills and difficult corners exist – I pity the horse power when that came on legs and not wheels driven by the engines of today!

Some of the Bremridge fields were actually in another parish – Upton Hellions. Perhaps the occupants of the farm many years ago would, like us, have had as much to do with Upton Hellions as with Sandford, for it was on the direct route both to Sandford and to the nearest town, Crediton.

It is a parish with scattered property, a few large farms, some workmen's cottages, a rectory and a church. The roads are narrow and hilly and from a distance the church, St Mary's, stands out on the hill a landmark to be seen with still another hill behind it. The rectory is actually some way off by the road but there is a short cut across a couple of fields.

Parson Gascoign retired and had a sale at the Rectory and I remember going to it with Mum and receiving an impression of a long passage in the house itself; there was a horse drawn carriage in an outhouse, for sale. I do not know if it was actually purchased by anyone; it was still a very usable conveyance but a superior sort of horse power was taking over by that time, 1928.

Every journey to and from Crediton Upton Hellions way meant that we had to pass the church, not so much 'pass it' as to go up behind it, going home. I think there must have been a couple of cottages which were removed so that there was a flat area where cars could turn and which provided a very welcome but all too short rest for horses. I have a recollection of a grey-blue wooden door almost opposite the church and a stone wall which was not in a very good condition – part of someone's garden, perhaps.

Lavinia and I were christened in this little church, at the same time, and there have been the Harvest Thanksgiving Services attended by neighbouring farmers, people from Crediton and Sandford – and us. The Heards from Preston would walk up over the Bremridge fields and after the Service Mrs Bedell and May would join us but I do not think any men from either family attended the Thanksgiving.

Past the church, on the level road, there was at least one cottage and one large property, and down over the fields there was Hellions Mill and Hellions Barton. Going the other way, leading to the Rectory across the fields, there was a house which I remember as always having been painted black. It was here that Farmer John Manning lived with his housekeeper, Mrs Bussell. This was often a stopping place for Grandpa on his way home from Crediton when he would call on Farmer John and enjoy a glass of cider with him and listen to any news of the local farmers – the Dickers, the Colemans and others. Farmer John seemed to know everything – so did Mrs Bussell, a lady with a mop of light gingerish hair which supported a dark hat. I went there once with Grandpa and was treated to a small glass of what seems to have been every farmer's favourite drink. The little courtyard to the south of the house overlooked a beautiful stretch of fields right down to the little brook and that sharp bend in the road with hills on both sides.

In 1928 Upton Hellions and Sandford combined for church matters, so some of the services were 'taken' by the Rev. Llewellyn and reduced in number – possibly one or, at most, two a month. 'Kip' Chudley played the organ.

I knew that Hellions Church was old because the steps leading from the little covered way, the lychgate, were somewhat uneven

18

and worn down as if they had been in place for many years and the many, many feet which had pressed down upon them had caused their foundations to move. Perhaps the big stones had been stepped on by heavy knights in armour – maybe they had even ridden their horses over the entrance and up the little path which led to the church door.

Then, too, all the grave stones or headstones bore signs of age. There was writing on them but of course I cannot remember any names after all this time. 'Sacred to the Memory of . . .', 'Beloved Brother' and 'Late of . . .' were phrases which have remained with me. There was one very big box-like 'monument' – in my innocence I thought that it would make a very good table!

Inside the church the Bremridge pew was in the 'off' portion and every time the Creed was said we turned towards the East. I wondered why!

Lavinia and I often went with Grandma to Hellions Church because as School Mistress of a church school it was expected. Oh no, she could not go to the Methodists down in East Village, nor did she until she had retired from teaching. She always tried to maintain the 'no work on Sunday' rule and she once told me that if a button came off a garment when she was young, if the day was a Sunday it should not be sewn on until the next day!

Many times I have dreamed about Hellions Church – I could hear the bell (there was only one). I have tried to climb the tower on the outside and have run up the ladder on the inside but I never remember reaching the top. One night, when I went to the church, I found the stairs and a bedroom so small that it fitted into the tower.

Suddenly all these dreams stopped. In October, 1980, there was an account in our paper of the young lady in Crawley who had won a cottage in Devon and it was near Hellions Church – she had entered some competition and been lucky.

A trip by helicopter had been arranged so that the location could be visualised and there it was – not only the church and cottage, the latter now bearing no resemblance to the modest dwelling we all knew 'on the other side of the church', but Bremridge Lane up behind the church. The view from the helicopter was fairly brief, but long enough for me. A wonderful treat.

People walked much more in Anna Maria's day than they do now, but I scarcely think that they would have all gone to

Sandford Church on Sundays. Like their ancestors the men of the family probably rode into Sandford while the women folk and the children would have walked through the lanes and visited the nearest place of worship, St Mary's at Upton Hellions.

The Rev. James Carrington was there from 1757 to 1794. He became ill and died. John Ley followed, from 1794 to 1805 by which time Anna's 'young people' would probably have gone to Sandford also!

The modern generation is so used to travel in all its forms that it is difficult to realise just how important the roads were, even before they had good surfaces. Think of this country – these islands – without any cars, without any railway, without any telephone, without any modern convenience of communication at all and you begin to realise why roads which had received a new surface brought new life to many areas and many are the blessings heaped upon the head of John Loudon Macadam for his invention of a new road covering which eliminated deep ruts and mud.

Although the good surface Upton Hellions way made travelling much easier the route still had hazards, as I well remember! Those bends and corners must always be approached with care but once 'young Joy', in a very new motor car, and Mum driving home to Bremridge nearly came to grief for they met on the 'brook' bend and 'young Joy' was so startled that he lifted his hands above his head and let the car go where it would. Mum and the pony and trap were only just clear but quite shaken!

Another incident, another day, another corner. This one was between Hellions Rectory and Lower Creedy Farm, when we were on the way home we met a mounted funeral procession with the two black horses wearing waving black plumes. I do not know who had died but it must have been someone in Upton Hellions – pony panicked and needed all the encouragement Mum could provide, first to pass the unusual sight and then restraint to stop it 'running away'.

I think we had to make a journey into Crediton about once a fortnight on a Saturday afternoon – all because of that new invention, the wireless set; it needed dry batteries and wet batteries and it was a marvel to be able to hear what was said miles and miles away and to listen to music, even from London! Our wireless, a Marconi with a horn bearing the picture of a white dog listening to 'His Master's Voice', was the result of a deal between Grandpa and the proprietor or owner of a property where apples in quantity were bought for making into cider, in Exeter, where the son was into the new fangled radio business. It was a case of 'I'll buy your apples if you help my son out by buying a wireless' – could have been 1924 or 1925!

The big block of batteries sat together in the wide window bench in the sitting-room – they were little trouble – no, it was the small rechargeable creatures which had to be fetched from 'Vigars', probably left there on the farm shopping trip earlier in the week.

I must say that Grandpa was none too keen on the 'contraption' after listening to the sermon one Sunday night from St. Martins-in-the-Field where the Rev. Dick Shepard was preaching about appreciation. The voice which came from the horn just behind Grandpa's chair asked, 'When did you last take your wife a bunch of flowers?' The answer was 'Flowers, be blowed' and Grandpa walked out, to sit in the kitchen until the service ended!

One Saturday afternoon was memorable for three things when Mum was driving the pony and trap into Crediton. I think I was the only other person, useful because I could get out and open the gates as we came to them Upton Hellions way.

The meat part of our dinner that day had been Lambs' Tail Pie and out in 'Q'm' meadow which we passed there were all the sheep and their lambs grazing, as usual. There was only one black lamb and even after cooking the little pieces of dark flesh had been obvious – and I had eaten them! I remember saying, 'I had a little bit of you today, Blackie.'

Two more gates to be opened and shut and the walk over the rough stones of the hill behind Hellions Church. That was all right, but 'Joe' stumbled rather badly further along the road and I bumped my head as I was pitched forward against the front of the vehicle. No serious damage, but certainly a fright!

Everyone in Crediton knows where 'Lords Meadow' is and we had a good view of it from Exhibition Road, our route, a long stretch of land outside the town, a green field, quite large. I asked why it was called 'Lords Meadow'. Was there a 'Mr Lord?' Mum said it was something to do with a battle or war years and years ago when the Lords and the Commoners were fighting, but you ask Grandma all about it when we get home.

21

When opportunity presented itself – not at tea-time with everyone in the kitchen – I did ask Grandma about why the field was called 'Lords Meadow' and I think that her explanation was about the first real history lesson in which I took any interest. She made it all sound so real and explained why it happened – because King Charles the First was not really a good and sound ruler and there had been many difficulties between him and another high sounding place – 'Parliament'. In fact he had ruled the country for some years without Parliament. He had done everything on his own and at last there was a crisis, something had to happen.

Oliver Cromwell was about the same age as Charles but he had quite different ideas. He managed to get an army together, in the name of the Parliamentarians, and his army and King Charles' army had many fights in different parts of the country. Sometimes one side won, sometimes the other side, but eventually the King was taken prisoner although he managed to send his wife, the Queen with her little daughter, Henrietta, across to France so they were safe.

Many places in the West Country had suffered form both armies and roads were even more churned up and deep in mud, for it was before tarmac had been invented. It was difficult to provide for men and horses, foot soldiers and all that went with them. I wondered if they had made their way into Bremridge, demanding shelter or food, it was so far off the beaten track it might have escaped.

Grandma said that the King was captured, tried and later beheaded.

Judging from my memory of what happened on a fine Saturday autumn morning many years ago I expect they did find Bremridge and commandeered supplies and horses. I had walked with Grandfather and his dog up over Quarrypit field and along the track beside Preston Down. Where it descends sharply again towards 'Q'm Meadow' we met a figure in a khaki uniform. I do not remember any preliminaries but the stranger said that he was looking for horses for the Army, to which Grandfather replied that he had none suitable nor did he expect to have any. After a few minutes somewhat one-sided conversation the stranger departed. Grandpa could be very non-committal! The stranger probably had someone with a car waiting for him near Hellions Church, our lane was too rough to encourage any motorist to use it. I suppose it could be an odd thing to remember but being only knee high to a grasshopper, people's legs and footwear came so much within my line of vision that the long khaki clad legs of the stranger became the most remembered detail – they were such a contrast to Grandfather's sturdy mud-spattered boots and leggings and my almost new navy leather laced up boots. The next time I needed new boots I had a pair of Wellingtons, made of that 'rubber stuff' and supposed to be not so good for the feet if they were worn for long periods!

As well as the exits out of the farm by the East Village road and the rougher Upton Hellions track still another route existed. This was up over a field called Barns Close and up to Higher Orchard and out on to the Broxfords Road.

Broxfords Road was really a narrow, steep track with two raised ridges and three depressions, the latter produced by the wheels of carts, wagons or traps and the track which the horses followed. There were a few places in Broxfords which were really steep, the longest being at the bottom towards Heath Bridge and past Rose Cottage. The shorter steep gradients levelled off into level stretches of only a few yards before dropping steeply again.

A very dangerous 'dip' exists towards the end of the Bremridge fields where an open stream crossed the road – merely a dribble in summer but something much worse in winter. Maybe it has been bridged over by now. The following steep little nap led on past Broxfords Cottage where the Bedells – and their donkey – lived, and on out to the road to Crediton. This, too, has some quite dangerous corners, is hilly in places, but joins the Upton Hellions Road at the foot of Park Hill at Creedy Bridge, and so on into Crediton.

By using the Broxfords Road it is possible to go right into Exeter in about half the time it took to go to Crediton and then up to the City by train or bus. Along by Shobrook Park, down 'Kemps Hill', out on to the Exeter Road at Newton St. Cyres or New Bridge – I have cycled this route and thoroughly enjoyed it.

Other Places

'Other Places' covers – among other things – the two modest properties which nestle against the hill known as 'Broxfords Hill': Rose Cottage and The Bungalow.

23

As far as I know, Rose Cottage has been there for many, many years but I think that at one time it was part of the village of Heath Bridge, where there was an Inn named 'The New Inn', all traces of which disappeared before the present generation was born, so that very little is known, or can be found out about it.

The cottage contains a large living room and a good sized kitchen, now in the modern style. There is a bathroom and two bedrooms and it has been a very comfortable home for many years. It was thatched, and re-thatched, and then when thatch became less popular and gave way to modern roofing it was slated.

The garden and orchard adjoining have been the pride and joy of many a dweller there; indeed it has provided vegetables, apples and all sorts of soft fruit, to the pride and delight of 'Mrs' in the cottage. The ground also offered opportunity for the keeping of poultry and pigs – and even calves several years ago.

'Rose Cottage' came into the possession of my family when we lived at Bremridge and when I was only about knee-high to a grasshopper! It was a ruin, and was sold by the Creedy Estate in Sandford to my Grandmother who thought that it could be made habitable, so she bought it and the adjoining land on which 'The Bungalow' now stands. She re-thatched it and did all that was necessary to improve it then.

It was on the 4th of November 1915 that a fire started at Creedy Park and the whole house was lost. (4th November, again, it seems to be a most unfortunate date and not only in my own family.)

By a stoke of amazing good fortune the Agent to the Estate had renewed the insurance, almost in opposition to the owner's wishes. Mr Pitts Tucker had telephoned from Eggesford Station to the Insurance Office with renewal instructions. He had visited Creedy Park that day, insurance had been discussed and had been thought to be an unnecessary expense.

Unfortunately many records of properties were destroyed but Mr Pitts Tucker was able to remember details of the most important documents, and no doubt reference to the tenants then existing helped.

I remember that at Bremridge – and for many years after we had left the country – we possessed a chair which had been in the Creedy Park House. It was an armchair covered in dark red leather and always known as Sir William's chair. It did not seem to me to be damaged or marked in any way but I know that some of the furniture rescued had either been sold or given away, they probably had to do something with it in a hurry.

I think it was because of the fire and loss of so many documents that the little property Rose Cottage down under the hills of Bremridge was sold to Grandma some years later, with land for gardens and rights to water in a Bremridge field, with a simple letter of transfer – no history, no pedigree, nothing – only a ruin!

Copy of Letter from:

PITTS TUCKERS,
SOLICITORS
Bridge Chambers, Barnstaple.

19th March 1923

Dear Mrs Stoyle,

Sir William agrees to sell the plot of ground together with the remains of the cottage with a free conveyance for £60, but he does not agree to let the Brake as he wishes to keep that in hand. Please let me know by return of post if you agree to this.

If you decide to purchase and send on the £60 you may take possession of the plot and you can also have the right to the water etc.

Yours faithfully,
C.H. PITTS TUCKER

Mrs Stoyle.
East Village School,
Sandford, Crediton.

I think there could be two reasons why the letter was addressed to Grandma at East Village School and not to Bremridge Farm. One was possibly on the part of Mr Pitts Tucker to be clear of a blot on the Creedy Estate before Grandma changed her mind. If it went to the farm she might be talked out of it by Grandpa who probably considered Rose Cottage beyond repair without too much cost. By giving her address as East Village School she could deal with the matter on her own – and she did!

Young as I was, I can remember looking up over the little gate at the bottom of The Bungalow garden and seeing a large space, almost another little hill in front of Rose Cottage. Then, one day,

25

b

there was another modest construction there – the empty space had been removed, if one can ever remove a space! This must have been when eggs and butter were brought down from Bremridge – the result of Mum's labours as far as the butter was concerned – to be collected by a gentleman who came periodically (once a week, I expect) to gather goods to sell in his shop. I think he was a Mr Tapp, and some distant relative to the Snells who lived at Pakeham.

In those days, the road to Bremridge from Heath Bridge was so rough that the baker or the baker's boy would walk up to the farm, over the stile and up through the orchard. People who did own or drive cars did not care to make the journey – perhaps they considered it too risky!

Broxfords Hill itself was very rough, too, but considerably better than our road, but, again, vehicles were left at the bottom of the hill and tradesmen and friends often walked up beside the Brake to the bungalow and cottage.

Of course, in those days there was no electricity and no 'running' water to come indoors and be available by the turning on of a tap. There was water in a well in Little Hill field belonging to Bremridge and this had to be fetched by the occupants of cottage and bungalow bucket by perishing bucket full!

There are still two more houses along the road, over the bridge which is part of the Heath Bridge area. These were cottages where the man of the house worked for the farmer at Dira Farm – a large farm up over another hill. I have seen water being fetched from this same well in Little Hill field when the supply in the well belonging to the cottages was not adequate. It was quite a long walk with a bucket of water though mostly on the level.

Across the fields there was another cottage where the Bennetts lived. Mr Bennett had come to live and work on Bremridge Farm in 1911, earning 11/-d (55p in today's money) per week – and Mr and Mrs had eleven children. Ivy Cottage was so much in the valley down over the fields and near the river that I do not think it could be seen or found by anyone who did not know of its existence. There was no road to reach it, and only a footpath from Heath Bridge to the cottage itself. It had an excellent garden and, of course, potatoes, eggs and milk free from the farm. Bennett always did the milking and many times I have seen him going home with his can filled with the precious liquid.

Ivy Cottage was thatched and larger than the normal farm workmen's accommodation in that it had three bedrooms and extra space downstairs. It drew its water form a well which had been built and bricked up but which supplied a pipe emptying into a kieve just beside the back of the property.

On the 4th November, 1930, my Grandfather, Mr Stoyle, was taken ill – an illness which kept him in the Royal Devon and Exeter Hospital for about a month. He died and life changed for us. 'Us', I should say, meant the women folk, Grandma, Mum, Lavinia (my sister) and me, and we had to find other accommodation after a sale of farming equipment and livestock.

For years there had been a horse drawn furniture van parked at the top of Bremridge Court and before we actually left the farm Henry and Bennett and Mr David Retter put 'Farmer' and 'Violet' to the front of the van and its destination was right beside The Bungalow. I did not see the operation – I was at school – but I can quite imagine that there were some fairly hair-raising moments. However, it did come to rest and it provided a very much needed extra store, but is now only a memory since it has been replaced by much more elaborate accommodation – but more of that later.

The Bennetts left Ivy Cottage and went into one of the Creedy Lodges in Sandford, I never saw them again.

Henry went to a farm on the other side of Exeter, got married and had one son. I met him or his wife several times in the Paul Street, Exeter, bus depot.

David Retter was a Brother-in-law to Grandpa – he had asked to come on holiday at Bremridge just about the time Grandpa became ill, and stayed to help in the clearing up operations – help which was very much appreciated.

Perhaps I can add a few more words about Grandpa and his funeral. Because the track was so rough and because The Bungalow was empty at the time it was decided that the coffin should rest there all night and not be brought right up to Bremridge, his home for so many years. Bourne, in Crediton, was in charge of the funeral arrangements but he did stretch a point and brought one of the large limousines right up into the courtyard for the convenience of the widow and other relatives.

One of the 'other relatives' was Uncle Harry Reed, and he just made the funeral procession by the skin of his teeth and the 'hell for leather' driving of Henry, who had been to Crediton Station with 'Netty-pig' to meet him and knew that the time was tight. Think of the date for a moment, Grandpa died on Sunday and the funeral was on Friday, the 5th December, so there could have been no communication with anyone until Monday, 1st December. No telephone but I expect the Post Office was busy with telegrams.

Uncle Harry was a tall, well set up man (as the saying went), working on the River Thames as a member of the River Police. Years later he became a complete invalid because of sustaining a head injury (knocked on the head by a thug, I believe). Lavinia and I went to his funeral and tried to comfort Auntie Nellie.

I can remember standing beside Bourne's big car and watching for the governess car to appear on top of the hill and watched it rattle down over 'with my heart in my mouth' in case a wheel should come off.

Why did Grandma have the bungalow built? I am not sure of the answer but I think there are several reasons and perhaps the fact that they 'were getting older' and may need to retire from farming and the hard work which Bremridge produced may have been the most important. Its neighbour, Rose Cottage, would not have been equal to accommodating 'The Stoyles' and my Mother and Father and 'me and Lavinia'.

Perhaps Grandma intended to live there herself so as to be nearer the School, actually treating the two properties down under the hill as part of Bremridge, which they certainly were then. I know that Grandpa planted the orchard with apple trees – the mix of cookers and eaters which still could have been used for cider!

I do not think Rose Cottage was the only ruin on that piece of land and I feel sure that the bungalow was built on the site of one tumbled down dwelling. There were big stones – not unlike some of those forming part of a wall actually in Rose Cottage – which had been used to form a rockery linking the steeply sloping garden to the veranda and supporting it.

In the early twenties there were not very many bungalows, and I remember a conversation where Grandma was speaking about the builder who 'put it up'. She was obviously not very pleased with it for she said that 'he practised on my bungalow!'

The pre-occupation with the Heath Bridge properties came soon after the death of Auntie Alma in Bristol and I think Grandma found relief in having something to concern herself with apart from the inevitable 'if only's'.

She bought the ruined cottage, inspected her purchase and knew that she would have plenty to do to make it into a house fit to live in.

Grandma said that there were no rooms upstairs, you went up a rough ladder and the upper area covered the whole of the length and breadth of the cottage. No doubt upstairs had been used as sleeping quarters, but there were no divisions. She had it 'walled up' properly, and the stairs became proper steps with risers and were safe, though I remember that there was one very deep step near the top!

New thatch made the roof waterproof and all the other repairs which were essential were carried out. The cottage had been turned into a home again, with its open hearth and its oven in the wall, and the fresh re-decorations on the walls, even if these were only distemper! A buttress had been added at the lower end, near the road, and this received a coat of tar, as did all the other exposed areas near the ground.

I looked back through an old 'property' file some time ago and there, staring me in the face, although I did not realise the significance of it, I found the enclosed bill from Mr J Drake over at Cheriton Fitzpaine for a total of £22.2/6d. This would have been for only part of the repairs necessary. There was a new thatched roof needed – an essential item – gates and the driveway seen to and the wall round the garden to be retained by stones. Some of these 'outside' jobs no doubt could be done with farm labour.

Beside the reason I have already given for the acquisition of Rose Cottage I am pretty sure there was another, and this may explain the urgency of the repairs. The Cottage was bought from Sir William Davie in the latter part of March, 1923, repair work started by Mr Drake on the 28th March, finished before the end of June, all paid for over a 2d stamp on the 6th July.

The first of the tenants in this second life of the property was my Dad and Mum and I can just remember living at Heathbridge for a very short period. I can only guess at the reason why they were no longer living at Bremridge, though I do know that they were still very much connected with it, going up the steep stony track with the gorse bushes on 'Little Hill' field side and Nannypark hedge on the other, every day. In fact, I can just remember sitting in a pushchair with carpet seating and wooden arms and being jolted along, particularly under the elm trees in the lane!

Grandpa and Dad did not agree any too well together and I expect 'the two children' were better off or thought to be, on their own with just their parents to be responsible. Being so near almost meant being on the spot, anyway.

I can only guess at the reason for the unhappy feeling between the two men. Dad had been injured in the First World War and had been placed at Bremridge under the scheme which released a fit man from working on the land for one who could do what was necessary, even if injured, although he may not be considered of further use to the war effort. Such men sent to the farms were known as 'Substitutes' and this became a derisory term at times.

Another cause for complaint – in Grandpa's estimation – could have been the fact that Dad became his son-in-law, when Mum could have had the son of other, and well-off, farmers. Not only that, there were two 'scrawling chilern' in no time – how many more were there going to be? Never one of the most patient of men, Grandpa would not have welcomed further additions to the family.

I know Lavinia and I had beds in the 'L' shaped room upstairs, and I can remember having a bath in front of the open fire, downstairs, of course! Dad possessed a dog called 'Nip' or 'Nipper' – a black and white terrier type, with black predominating, a 'proper ratter'. I do not know what happened to him, but do not recall his presence back at Bremridge, so imagine that he had been found another home somewhere – or a load of shot!

If I can find out anything about any previous tenants of Rose Cottage of course I will add it, but Bremridge Farm was occupied from the time we left in January 1931 until well on into the 1940s by a young farmer and his wife and their four small children. It is, I believe, somewhat unusual for people who leave a farm to be friendly with the in-coming tenants, but in our case there has been a very warm friendship which has lasted all these years – and still continues.

In those days, before the stringent rules and regulations brought in by the Milk Marketing Board it was possible for farmers to sell milk to any neighbour, so it was soon my turn – or Lavinia's – to take the large blue and white patterned pitcher shaped jug which had belonged to my Great Grandmother, go up the hill to the farm and fetch the milk before we went to school.

Farmers were really becoming interested in the increased profits which selling milk in quantity to the Milk Marketing Board could produce, so soon the everlasting job of making the butter, packaging it and taking it to Crediton to sell became a thing of the past, one everlasting 'chore' had been removed.

When Bremridge also became a supplier to the big concern even the milk lorry did not attempt to go up the rough track. No, the milk had to be brought down in churns in a cart and 'Farmer' was still used to do that job – among many other purchases – he had been acquired at our sale by the young farmer.

The Brake or 'The Hump'

This is an area of land actually in Shobrook Parish. It extends from Heath Bridge to about half way up the first part of Broxfords Hill and is just across the road from The Bungalow and Rose Cottage.

When I went to school the lady who lived 'on the corner' up at East Village wanted blackberries to make some jam. There were plenty of brambles in part of the Brake and I picked and I picked until she was satisfied that she had sufficient – I earned 7/6d (37½p) a princely sum in those days. I know that I went up there on my own, never feeling for one moment any sense of insecurity or apprehension that there was anyone about. It was lonely, yes, but not threatening.

There were two definite areas in the Brake – land which could grow crops or support livestock and 'The Quarries' opening out on to a flat plain, the latter was thought to have been used years ago – many years ago – as a skittle alley. This was possibly when Heath Bridge actually was a village, and the inhabitants found some sort of amusement for themselves.

Beside a few good oak trees near the quarry area but on the grassland above, there was one apple tree which still bore fruit, more a cider apple than eater or cooker. Nevertheless, it was cooked by those who had access to it!

The stone from the quarries had probably been taken to make better roads in the district – I can remember seeing an old man sitting beside a large 'tip' of stones where the road widened near

East Village and cracking them with a hammer!

It was the widest part of the lane and not causing any threat to the small amount of passing traffic.

Periodically – or when it was essential – there would be a road mending 'gang' with their watercart, means of producing hot tar, and a heavy roller, horses and carts, and the stones would disappear.

Grandma never owned the Brake for it belonged to the Davie family at Creedy Park and was kept by them as cover for any game birds; Sir William retained it and it was visited very infrequently by him with his 'shooting party'. On those occasions he would bring his friends to Bremridge for luncheon – provided 'exactly so' by Mum in the sitting-room and I remember that potatoes had to be cooked whole in the ashes of the kitchen fire, while his Keeper had to be accommodated in the kitchen!

When part of the Creedy Estate – several farms and 'Accommodation Land' was sold by Sir Patrick Davie some time after Sir William died, the Brake and 'The Garden' by the river were included, both of which had been rented by the tenant in Rose Cottage for some years. The land had been much improved and carried at least two cows and their calves, and poultry which usually provided Christmas dinners – and helped to pay the rent.

It was then that I became the owner and the tenant was able to continue with no interruption to his plans.

Some years after this tenant died and new tenancies had to be arranged the land was left 'idle' again and was eventually let to the then owner of Bremridge who christened it 'The Hump'! He wintered cattle there and it became deep in mud.

2
Anna's England

Anna Maria married Richard Melhuish of Poughill on the 30th November, 1775, and their first baby, a son whom they christened John Bremridge, was born on the 13th November,1776. Another son, Thomas, came into the world about eighteen months later, on the 18th June, 1778, and yet another son, Richard, made an appearance on the 13th October,1779. There is then a longer gap before Mary was born on the 29th July, 1783.

Anna's mother, Elizabeth, had died in 1781 so she would not have known anything about this last little child. No one knows how much she was able to help with the three little boys, but I'll bet they were quite a handful in spite of there being apprentices and help from any of the residents of Heath Bridge. 'Residents', I can almost hear them saying, 'We're not residents – us lives yere' – it was only the gentry who 'resided'.

It was much harder to look after babies then – think for a moment of how to manage without little rubber pants, without disposable nappies and without so many of the conveniences which have been taken for granted now for years. There were not even safety pins to hold the nappies together but no doubt they had their own methods of overcoming the problems. No wonder all the servants and apprentices were needed 'just to keep up-sides with what we take for granted'.

If there were cases of illness then homely cures were employed – boiled onions with milk I remember were recommended for colds and many times I have been treated with the old fashioned recipe! Camphor oils, and goose grease were rubbed into little chests, clothing being protected by a piece of old flannel or a piece of brown paper. In cases of serious illness a small light would be left burning all night, of course placed well out of the reach of the poorly child and an adult would have a bed placed fairly close to that of the sufferer so that any attention necessary could be given immediately. Certainly all the fussing and care would give the patient the idea that they were valued and wanted and if it was thought necessary to call the Doctor, oh dear, he had to be paid. He, poor man, must have often wondered whether journeys on horseback to outlying properties in all weathers were sufficiently recompensed by the amount of the bill he could charge.

Without any telephone it must have been difficult to communicate with any form of assistance but neighbours played a much bigger part in life than they do today. Anyone going 'to town' would always ask if there was anything to be brought back, even in our day and in this way the feeling of isolation was much diminished.

As the three little boys grew into children and began to show interest in everything their first guide and mentor was probably their Grandmother but only the elder child would have had any real appreciation of her as he was five years old when she died. There was Grandfather, probably not nearly so approachable, very interested in the church in Sandford.

There does seem to have been facilities for a school in East Village when the children were of an age to receive some education. How good it was, where it was, is not known to me so I am not able to say how much 'book learning' John Bremridge, Thomas or Richard actually received. I do not think that the little girl, their sister, several years younger, would have been allowed to go down to the Village every day with them. After all, education was thought to be more important for boys than 'maidens' and schools intended for all children were not generally available until the State Schools were established toward the end of the eighteenth century. There was, of course, a bigger school in Sandford and it is possible that the boys as they grew older might have gone there, that would still have been quite a long walk every day.

I have discovered several references to the fact that children did not always go to school when they were expected to do so — probably not because they were just staying away 'mitching' but

34

because they were expected to help with harvests, both hay and corn! When you realise that there was no mechanical equipment, only work by man's labours alone, you can see that any help was welcome. If the children received payment, so much the better for the wages were meagre, being made up in part by the amount of cider allowed for working in the summer. If 'full' meals were provided the wages were less still – one can only hope that the meals were good, well cooked and substantial. 'Cider allowed' no doubt accounts for the number of apple trees in the old orchards.

Water, at Bremridge particularly, and many other farms to some extent, must have been one of the biggest problems. I very much doubt that there was a piped supply from the well in Little Meadow when Anna and Richard lived there, so it was fetching water from one, or both, of the wells at some distance from the house in buckets for everything they needed. 'Buckets', what were they made of then? Probably wood, heavy before any quantity of water was dipped up, possibly animal skins were also used. I am sure I have seen a leather bucket somewhere.

If such containers also had to cope with a quantity of milk what a nightmare that must have been to be sure that they were clean. No detergents and even soap of doubtful quality meant a reliance on soda – awfully tough on one's hands, especially in winter. Butter would have been produced but I expect there was a much greater reliance on dripping and lard – margarine was not generally accepted for human consumption until later.

With a housekeeper and four apprentices, themselves, and four children, also Grandparents when the children were very young, there must have been many problems of how to feed them all. Sandford would have been the nearest village, with limited choice, while Crediton would have offered a wider selection if Scratchy-face Lane and the rough, muddy conditions could be overcome. Wherever they went for shopping the roads were awful and horses could be temperamental if the mood took them to be awkward.

Each season would bring its own problems. Spring could be very cold and wet so that working the land was difficult.

The cultivations and the sowing of the seed 'catching the weather just right' – a phrase I have often heard used – was followed by 'dashiel stabbing' when thistles began to show their unwelcome heads in the corn crops. That tool seemed to be the only defence against the obnoxious weed. If the dashiel stabber was resting beside the back door at Bremridge in our time then Grandpa was indoors. It was a long handled tool with a small piece of metal at the business end. This was very sharp indeed.

Then there was the hazard of the birds with their hungry appetites. Boys – the apprentices – were often given the job of bird scaring with something which made much noise. I have seen a scarer which looked like the front of a drawer with a loose handle which rattled. The sound travelled some distance in the empty fields, and did its job well. An old tin tray beaten with anything which would make a noise was also effective.

A boy with a good voice might often be heard singing – years ago no doubt he would be encouraged to sing hymns and not the rowdy songs of the day.

At the time of harvest the birds must have had a feast! Grandpa's saying that the corn should hear the church bells three times before it was brought in gave every species of feathered foe the opportunity to pick the grain from the standing stooks until all feathered crops were full.

I expect that even Anna's sons were encouraged to spend some time protecting the corn for conditions would have been even more primitive in her day than in ours.

Before the introduction of potatoes into this country somewhere about the time of Sir Walter Raleigh – he is said to have grown some experimentally at his Devonshire birthplace, Hayes, and elsewhere – bread and meat would have formed a large part of the diet, particularly in the country. When potatoes became popular they must have been a Godsend but they did require proper cultivation and storage. We always had a big 'teddy-clamp', often out in the garden beside the big barn. I wonder if Farmer Richard Melhuish was the first one in the district to do this – after all he had quite a family to feed with his four children and the apprentices and servants. Woe betide anyone who went to the teddy-clamp and did not cover it up properly, so that frost destroyed the store.

In our time it was customary to grow a couple of rows of potatoes for the workers but it has been known that, although the crop looked perfect, when lifting began some of the tubers had already been removed! Hungry men did not wait for large specimens.

A gentleman called Townsend, nicknamed 'Turnip', imported a very useful vegetable from Flanders, again a very welcome addition to the diet of both humans and animals, and it became quite widely grown and stored.

Then, in 1786, yet another root crop was introduced. The mangold was a food for animals but not humans. It took some care and attention to grow, having to be hoed and singled out by hand, but good soil and good storage ensured that at least the animal inhabitants of farms had something for the winter months when grass was scarce.

I have recently seen some programmes on T.V. on some of the remote areas of China. Children were speaking about the hard work that their mothers did in harvest time. It appears that long grass has to be cut with a small hook, bundled up and removed to shelter ready for use when bad weather comes.

How similar it must have been in the days before the scythe was invented, in the western countries, in England, in Devon and, in particular, in some of the steep fields belonging to Bremridge! The farmers, the workers, the apprentices, how the weather ruled their labours and no doubt some of the more irresponsible of the workers wished for rain when 'Maister' needed just the opposite – aching backs and aching muscles had no place if there was a threat of rain about. It would have been the small hook in wide use (in wide use? – more likely in 'narrow bands') when all the masters of Bremridge were Bremridges and even when Richard Melhuish was in charge.

Perhaps it is just as well that the fields were smaller then – it is only since the advent of the modern tractor and big machinery that hedges have been removed, two, or even three, fields put into one and some 'semi-prairies' created.

Speaking from my own experience of many years ago, the women folk would only have been involved in harvest time to the extent of taking drinks and food out to the workers. Cider, cider, and more cider, would probably have been fetched by an apprentice boy, while tea and 'something to eat' would have been provided by the girls and 'women-folk'.

Workers in the sun nowadays often strip down to their jeans – some even wear short trousers of varying types and they are not always what would in yesteryear be termed 'neat and tidy' for the lower edge is just left 'raw' and not turned up to form any kind of hem. The sun must have been just as hot years ago yet workers were covered from head to foot. Hats of all kinds, particularly old felts, protected the head. Shirt sleeves were never rolled up in harvest time so that the arms were protected, woollen socks took care of the feet in leather boots, I do not think they could have ever heard of sandals!

The women were equally wrapped up against the sun. Dark dresses – navy, dark brown or black – were the usual and again the sleeves were not rolled up unless it was washing day and then they just had to be. They wore long white aprons – and they were 'white' – in fact ladies took quite a pride in having their aprons 'spotless'. How many changes of apron that would involve in one day is not known but certainly it was the custom to wash and clean up before tea and put on a fresh apron.

No wonder so many servants and apprentices were needed. Just to be equal to today's modern standards: there was always 'the fire' to be seen to, always the oil lamps to be filled and lanterns to be ready for outside work at night. The modern farmer can call a vet quickly by telephone but help for animals was very difficult years ago and very few drugs existed.

A journey to Exeter would, indeed, have been an outing. It was quite a different Exeter, very much smaller – in fact from the Crediton direction the town did not start until near the Sir Redvers Buller statue – and that was not there in the time of Anna Maria and Richard Melhuish!

Exeter without street lighting must have been a dismal place after dark. With so much horse traffic one would almost need to look where one was going just as carefully as today, for a rider could very quickly round a corner and present a hazard to the unwary.

There are districts in Exeter where terrible things have happened – people have been put to death at Livery Dole, in Southernhay, at the Castle, even near the Guildhall. Life seems to have been very cheap.

I have seen an account of deliberations about the Hospital many years ago, when it was thought that the keeping of pigs by the Hospital should be discontinued. Why would a Hospital wish to keep pigs – to feed the inmates on pork or for the pigs to eat any rubbish produced?

Is it possible that ghosts from the past exist even today? I remember the old Paris Street and some of the houses reached by entering a covered way – almost like going through a tunnel to reach a few steps somewhat roughly constructed which led to a couple of cottages. A girl who attended St. Wilfred's School when I was also a pupil there lived in one of the houses – until Hitler's bombers came over on a night in May 1942. She was killed, and her sister and mother also. Yes, Hitler did much to redesign Exeter.

Crediton also had its difficulties. There were two terrible fires right up top of the town in the area known as 'The Green'. No doubt all the houses had the traditional thatched roof. They were close together and when fire starts it does its best to spread. The first big fire was in 1743 and 450 houses were destroyed. Some of the new houses erected as replacements went in 1769. What a disaster!

The Crediton I remember had one very long, very wide street. Little traffic. Plenty of room to park and even the odd horse drawn vehicle – sometimes a farmer's trap would be just outside a shop, usually guarded by a young member of the family. There were side streets off this bus route, of course, some of them could be described as 'Courts' being very narrow with doors opening directly on to a passageway providing a safe haven for young children.

The bus came from Exeter and went to The Green to turn – a very welcome sight to see it was stationary up there when any intending passengers joined other hopeful passengers waiting further down town.

There was a bus service out of Sandford, naturally not a very frequent one but very welcome all the same.

People who motor through Crediton just catch a glimpse of the beautiful church – I hope some of them do find the time to stop and appreciate the sense of peace and quiet which such a solid, substantial building induces. I remember going there once in the autumn, when the mauve Michaelmas daisies against the stone pillars looked just perfect and so restful! I stayed, almost alone, until I remembered that I ought to go to Exeter!

While I was in the quiet church I thought about my Confirmation there – 'my' should have been 'our' for Lavinia and I were confirmed at the same time. I remember standing in the kitchen at Bremridge and trying on the dress which Mum was

39

making especially for the great day. The kitchen was always the warmest part of the house unless the fire had been lit in the sitting-room – and there was hurry to get it fitted before Grandpa came in for tea. It was quite a plain and simple white muslin with a bodice to the waist and full skirt for easy movement – long sleeves. There was also a white petticoat and a plain length of the same muslin made a cover for the hair, pinned back at the nape of the neck. Just a little lace edging had been added to the neck and sleeves of the dress and this took off quite such a plain appearance.

All I remember of the great day was the journey there and back and the big stone squares of the floor where I believe we had to await our turn before being called in before the Bishop – indeed a very austere personage in his long robes and the mitre which added several more inches to his height!

Having been prepared for Confirmation so carefully by the Reverend Llewellyn we were conscious of our serious undertaking, and determined then to abide by it all.

I wonder where Anna Maria was confirmed; Sandford Church and this 'Mother' church in Crediton had been connected for many years – probably still is.

I don't think you could call the world a very happy place in the reign of George II. It was quite a long reign, from 1727 to 1760, and saw the War of the Austrian Succession, the King and the British Army being involved and ending in a notable victory at Dettington. In 1745 there was a Jacobite Rising, which was suppressed, and there was the beginning of the Seven Years War towards the end of George's reign.

There was difficulty with America, resulting in the election of their own President George Washington – in 1789. That four year system then established seems to have lasted ever since.

The Indian Empire came about after some battles (Plassy in 1757 was one) and so began a very long association. I wonder who has derived the most benefit!

George II had to rule for many years without his wise companion, Caroline of Anspach, for she died in 1737 and it was she who had prevented the dismissal of Prime Minister Walpole, Sir Robert, Earl of Oxford.

There was the excitement of the marriage of George III to Charlotte on the 8th September, 1761, the year after he became

King. His reign was another very long one, 60 years, and he was father to fifteen children. Queen Charlotte must have had her hands more than full as poor George started having fits. In fact for the last ten years of his life his son George IV acted as Regent.

News came out from France about the state of that country. There were great fears for the safety of the French Royal Family with all the plotting which was taking place. Louis XVI ascended the throne in 1774 but he and his Queen, Marie Antoinette, were not popular – aristocrats hated by the poor people of France who listened to what such leaders as Mirabeau and Rousseau spoke and wrote about. A lady who also had a great influence in French politics was Madam Pompadour, a very evil person if everything known or written about her was true.

There was indeed a Reign of Terror in France. This lasted for 420 days from the 31st May, 1793 to 28th July, 1794 when over 30,000 people died by the guillotine, Louis and Marie Antoinette among them.

Rumours of old women knitting while these executions were taking place spread throughout England. The song of the Revolution stirred up more feeling, people were afraid to mention any connection with France and, indeed, that country must have suffered greatly through it all.

All this while country people, such as the family at Bremridge, the Melhuishes, tried to get on with their everyday life hoping and hoping that the trouble would be contained within France, almost fearing to hear of the latest number of victims.

Ultimately it did come to an end and there was much rebuilding to be done – even the great Cathedral of 'Our Lady', Notre Dame, in Paris which had been founded in the twelfth century had to be restored. It seemed that for a while certain elements in France could not be satisfied until so much had been wrecked.

3

They Went – or Came – A-Courting

With the ease of travel today, with the good roads and very convenient cars it is difficult to really have an appreciation of what it meant years ago when a young man wished to visit his 'intended' who did not live very near to his home, or lodgings.

It must have been even worse for the young lady to attempt any journey to visit him. Think for a few moments about the state of the roads and about the unsuitability of the young lady's mode of dress – how did they cope with muddy skirts and soaking coats? All I can say is that both sexes must have been pretty persistent to travel far in search of a mate of suitable social standing.

There was, of course, the horse to make travel a little easier and it would have been the young man who saddled up and made a journey of miles to see his 'intended' and the frequency of his visits would indicate the strength of his passion! Depending on his reception and enjoyment of an evening with her, and her family, his decision would be made as to whether it was worth coming again. 'Getting to know you, getting to know all about you' must not have been too easy as convention played a very important role years ago.

I am not speaking about 'the gentry' who had their carriages and servants who undertook all the hard work of making the journey possible and waiting to take the passenger back home, however long the visit lasted.

No, lesser mortals living in hilly farms stood a much greater chance of remaining single – many of them did.

I have been able to trace the marriage of a few of the

'Bremridge' lads and if I am right the first one, the Grandfather of Anna Maria, chose a young lady who did not live very far off. She was a Mary Reed of Priors Town and the wedding took place in 1713. 'Priors Town' no doubt refers to a farm we always knew as Priorton and, if so, then their courting could have been comparatively easy because the fields of the two farms adjoin, although the boundary was altered many years ago when more land was purchased by the owner of Bremridge from the owner of Priorton.

It could have been a case of the young man crossing the river – on foot when the water was low in the summer but by horse power when there was any quantity flowing down stream. Who knows how long they walked by the quiet, peaceful little waterway before they could plan their wedding? I know that John had reached a good, sensible age; he was 28 but I don't know how old Mary was then. There were, as previously stated, four sons, the eldest was John, followed by William, Richard and Samuel.

Their childhood would have followed the pattern of the times for the children of Church people – as all the Bremridges seem to have been. I imagine them all as very straight-laced, very proper in all their dealings. It is certain that religion and the medical profession were very much favoured, with the influence of one of the descendants of William being acknowledged even today!

This same William also went courting in due course. His wife was Elizabeth, daughter of John Reed of Chawley and they married in 1751. Quite a puzzle as to how those two met and became friends but William is described as being of Kenn – a village not too far from Exeter. He was the father of William, John and Mary. There was another child, signified by a very small 'd', so I suppose it died at birth, or even before.

This last William followed the pattern of the human race and although I do not know who the mother was there was born to these Bremridges in 1810 a little son who was christened Elias and it is this child who became so famous. William and 'Mrs' had moved to Whetstone in North London and as he was the youngest of a large family it was thought that outdoor work was beyond him and he should take up a different career, so he chose to come back to Exeter and serve an apprenticeship under Mr William Froome, an apothecary-druggist. This lasted for seven years.

Then he returned to London and became one of the founders of the Pharmaceutical Society in 1857. He became Secretary to the Society and he secured exemption from Jury Service for Pharmacists in 1862.

Elias married twice, and his son Richard took his place when he eventually retired. There were also two daughters but I know nothing of them. I do know that Richard had old fashioned standards – a typed letter would not be read, it must be hand written!

I thought that I would obtain a little more information from the Pharmaceutical Society about both Elias and Richard so I wrote to them – and there it was at the head of the letter just under the heading and address and after the telephone number, 'Cables, Bremridge, London, SE1'. The Society enclosed copies of extracts from the Pharmaceutical Journal, dated the 18th June, 1904, showing Elias from a photograph with hair receding from a broad forehead, two bright eyes under white, bushy eyebrows and a white moustache and flowing beard. He has a long, straight nose and I think his face was long rather than round.

The journal speaks in glowing terms of the good work done by Elias, sadness at his death on the evening of Wednesday, June 15th (1904) and arrangements for his funeral on Saturday at 12.00 noon, the 18th inst. at Norbiton. No flowers, by request. Certainly his is a life which appears to have been 'well lived'.

Another page from the Journal, dated June 7th, 1913, outlines the career of Richard, son of Elias, and speaks with regret of his retirement after forty-five years of service. There is also a photograph of him, perhaps with more of a round head than his father had, short beard and moustache, receding hair.

There is still a further page, showing Richard with his Grandson, Eric, in 1913, quite a small boy, possibly four or five years old. On the same page there is a family group – a posed photo – showing Grandfather Elias, sitting down, son Richard standing behind with his left hand on the old man's chair, and Grandson, Richard Harding Bremridge, aged 21, standing beside his father.

Richard Harding Bremridge was in the First World War – I believe Eric (his son) told me that he became a Captain then and when hostilities ended there were several posts to do with medicine in one way and another. Eric had one sister, but she died many years ago somewhere around middle age. There was also a brother who went to Canada and with whom there is now very little connection, very sad. I think he was born in 1919 (David).

Now that I have explored the connection between the well-known son of the Bremridges as far as I am able to, I will get back to John Bremridge, brother of the first William I mentioned. He married Elizabeth, daughter of William Smale of Witheridge, Mercot. He died in 1784 and she died in 1781. They had two children, John and Anna Maria.

As previously mentioned, some illness must have caused the death of this last John, for he died on the 4th November at the age of 22. Records for coroners papers do not show that there was any accident or foul play of any sort. At the time of his death there were outbreaks of smallpox mainly, so it is possible that he became ill after a visit to Crediton or Exeter where the infection could be spread, unless he was an invalid 'from the consumption.'

The 4th November, 1769, is the date given but it could have been when his funeral took place. In any case, the 4th November has been a very notable date in my own family for both Grandpa at Bremridge and my mother when we lived in Worcester Park, Surrey, were ill and taken into hospital on that date in the dreary, dark month of November.

What is certain is that Anna met someone she could love and trust and in time she married him. He was Richard Melhuish of Poughill, though other than that I do not know which farm was his home.

Poughill is a village up over the hills towards North Devon, quite high and somewhat bleak in winter. In good weather you can see for miles and miles and summers in such a place bring many compensations. If you work out the distance from Bremridge, as I have done, it would appear to be a good three miles off as to go to East Village is one mile, up to Stockleigh English from there is about one mile and there could be another mile up over the hills before Poughill is reached. I think it is doubtful whether Richard actually lived in the village – I expect he came from a farm somewhere within that parish. He must have had a farming background to consider being concerned with farming at Bremridge, whether on his own or under the influence of the gentleman, John, who became his father-in-law.

From records I have seen I am sure that Richard and Anna went over to Pakeham to live for a while and only came back to Bremridge when Anna's mother died in 1781. Her Father died in 1784 and I am sure there would have been many journeys over the grass track, along the road and over the bridge before the hill with its large oak tree was reached, round by the orchard and up the lane.

I wonder if the stile at the bottom of the orchard existed then – it would scarcely have been of use to anyone wearing a long skirt! It was a recognised and well established stile by the time Grandpa lived at Bremridge but, of course, the men from Heath Bridge or East Village all those years ago might have been glad to 'cut' up over the orchard, especially if they were a little late in getting to work, harvesting some crop or other.

I remember that stile with great affection for many times I have perched on the top rail and enjoyed a few minutes to myself looking over the fields. I have seen a lady from Priorton with two buckets going to a house with feed for housed poultry which would soon be running around freely outside. I have seen Mr Miller's Knole field with the large oak tree in the middle, part grass with sheep grazing, and part growing a crop of some description. Further in the distance there was Prowse and Downhayne while the school roof was nearly always visible – 'nearly always' because sometimes the growth on a hedge would hide it. Hedges in my young days were not shorn or trimmed to the extent common on most farms now.

The road below the stile was not too muddy most of the time but it had two or three very large dents which very soon filled with water in wet periods – puddles, always to be avoided on your way to school otherwise your feet would be wet for a very long time – no wellington boots!

Of the four children born to Anna Maria and Richard Melhuish I can trace that Thomas, the second boy, married his cousin, Elizabeth, daughter of a clergyman, the Reverend T. Melhuish who had a living at Ashwater and Clawton. Now that really was some distance away and in the days of poor roads and pony travel it probably meant a visit which could last at least overnight – probably a few days.

In time, the farm, Bremridge, belonged to them. There is a

record of the Melhuish family living at a farm much nearer Crediton in the Upton Hellions parish, so I think that elder brother John might have married and gone there.

In 1822 Richard Melhuish, Esq. of Bremridge is mentioned in some official record; he could have been either Anna's husband or the third son.

What is known is that Thomas and Elizabeth had a son, born in 1812. They named him Thomas Bremridge and in due course he became the Rector of Poughill. And, of course, it was this gentleman's name I found in Poughill Church so many years ago and no doubt he was also the 'Parson' who used the little house built into the wall in the back garden for study purposes. One wonders why, for by the time he was old enough to study seriously his Aunt, his Father's only sister known as Meg, had died, and so had his Grandmother, Anna Maria. Thomas would have been ten years old then, certainly not able to concentrate on writing sermons!

Time passes and Thomas Bremridge Melhuish also married and had a son, John. John became a farmer, but it seems that he preferred to live on a farm at Poughill, and not at Bremridge, for a tenant by the name of William Densham is known to have occupied the farm where his maternal ancestors had lived for hundreds of years, yes, hundreds of years. When it was realised that his Father had a living in that parish and that his Grandfather had also been farming in Poughill perhaps it was difficult for him to choose.

Eventually, John Melhuish sold Bremridge to the owners of the Creedy Estate, the Davie Family living at Creedy Park in Sandford. This seems to have been only one of several farms bought by the Estate for it is said that they owned 67,000 acres but I am not sure it was all in Devon since the family had connections with property in Somerset. Certainly more and more farms had been acquired in Devon.

William Densham must have been the Father of the w3icked John Densham who fell out with Grandpa – Mr Stoyle – when he had applied and been accepted as a tenant to follow him. I think I can remember being told that it was something to do with the Valuation – often causing poor feeling between the outgoing and incoming tenant. In this case John Densham stood at the Court gate and cursed William Stoyle, saying that he would never do

47

anything as long as he lived there, meaning that he would never make money or make a success of farming. John Densham made sure things were difficult for the young Stoyles by setting fire to the buildings at night before they had actually moved in.

Me – Dorinda, 1938/9.

Bremridge Farm
Drawing by my sister Lavinia.

My mother, about 1936 in Exeter.

Rose Cottage and The Bungalow, Heath Bridge, 1966.
Cottage later had to have a new roof, so no longer thatched.

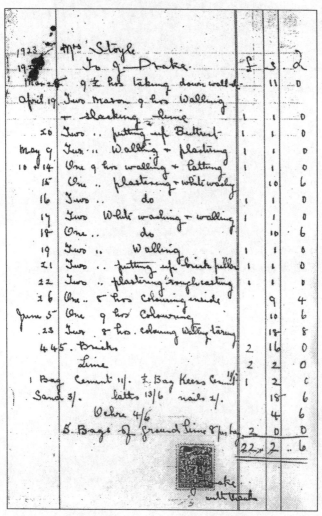

The receipted bill for work on Rose Cottage in 1923.

Lavinia's wedding emerging from the church in Salisbury.
The young man on the left was killed the next day!
I am just behind Lavinia the bride.

Heath Bridge.
Drawing by my sister Lavinia.

4

My Bremridge Days

I look back on the period when I lived at Bremridge as a very happy one for all through the 1920s. Lavinia and I thought the security of the large farm house with its thick cob walls would last forever. Open log fires and oil lamps gave warmth and comfort during the long days of winter, and in the summer there were always the harvest fields where helping to carry tea to the men out in various parts of the farm provided us with what we thought of as 'picnics'.

We had our animals – twenty tame rabbits housed under the shelter in the back court. There were as many as eighteen chinchillas, so much alike you only knew which was which because of the houses they lived in. The two foreigners were Angoras which were said to be able to provide enough wool to make all sorts of things. I think Lavinia succeeded in getting a small quantity, about enough to make a scarf for a doll.

In season tame lambs were fun for us – one we cuddled in an old wooden wheelbarrow. That lamb would follow us anywhere – had to be shut in when we went to school or else there would have been trouble.

Puppies were favourites but too many of them could not be encouraged. When the drover living in Crediton wanted a young dog he had my Ben and Grandpa told me I could have the whole half-crown – the purchase price – all to myself. I would rather have kept my Ben, but even Grandma thought he should be given another home, so he went.

In summer, when the horses had to be taken up to

c

Wedgiecleave or Brake, it meant a walk up through Barns Close, Higher Orchard and out into the Broxfords Lane. Usually there were three animals and three riders. Henry was in charge and the halters were linked by a rope — we took up the whole width of the Lane. Henry rode the colt, my mount was Smart and Lavinia had either Farmer or Violet.

The way home was back through the farm fields; often we could persuade Henry that we wanted some grass for the bunnies and he would pick a good armful. If he had no grass, then he gave me a piggy-back all the way home and I thought I was favoured because I was much lighter and smaller than Lavinia!

I do not remember very much about Annie Furze except that she was thin and had big feet, large hands and a red nose. Years later I heard that it was because of her that my Father left Bremridge, she became pregnant 'by someone over Cheriton Fitzpaine' so she had to leave and was returned to the Institution in Crediton. Edith Spear then came to help. I think that she had only just about left school herself at New Buildings; she was very scared of Grandpa and went home after a few days. Grandma drove the governess car and went over to bring her back gently and kindly. She stayed with us until we left the farm.

The cobbled stones in the court must have been trodden on and walked over by many generations of Bremridges before the Densham era and the coming of the Stoyles, for the stones near the back door were very smooth and shiny. They must have been selected with care originally for they were all much about the same size and shape, rather long, but they did not cover the whole area for there was a large square in the middle of the courtyard where wood for that hungry open fire was stored as in a rick. Part of it contained heavy logs — fallen trees and branches — perfect for 'back sticks' in the open hearth in the kitchen which could lie and smoulder to itself for hours and then be resurrected into life when needed. Smaller material must have been the result of hedging and fencing and the cutting of gorse.

The woodrick was ideally placed not far from the wood shed where a store of dry wood should be kept.

The afternoon sun shone into the kitchen from the front lawn. That was said to affect the fire — 'T'won't burn while the sun shines on it' is an expression I've heard many times. The remedy was to place a towel over the back of a chair so that the fire was

50

shaded. If it had really gone too low then a drop of oil, paraffin, thrown on by a grown-up, of course, usually produced a good blaze for a few minutes.

I remember seeing a toad in the bottom of the woodrick and watched it as it sought shelter away from danger. I have wondered why there was such a stigma attached to the poor little toads; in any case, why toads and not frogs, or spiders? I was glad I had let the toad escape but I did not tell anyone about it or they might have ferreted it out to be rid of any risk of ill-fortune.

Grandpa did have much bad luck, though, at Bremridge. One cow got down too near the river to produce her calf and dropped it in the water! It was a Sunday afternoon and a certain amount of blame was put at Bennett's door for not being aware that she was so near either to calving or to the river.

'Madam', the colt, came in from a field in the morning with an injured head – something had badly grazed her forehead. It healed satisfactorily after much attention with homely remedies, for vet's bills had to be avoided.

Calves down in the orchard drank from the sheep dipper; they died. If the old black sow had a good litter of pigs she would invariably crush one or two, even more.

What caused 'Smart' to jump a ditch out in the field one morning will forever remain a mystery, but she twisted a gut and within a short time in spite of 'nursing' all night by Henry, she died.

I thought several times of the little toad. If I had killed it, would there have been such bad luck? Bad luck brings despondency and recriminations – I am sure it cannot all be because of a little toad!

5

Plucking Poultry in the Woodshed

It is certain that this shed, adjoining the house as it does and being near the kitchen with any utensils necessary, or water, or whatever, has been used all down through the years for the plucking of poultry. At Christmas when more birds had to be ready for market local help was necessary and it was then that there would be several women sitting on the old chairs and the chopping stool as they worked skilfully denuding the birds of their feathers. (Nearly wrote 'fathers'!)

Of course the women talked, they always seemed to know everything, to be apprehensive about many things which they could not control – love-making in their offspring, for instance, the problem of the drinker, the difficulties between husband and wife, what 'so-and-so' was going to do, how to make a little more money, how to try to save any for the rainy day they all knew was coming. Perhaps their most interesting subject of all was who was going to have the next baby. When a couple were newly married, one of their favourite expressions was 'Well, wait and see – you just watch the clothes line! That will tell 'ee.'

When I first heard that remark I had no idea of what it meant – why should a clothes line with a week's washing tell anyone whether a baby was due to come into the world after months of waiting? In time, I found out – and so must you!

One Christmas Grandma asked me to go to the wood shed and see if I could get two grey goose wings because she wanted them for 'doing the stairs down'. In fact, we used goose wings for years and the end feathers made getting dust out of the corners of the steps quite easy.

As usual, the women were talking and I heard a remark about 'a love child'. I was sure that they had meant it was a lovely child but had overlooked putting on the last part of the word. I do not think that they had noticed me looking for the grey goose wings, but suddenly there was a silence which was broken by a sort of a giggle and someone said, ' 'Er does not know what it means.'

It was then that the puppy appeared and scampered round the wood shed with its nose very soon covered in feathers. 'Get that animal out of here' was an almost universal chorus and I was so busy in trying to do that I forgot all about the lovely child. Queer, how things come back to you years and years after they were first said and in my mind's eye I saw much the same scene again only the women were quite different. Their clothes were much longer and very much darker but the work-roughened hands showed that they did much the same work as the ladies I knew. The conversation seemed to centre around two young people, a boy and a girl and something about telling them all that they ought to know. If there was trouble they could be made to sit on the Stool of Repentance in church on a Sunday in view of all the congregation. It would not only be a disgrace to the two people concerned, it would also reflect much discredit on the house where they lived.

The Bremridges and, later, the Melhuishes, all had duties to the church as Overseers, therefore they and their households must be above reproach and human nature must be subjected to strict codes of practice!

Even more than that, there are several Bremridges who became 'Parsons'. Father, and then son, became clergymen at Winkleigh, and I remember going with Mum to a Church Service at Poughill — I expect it was a Harvest Festival — and seeing a tablet on a wall with the name Rev. Thomas Bremridge Melhuish engraved on it. I know I asked why he was called 'Bremridge' but Mum did not know and could not explain the connection.

Another tale of the Woodshed was supposed to be an account of what actually happened.

One of the women who lived at Heath Bridge put on an old apron and went up to the field where the turnips grew with the intention of helping herself to one or two. They could be covered by the apron and no one would ever miss them when the crop was

53

dug up. Over the growing season she had done this more than once and not been seen, until one day – Oh Lord, Oh Lord, there was the master coming up on his horse and with his dog trailing behind. Her apron had collected enough for two or three meals and if she turned them out he would know she had been stealing. She must have been quick witted, for she assumed a position as if she was sitting on something and muttered, somewhat shame-facedly, 'Must be done, Sir, must be done.' Sir did not really look at her but said, 'Quite right, Mary, quite right', called his dog and rode on! Mary went home with the turnips.

It seems that the bigger the farm and the more prosperous the more apprentices would be needed there. All these apprentices were allowed to go home now and again and no doubt passed on to their own families much news about the life with the farmer or the doctor, or whoever, to their own immediate circle of friends. In return they would receive all the local gossip which, no doubt, some would be only too anxious to pass on to anyone who would listen. Here, again, it was the woodshed which could reveal secrets told in confidence to whoever was working there and had the time to listen.

Some apprentices were lucky enough to have employers who would see to it that there was something useful which could be taken back home – perhaps a freshly baked loaf of bread or chunk of cheese. A number of farmhouses had cheese presses and could make their own – we did at one time at Bremridge. A cake was another gift which was sometimes made by the girl herself. Times were hard and these gifts were very much appreciated.

Woe betide any apprentice, boy or maiden, who deliberately made mischief or carried what was known as 'tittle-tattle' to belittle her employer – even her own relatives would be against that and fearful that anything she said would get back to her employer.

Perhaps it was thought by apprentices that they were actually owned by the occupants of the house where they worked but it was preferable by far to going 'on the Parish' with 'Officials ' in charge.

It was not only at Christmas time when all new snippets of information were passed on or old tales resurrected, that the woodshed was the place where a modern microphone would have picked up items of praise or blame, for most of the apprentices seemed to make good use of that space. The seats were not all that comfortable, but they were in the dry and sometimes it was not well to advertise to the world that you had little to do – after all, you could be breaking up a few sticks to help a reluctant fire on its way – and for that the ladies in the kitchen would thank you.

One piece of information which came from John Melhuish on a hot day in the summer, was imparted to both his brothers in the woodshed. He said that he had been walking along down by the river and had met Adam Quick, and that he had tried to talk to him. Adam 'looked queer' he said, 'just as if he was looking through me'. John said that he had met him there before, several times, and that he had always stopped to talk although he never said very much more than a few remarks about the weather, or about some farming operation which was current.

Some time later the body of Adam Quick was found. He had drowned himself in Priorton Mill leat. He had been 55 years old.

The Upton Hellions road to Crediton runs close to a stream in the 'dip' between two steep hills. It was here that the awkward husband of a patient, long-suffering wife drowned himself in more modern times. A farmer who had been riding his pony just could not make him pass the spot and had to go miles out of his way to get home!

6

The Sandford Parish Magazine
(January, 1888 and 1890–1895)

I rediscovered these magazines recently, the paper now bearing signs of being very old, of fairly good quality if slightly discoloured. Obviously they had belonged to Grandma for there is a pencilled note up in the right-hand corner in beautiful writing – 'Mrs Stoyle, Bremridge'. All of them follow the same design and layout with 'Church and Mission Room Services' for Sandford itself and also for New Buildings and East Village Schoolroom Services, 'On alternate Sunday evenings from April to December at 6.30 p.m.' and give further information about the Services in the Parish Church. That must be classed as Page 11, for Page 11 begins with a message from 'Your Pastor and friend in Christ, and signed 'GEO. T. LLEWELLYN'.

It is obvious that 1888 is the first year of its production and although it is rather long I think I will quote his message under his heading of A HAPPY NEW YEAR TO YOU!

My Dear Parishioners,

For the first time, after nearly seven years' ministry amongst you, I can give you a New Year's greeting through the medium of our own Parish Magazine. And I do so most heartily; praying that, whilst you may abound in all earthly things good and expedient for you, you may also, day by day, and year by year, 'GROW IN GRACE, AND IN THE KNOWLEDGE OF OUR LORD AND SAVIOUR, JESUS CHRIST'. We want a motto for the New Year: I will offer one for you. Let it be 'FORWARD'! 'FORWARD' through the weal and woe of this world; FORWARD in the spiritual knowledge and experience, FORWARD in Divine grace! But I warn you against two great obstacles we must be prepared to overcome – SELF-WILL AND NO-WILL-AT ALL. It is chiefly through these that world, flesh and devil punish us so severely as they do. Do help me in the fight against them in yourselves, and in those around you. Do help me with your prayers; with your more regular attendance and your keener interest in your Parish Church; with your more earnest heart and voice in its Public Services; with your really Christian lives; and with your help in our Sunday Schools, or among our poor, and aged, and sick. Make a good resolution, according to your abilities, at the beginning of the New Year. Meanwhile I owe a deep debt of gratitude to those who have been already helping me as Sunday School Superintendents and Teachers, or as District Visitors. But there is still room for many more helpers.

I trust that every reader is pleased with our Magazine, 'The Dawn of Day', and that every household will have its readers of it. There is something good and useful, sound and instructive, in every number. I can always myself learn something from it; and I do not think it is too difficult – nor TOO SIMPLE – for any reader amongst us who will ONLY READ IT. If those who have already taken it in have not had a thoroughly good six-penny-worth in the past twelve months – well, I cannot believe it is altogether for fault of the Magazine.

I have added a record of some chief parish events of the year just ended, and of other facts you may find desirable to know. When the sale of the Magazine gets larger, I may be able to print it in a Monthly, or, at least, a Quarterly record. If those of its readers who are quite able will offer to pay one shilling a year for it, instead of the trifling sum asked before, it will help me to carry out earlier this improvement.

I think I have filled now all the space which can be allotted to my address to you in this number. The facts which follow will speak for themselves. In conclusion I will again ask for my parishioners' prayers for me as earnestly as I desire and pray for their spiritual and bodily well-being.'

Mr Llewellin signs himself 'Your Pastor and friend in Christ' after this letter and for two or three years more, then he drops the last two words.

There are several letters where Mr Llewellin concentrates on the passage of time and how quickly it goes; how easy it is to waste it. He said 'It is a real crime to idle and waste and throw life-time away' 'NOW is our sowing time. Don't we know that "Whatsoever a man soweth, that shall he also reap"? This is God's decree; no one can alter it. The fruit of our life-time shall be according to its sowing.'

Perhaps I have quoted just enough to show how he considered life should be lived – straight and upright. He concludes one letter with an excellent bit of New Year's counsel from a great poet:

> 'Have more than thou showest,
> Speak less than thou knowest,
> Lend less than thou owest.'

The church 'offerings' seem to amount to about £30 per year, even including just over 8/-d each (40p) from East Village and New Buildings Schoolroom Services. There were other monies not 'made' in church for the support of various things, even including the Day Schools – a voluntary rate – realising somewhere about £100.

In each magazine there is a report on the Schools, Sandford (I suppose you could call that 'the parent school') with the outlying New Buildings and East Village Schools as accommodation for the children who live in or near those villages when Sandford would be too far to walk every day – 'Shanks's pony' was your only means of getting there.

It seems that there were problems with school attendance about 100 years ago and mention is made more than once of the importance of attending regularly and so one magazine states that 'Parents forget that EVERY TIME a child is absent from school, about ONE HALFPENNY IS LOST from the Government Grant for the support of the school. Taking the Girls' School as an example (Sandford School); in the last year there were present 46 girls in all; and the school was open 437 times. But no less than 15 girls lost more than 120 attendances each; while 3 of them lost more than 240 each. This really means that 12 of these girls lost between 5/-d and 10/-d (25p and 50p) to the school funds; and the other 3 lost 10/-d (50p) each or more. Of course this is a serious consideration, because the Managers are bound to let these girls come to school; and each one's schooling costs on an average 32/-d (160p) a year while her parents only pay as school money about THREE AND SIXPENCE (17½p) towards this expense.

'For the remainder, the Managers depend on three or four small endowments, a voluntary parish rate, and the Government Grant earned for the secular instruction given. The Government Grant would reach nearly one-half as much again as it does, probably, if the attendance were as perfect as it could be. Under such bad circumstances it is most creditable that the respective mistresses should have passed, at the Government examination in last July, in the Girls' School 96 per cent, at East Village 95 per cent, and at New Buildings 92 per cent of their children in Reading, Writing, and Arithmetic, the chief secular subjects.'

When East Village School is mentioned, it reports 'Miss Slade's good and careful work continues, and she has her school in pleasing order; and her children are well-mannered, and interested in the work. Discipline, tone, etc. good. The school is classed 'Good'.

What a hope in those days and equally in these: It says 'The Managers trust that parents will co-operate with them as much as possible to make the schools thoroughly efficient – religiously, morally, and educationally. For the encouragement of regular attendance they intend, at the end of each school year in July, to give every child who has made more than 400 attendances during the year, a reward of one halfpenny (480 to the pound of today) for every such extra attendance. Last year the schools were opened about 437 times.'

There seem to have been extra problems at East Village School during the harvest time for the attendance was low and it probably meant that 'Junior and his brother' were helping Dad – probably driving horses with some of the more simple mechanical machines which were still somewhat of a novelty.

From the Church Registers

Grouped under the three obvious headings 'Baptisms, Marriages and Burials', I find these entries most interesting and I have looked thoughtfully through the lists for each year and I have found many names very well remembered. I have underlined them.

On the 24th December, 1888, William Stoyle and Alice Sophia Slade were married in Sandford Church. Grandma told me she had a grey outfit – I do not think any bride wore white in those days. Little is known about the weather on that particular day except that in the middle of winter there is little hope of the sun being brilliant! No doubt it was a very quiet wedding, with the few relatives who attended being on the side of the bridegroom, though it is just possible that Grandma's relatives from Bristol or Bath did get to Devon. I think that Grandma must have had lodgings at Doddridge Farm in East Village, or even at Prowse.

When she had first arrived at the little village school she had earned for herself a reputation of being very strict, having taken over from a lady who had not been nearly sharp enough – had, in fact, allowed the children to 'play her up'; she was a Miss Meyer, or Mair, or some such name – I have not been able to check the spelling, I think she was only a 'Supply Teacher' in any case. Grandma found that the novelty of a young mistress who meant what she said and did, was resented by the boys and they decided to 'play her up' with the result that she used the cane pretty liberally. They had worn boots – hobnails – so she had bruised legs and it was then that she decided it is either them or me. Her father had been in the Army and been in charge of a Boys' School since retiring and he was a very strict disciplinarian even with her and her brother when they were children, and she knew she must maintain a good discipline if anybody was going to benefit from being in school. 'I'll tell my Mother of you' was the general chorus, so, quite soon there were several women waiting for her as she came out of school.

She raised her skirt enough to show them the bruises their sons had produced – her side of the story was accepted. Perhaps they knew their sons only too well!

I think that it is probably because of the somewhat 'difficult' start she had at East Village School that I value very highly the good reports she received for as long as Mr Llewellin produced his Church Magazine. Also, I have heard Grandma say that when she had big boys in her class – consisting of several 'Forms', as I remember them being called, in the big part of the Schoolroom – there was never any more trouble. Her word was law. In fact, one of the school inspectors waited outside for whoever he thought was visiting the classroom to finish a conversation and emerge. Only 'he' did not and in the end the Inspector had to go in himself, explaining his reluctance to interrupt a conversation with a young man.

Perhaps because of that reputation there were two suitors for the hand of the young mistress – Grandpa, William Stoyle, and his brother, Richard Stoyle. Time has shown that the families grew somewhat apart, but girls in the Stoyle family seem to have married away – there were ten children in all and their mother died very suddenly, expecting the eleventh child. I believe it was Mary Ann – the eldest girl – who acted as 'Mother'. Grandpa never forgot that once when things were 'not too good' Mary Ann had made a barley-meal pudding! Then there was Sarah – Grandma maintained a friendship with her until she died, then with her daughters.

Apparently one of the Stoyle boys was an invalid and, for a joke, some of his elder brothers organised the arrival in Prowse courtyard of the hearse, horse drawn of course! I believe he was Phillip. What the 'Old Man', Father John, thought of that is not recorded, anywhere!

I know a little more about Phillip and his brothers now than when I started writing this chapter. The circumstances of finding out this information are sad – it is a pity it takes a death in a family to bring relations close to each other but it does happen.

In this case I think I am right in saying that Mr Peter Stoyle and I are such distant cousins as to be 'third or fourth time removed'. Be that as it may, when I heard that his wife, Mary, was very ill I wrote to him.

When she died I wrote again and enclosed a copy of 'A READING' by C.S. Lewis entitled 'A Voyage'. This had been sent to me by Mrs Agnes Bremridge when my sister, Lavinia, died and it has given comfort to many since.

One night I received a telephone call from Mr Stoyle and we had quite a chat.We referred to some of the difficulties there had been years ago and I mentioned his Great Uncle Phillip, and so heard what was probably the truth of the matter. Phillip had been a very strong lad until he 'overdid' himself by carrying a 2½ cwt bag of grain in a very steep, muddy lane – (I know it). Peter said he never worked afterwards!

His brothers – William, Richard and John – probably thought

61

he was 'skiving' maybe his father, too!

Therefore the calling of the hearse was probably not a joke but a crude attempt to shame Phillip into trying to work!

Peter referred to the difficulties between the two branches of the family by saying that he thought the trouble was with the two Grandmothers.

Yes, I believe he is right, for I can remember Grandma saying that things were happy between the brothers until 'the old man died.' She referred to John Stoyle, of course, and apparently by the time he died William and his bride were occupying Doddridge, the adjoining farm down in East Village. By the old man's wish they shared farm machinery until it was made plain to William that the arrangement could not be continued. That being so, William must have considered there was no further point in remaining such a close neighbour, hence the move to Bremridge.

Grandma could not have been entirely happy about such a move when you consider that Doddridge was only a matter of a few minutes walk from the school, but from Bremridge with its rough lane it was quite a different matter and there was always the river, Holly Water, more or less guaranteed to flood every year. Then pony and trap transport was essential if Governess was to get to school.

I do not know how long was the period when she had to take over the milking early in the morning but she said more than once that a gypsy telling fortunes had prophesied she would be dealing with liquid all her life. Her thoughts had turned to beer and spirits and she had dismissed it as being extremely improbable.

The only hint of criticism I've heard from Grandma of Peter's Grandmother was in relation to 'old Aunt Brooks'. Now, who Aunt Brooks was is still a mystery for we have not been able to trace her relationship to the Stoyle's side of the family, so she may have been related to 'the Mays', since Mrs 'Prowse' had been a May.

Grandmother Stoyle perhaps voiced her concern for Aunt Brooks a little too loudly and it could have been repeated and come to the ears of the mistress of Prowse. Grandma said that she had been vexed to see the old lady struggling towards the dairy with a large pan of milk and thought that someone younger should have been given that job.

In this day and age it is difficult to realise just how hard people had to work with dairy duties – scalding big pans of milk were 'the norm' and I suppose everyone was so used to it that it was taken for granted that the pans were removed by whoever was available. Perhaps Aunt Brooks was a very willing person.

I do not know the order in which these events happened, the death of Auntie Alma the deaths of Richard and Lilly Stoyle. Auntie Alma, my Grandmother's very dearly beloved younger daughter died in Bristol, so the funeral was there and exceedingly quiet.

Brother Richard and daughter Lilly died at Prowse and I think they rest in Stockleigh English Churchyard and no doubt the Bremridge Stoyles were mourners. From that time on Grandma understood that she would not be welcome at Prowse, and did not visit the farm again.

When you remember that Richard and my Grandma had been courting before she actually married brother William it could have been only too easy to have said the wrong thing at such a sensitive time as a funeral.

I can remember going to Prowse myself. Lavinia and I had the task of collecting for some charitable effort at school. I have forgotten how the districts or areas are allocated – probably we were told to do what we could to collect as much as possible. We set off with the scantiest of knowledge about the Charity concerned so it was fortunate that the people we saw did not ask too many questions, and a couple of coppers usually pleased us – and got rid of us!

We walked to Prowse from the lower road, the Copper Oak road which was just opposite the Heath Bridge Lane. The farm lane was muddy, with a five barred gate out on the road beside a couple of cottages. It is where the Garnsworthys lived – it was their eldest son, Leslie, and Lavinia who had a fight over the 1928 Election, and neither of them knew anything about 'politics'!

Incidentally, this is the lane which, years before, must have been the downfall of Grandpa's brother, Phillip.

I am sure we approached the back door of Prowse which was answered after a few minutes by a lady in dark clothes wearing a black waist apron. Lavinia would have done the talking – she always did – while I stood by, all eyes and ears. We must have collected some money from our visit or I am sure Lavinia's disappointment at having to return 'empty-handed' would be

63

something I would have remembered.

On February 16th, 1887 Edmund Ford and Emily Jane Stoyle were married but no information ever seems to have been given as to where couples went to live.

I have some vague recollection of Grandma saying that one of Grandpa's sisters married a Mr Veysey, or Voisey, and lived at Cheriton Fitzpaine but that she had died at a fairly young age.

1887 was Queen Victoria's Jubilee Year and there is quite a long account with names of the Committee Members who were to undertake the organisation of all the festivities. The church bells were rung and there was a special service in the church at which the Te Deum and National Anthem were sung. Sandford village was well decorated. 'On leaving the church at 3 o'clock a procession was formed; and, headed by the band under Mr R. Hatten, all marched together to Creedy Park. On the flat top of the hill facing Sandford village, ten huge tables had been fixed, east and west of fine oak, each calculated to take 100 people at least. Carvers, waiters, and diners were all in position within five minutes after the tail end of the procession reached the Park. And who shall tell the awful amount of prime roast and boiled beef, plum pudding, tea, cider and beer which disappeared during the succeeding 45 minutes? Appetites were royal that day!'

Dinner over and Sir John Ferguson-Davie proposed the health of the Queen, honoured with 'Three times three' while the Vicar proposed a vote of thanks to Sir John; tables were cleared and the rest of the day was given to music, athletic sports and dancing but by 9.30 the Park was cleared, people went home thoroughly delighted and loyal 'to the backbone'. 'When will Sandford see such a day again?'

In this first magazine under 'Burials' the date is given and the name of the deceased. In the next and subsequent publications the age of the person concerned is given. Many babies and young children are noted but some of the population of Sandford lived to a very great age, well into the 80s and one or two were 90.

There are two little burials which must have been very hard for Mr Llewellin to undertake. His own sons apparently lived but a few hours and John was buried on the 7th April, one day old, while Harold Deanes Llewellin was christened on the 31st October, 1895 and buried on 1st November of the same year. The

64

first little boy was buried in 1893.

In nearly every issue there is a message from Mr Llewellin urging parents who have children to be baptised to consider the first Sunday in each month. I expect he thought 'he could do 'em all at the same service' but it is obvious that this did not happen and he had to officiate through the month, sometimes only three of four days apart. I wonder whether his thoughts were as kindly disposed to his flock then as they could have been!

A James Gale, aged 64, was buried in Sandford on the 26th January, 1892. I wonder if this is the 'Gale who was killed on the Upton Hellions road when he turned the trap over'? I know the corner where the accident happened, almost a double corner and always considered by us to be dangerous. Perhaps he was going too fast, perhaps the wheels of the gig just caught the bank, frightened the horse, and that was that. The banks did slope a little but not enough for sight around to see what was coming.

Under 'Baptisms' from the Church Registers, 1894, on the 21st February, another James Gale is brought into the church, so the family goes on.

In 1889 there is a 'Memorial to Lady Ferguson-Davie' headline and this covers much discussion as to what would be appropriate and something of which Sir John Ferguson-Davie could be 'in accord'. One of the Committee members for collecting subscriptions, etc. was John Stoyle, Grandpa's Father at Prowse. The memorial finally chosen was a painted window in the Parish Church.

Something which affects us all was introduced in 1894: 'The New Parish and District Councils'. Their functions and aims are fully described, who could be elected, term of office, and when the Annual Meetings must take place, within seven days of the 25th March.

These Councils seem to have been very much welcomed by 'The Church' – it relieved the Vestry 'Wardens' of much work and responsibility in several areas of good management. The article in the magazine also describes the election of the first Parish Councillors for Sandford as follows:

'On Monday, Nov. 19th, at a public meeting in the Central Schools, the Vicar in the chair, Mr W. Augustus Ferguson-Davie, J.P., gave an excellent address on the new Act, and answered questions respecting it. A small committee was chosen to receive

65

names of candidates, and to select and recommend a representative eleven to the electors; but it failed to do this.

On Tuesday, Dec. 4th, the first Parish Meeting under the Act was held in the Central Schools, and Mr Augustus Ferguson-Davie was elected chairman. The nomination papers of candidates, 23 in number, were received, and a show of hands for each was made in the room and carefully counted by the chairman. Eleven well known names were chosen in the room in the order of votes, but a poll of the parish was then demanded by one of the other candidates and on Tuesday the 18th December a poll by ballot was held in the Central Schools from 8 a.m. to 8 p.m. About 11 p.m. the Presiding Officer, Mr Palmer, solicitor, of Crediton declared the result. With one exception all the former candidates were accepted and the first Parish Council meeting for Sandford was held on Tuesday evening 1st January, 1894. Sir John Ferguson-Davie was proposed as Chairman but withdrew as he was so often away from the Parish, so Mr E.C. Norrish, of Gays, was unanimously elected Chairman, with Mr Henry Hattin as clerk and Mr L. E. Auber of Messrs. Fox, Fowler and Co's Bank, Crediton, Treasurer.

I find the article headed 'Churchyard Improvements' gives some interesting information. It says 'At last the old unsightly building at the north-east corner has been removed, and the church and yard look better than they have done for the past 150 years. It was probably about that time ago that Mr Bremridge, of Bremridge, Mr Read of Priorton, and Mr Kelland, of Yelland, with two others, are reported to have built part of the lower storey as a stable for their horses on Sundays; another part being added later by the then owner of Creedy for a similar purpose. Later again a room was built above the stables along their whole length of about 50 feet for a schoolroom for Mr Morgan, once schoolmaster at East Village; and there are still a good many parishioners living who were educated there, under the late Mr William Morgan's father, before the new school was built by Sir Humphry Davy in 1825'.

The fact that the gentlemen rode their horses to church makes me wonder what the ladies did. Perhaps those who were near enough made the journey on foot, although that would still have presented some difficulties in inclement weather. One hundred and fifty years before 1890 would have brought the date back to 1740 – in the time of the Grandparents of John and Anna Maria

Bremridge – and, indeed, the roads were very bad.

Another bit of information this item provides is about the East Village school where Mr Morgan was the Schoolmaster. The school I attended had certainly not been built in those far off days, so I wonder where the children went for their instruction as there seem to have been very few houses in the village itself which would be capable of accommodating more than a very small number of scholars. Although encouragement would have been provided by many families for their younger members to be taught and achieve good results it was by no means compulsory for children to go to school – I remember Mr Lee of Land telling Grandpa that he never went to school and that he could not read or write. He could count though!

I do not think that there is very much more to tell you from information given in the Sandford Parish Magazines – elsewhere I have referred to the very long years when the church was closed because of a great fight when the two men concerned killed each other, but apparently the church was closed again for a while about the time of Henry the Eighth's reign for the re-opening took place in 1523. Possibly major repairs, or even rebuilding parts of the structure made the closure necessary.

There was one other occurrence – a terrible fire in some old thatched cottages in Fanny's Lane across the road from the church. No one was actually killed and everyone around worked 'like mad' to save what could be taken out. The whole row of houses was evidently doomed for no water could be got at in time to supply the Sandford engine to be of service when necessary, except by bucket or barrel. The Crediton engine arrived about eleven o'clock and the Vicarage well was ingeniously made available for it about midnight.

A list of the occupants of the houses is given – no doubt all accommodated somehow, somewhere in the parish – and on 23rd January 1891 the Vicar called a Public Meeting and a committee was formed to collect subscriptions to provide some of the necessaries lost by them – I see Grandpa's name, W. Stoyle, is included, and £58.2/9d was received, of which £54.10/10d was spent and the balance divided between the Church and Chapel's poor boxes. How different, how very different, is the value of money today!

So I am shutting up the Parish Records, January, 1888 to January 1896, with so many names underlined which have meaning for me. The Gallins: I'm sure it was a Gallin boy who lived in Upton St. Hellions and had one of the goat kids which was the offspring of a goat specially kept for me to try to improve my weak chest and cut down the colds I caught, one after the other. I do not know whether the goat's milk did any better than ordinary cows milk. Goat would jump on to a special stand – with a little food in front of her – while Mum did the milking, and Grandpa said that he could not abide the goats or their milk!

There was a family of Horrell boys who went to East Village School. I believe they lived in one of the Dira Cottages. There are entries of Edith Spear – probably an aunt of 'our' Edith – and other Spears, James Gale and other Gales, yes, many names I recognise, but I am only going to mention two or three more – the Fishers 'Up Shop' in East Village, for over the door it said 'Maria Fisher, Licensed to sell tobacco'. There is a marriage notice of December 26th, 1892, of James Fisher and Maria Hamilton and about a year later a Baptism notice for Emily Elizabeth Fisher. Emily, when I knew her, was such a quiet, gentle person, living with her brother and sister-in-law 'Up Shop'. She became so ill, the last time I saw her, in bed, I could scarcely wait to go back to The Bungalow at Heath Bridge – and cry all the way back! She had been so pleased to see 'Miss Stoyle' as she called me, and on my next visit to Sandford Churchyard when I went to Devon again there was only a black painted vase to mark where she lay with the words 'Emily Fisher' on one side, no dates, no regrets, no nothing. I cried again, could not help it.

Under the heading 'Various' in the 1895 magazine I have just found an entry which puzzles me somewhat. Perhaps there is a simple explanation, but taken at its face value, it reads:

'July 14th. Saturday – St. Swithin's Guild Excursion by road to Exmouth; thence by the steamer 'Duchess of Devonshire', to Torquay or Sidmouth.'

Were there two ships of that name, perhaps I and II, one going one way, one the other, for Sidmouth is in the opposite direction to Torquay, or perhaps that should be 'a round trip' to Torquay and Sidmouth. The Sandford boys or young men would have been strangers to the sea in those days of restricted travel and their enjoyment would have been much less exuberant then than if the excursion or treat had been arranged even after The Great War. Did ice cream exist in those days?

7

Sandford and District Census

The Church was very much more important years ago and not only in the matter of teaching and preaching Christian values. It had a very important role in looking after the people in the parish before the days of the Parish Councils and of course the District Councils.

A family had to be 'of the Parish' and I know that 'outsiders' in some cases had difficulty in becoming recognised as belonging to one particular area.

Therefore, the system of 'Overseers' and 'Wardens' had much to recommend it and it seems that it was only men who held those positions. It would not have been seemly for a lady to undertake the duties of investigating 'new' families. It must be remembered that some of the 'travellers' were exceedingly poor, often having too many children to be catered for properly.

The Church also seemed to be very much involved in providing shelter in the 'Poor Law Homes' for unfortunates who were perhaps not well enough to work, often children and young people, and conditions in some of the Homes were spartan enough! Food and shelter was given and as soon as possible and as often as possible young people were sent out to work on farms. Apprentices could, therefore, be provided by the Church and no doubt the Overseers and the Wardens kept a sharp eye both on the apprentices and on the farm, or other establishment, where they had been sent – the bigger the farm, the more apprentices! Some did go to shops or harness makers, even string-makers!

It was the Rev. George Bent, the Vicar of Sandford, who

organised the first Census in 1790. The next record is dated 1793 and the final 'Parish Numbering' took place in 1800.

Thanks to Mrs Munday I have photocopies of pages referring mainly to East Village and district and it is obvious that numbering his flock had given the Reverend much work. It appears that he used pages from a big book with nine columns and it is extraordinary the amount of information he has managed to collect, for the name of the village, or large farm, even down to smallholdings and cottages, is the first entry. Then the properties are numbered, with the same number following through each year. Where there is a husband his Christian name is given, followed by his wife's Christian name and also her maiden name in brackets. One or two ladies have had two husbands and both names are given. Yes, he was very thorough.

Then all the children are included with their Christian names and he completes each page by entering the numbers under the heading as appropriate, i.e. 'Children. Servants. Apprentices. Inmates. Total.'

Some of the spellings are a little odd, 'Eastern Village', Heaths Bridge', Lithybrook' (Lilleybrook), and the property we always knew as 'Whiterose' (over Preston where the Heards lived) is given as Whiterowes'.

I can imagine the Reverend Bent riding around his parish collecting all this information day after day. Was it exciting, was it resented by some? We shall never know.

Therefore, at Heaths Bridge – and this seems to be the only entry without a number – there was William and Mary Smith (Glass) with their two children, John and Mary. Two servants, Ann Pope and Elizabeth Hawkins, plus one inmate, John Drew. Perhaps he was a relative.

New Inn, No 297: Robert and Sarah (Down) Holcomb, two children, Sarah and Mary for the first two census years. The 1800 entry is for Robert and Mary Morris, Robert Joseph Morris and one child, Elizabeth.

298: Francis and Joan (Welch) Yard, two children, Elizabeth and Ann. By 1793 there was also one inmate, John Yarde, but by 1800 there is no mention of Francis.

299: John and Elizabeth Whitton, with two previous names, 'Drake and Tremlett'. Inmate, called Francis Tremlett. By 1800 that family had disappeared, with William Quick and Mary

70

(Holmead) living there with their three children, Abraham, George and William.

300: William and Mary (Venn) Yarde, their children Ann, William and Francis. By 1793 Ann is not mentioned.

301: John and Agnes Bond. She was formerly a Pope and Labdon, so one husband had died. There were no children. They were still there in 1800.

302: Joseph Morris married Elizabeth Tapp and lived there for the two first census years. There were no children.

303: Robert and Thomasin Jason. ('Giles and Tucker). By 1793 William Ford and Mary (Shorland) lived there with one child.

304: William Densem married Mary Bradford. There were three children, William, Elizabeth and John for the first year, but no mention of the boys thereafter.

305: Robert and Thomasin (Gosland) Fursdon, three children, John, Robert and Sam. In 1793 another child was added, Richard. In 1800 Sam, Richard and Ann are listed.

307: Ann Elstone (Perkins) was now living on her own with two children, Sarah and Ann. No record exists for 1800.

Perhaps one of these numbered entries refers to Ivy Cottage on Bremridge Farm, but Bremridge is mentioned . . .

296: Richard and Anna Maria (Bremridge) Melhuish, four children, John Bremridge, Thomas, Richard and Mary, one servant, Ann Haydon, four apprentices, Thomas Grant, John Haylows, Mary Parker and Henry Frend. That makes a total of eleven people. In 1793 there were only two apprentices, Mary Parker and Henry Frend. In 1800, Mary Venner was a servant and there were three apprentices, John Bradford, John Shilston and Sarah Edwards.

Priorton Farm seems to have a total of 13 individuals living there in 1790, 16 in 1793. That was in the time of Richard and Mary (Tremlett), but when Phillip Kelland and Ann (Morrish) took over that large farm the number had gone up to 18, there were ten children.

Doddridge, Dira, Prowse, Cross – all have their families listed and their servants and apprentices included.

The property I always knew as 'Pakeham' but spelt 'Pacombe' in the census papers lies between Preston Bridge and Heath Bridge, with its main roadway out towards the first bridge while

71

the exit which comes out beside Dira Cottages is still only a hard track. When the Snells lived there I have seen members of the family driving a pony and trap out on to the Heath Bridge road and up toward East Village. If they needed to go to Sandford it must have been much nearer than using the proper road, probably full of potholes anyway, and going all up around Cross.

The occupants in 1790 were Daniel and Mary (Eveleigh) Newton with two children, John and Mary. In 1793 Daniel Tremlet and Mary (Eveleigh) were there with children John and Mary. By 1800 William Norrish and Elizabeth (Densem) and two children were listed. They all had the valley to themselves, with the lush meadow beside the river and a good view of Hill Farm and the wooded area at Heath Bridge.

Later still, an elderly couple lived there, kept some livestock, kept themselves to themselves – how could they do otherwise as they were both as deaf as 'postes'? They could be heard shouting at each other, so I have been told!

Pacombe is interesting though for several owners or occupiers of Bremridge have bought the property or tenanted it. First, the Melhuishes in the 18th century, then tenants of Bremridge Farm, and, lastly as far as I know, it was owned by the Thorne family when Bremridge was their home.

There could well be another and completely different reason why some names of the children were missing from the second and subsequent census lists. In spite of the hard times they were living in some families did produce strong offspring and when they were old enough to be of some use on a farm they were 'placed' and became the apprentices, the number varying and consequent upon the size and status of the farmer and his business.

Some of the children were lucky enough to have found 'a good billet' – I would like to think that Bremridge was such a one. There was always the threat of going 'back to the Parish' – a stigma indeed – if for any reason the young person could not get on with 'Maister' or 'Missus', or were unsatisfactory in work.

Money seems to have been extremely scarce and even the old penny, when it needed 240 to make the value of our present pound, was considered to be worth working for, so with clothes and keep and work to occupy their time perhaps the children of the Heath Bridge village population were not doing too badly, if, in fact, they were working for Sandford farmers.

From 1733 to 1778 men on farms earned 1/-d (5p) per day all the year round, but with food and drink that was reduced to 5d in the winter and 6d for the rest of the year, with one quart of cider per day in winter but an unlimited quantity in the summer. This dependence on cider explains why there were so many orchards, good ones, too! There was also a cider tax and in 1763 the Bishop of Exeter had an apple thrown at his head by an irate farmer!

The Sandford Census figures give no indication of just who lived where in the Heath Bridge Village, so there is no knowledge as to the identity of the occupants of Rose Cottage. That period is finished, gone, done with and I must concentrate on the scrappy information I do possess.

Somewhere from my Bremridge days the name of Labbett seems to be connected with Heath Bridge and I have found another connection recently. I have been looking through the list of people who subscribed to an appeal for funds for renewal of Sandford Church bells. The people who gave most are listed first and foremost (as would be expected), then come many names of farmers. Most of them stumped up to the tune of 10/-d (50p in today's money), including 'W. Stoyle' and 'H. Stoyle' and the list continues until people who gave 6d each are listed together.

Last of all are two names contributing 3d each, one is 'Fisher' and the other 'Labbett', and I think the first one is a contribution from the people 'Up shop'.

When I read this list I felt that 'Labbett' would have been in Rose Cottage for it rang a bell with what I am sure I heard someone saying years ago about the 'Labbetts' at Heath Bridge.

The date of the list, apparently audited, was the 2nd March, 1901, but probably begun some time before.

If Mr Labbett left Heath Bridge shortly after that date it gives a good twenty years for the property to decay and become the ruin it was when Grandma became the owner.

I know the names of most of the tenants from that time onwards and until I became the owner in 1945 when Grandma died.

There were the Stickings, Mr and Mrs I do not think there had ever been any 'Baby Stickings' but I know that he had been in one of the Services in the First World War. Lean, bronzed, and healthy looking he had been recruited in harvest time to help Grandpa. He

d

did not speak like a native of Devon though where he came from was never discussed. Mrs Sticking was plump, always smiling and good natured. She cleaned the school for a while and they left Heath Bridge – if I remember rightly – to go up to the village to live.

The next tenant was a complete contrast to these good tenants for 'Mr' could only be described as a pig of a man. He had a very pale-faced, long suffering wife who would do anything to keep the peace. To be fair to him, he must also have seen war service for he was described, somewhere, as being 'shell-shocked' so perhaps one should feel sorry rather than seeking to lay blame at his door. Dark-haired, ungainly and ugly, with a permanent twitch in the side of his face, he strode along with a jerky movement.

I can remember being horrified at his action in killing all the chickens his wife was rearing because she had been attending to them rather than getting his tea ready.

They left the cottage and went to live in Upton Hellions next door to the Chudleys. It was, in fact, this miserable man who drowned himself in the river at the bottom of the hill, the 'dip' referred to elsewhere.

I think we must have been the next occupants of Rose Cottage and no doubt we quickly moved across from The Bungalow as the cottage became vacant.

After the large rooms at Bremridge and the comparatively small ones in The Bungalow, certainly the larger areas in the cottage were very welcome. Not that we could really spread out all that much and I know Grandma still kept the shed high up on the slope. It had a good pebbled floor and her boxes rested in the dry and she could 'turn out' in comparative comfort when she felt she could face the task. All my *Chambers Encyclopaedias*, *Culpeppers Herbal*, the *Women's World* must have travelled that way!

Lennard Matthews then became tenant of The Bungalow, with his wife, Cora. He used to cycle off to his work, which I believe was on Priorton Farm, for Farmer May.

The people who followed us at Rose Cottage were the Hammetts. Mr (Frank) was a brother to Mrs (Mary) Heard at Whiterose over Preston. Frank was a very useful character to the farmers around, sheep-shearing, harvesting, rabbit catching, he could turn his hand to almost anything.

From about 1932 or 33 until 1959 was a very long let – we were always very good friends.

For a little while the property was empty and then young Bill Hammett and his wife, formerly Amy Garnsworthy, became tenants and remained at Heath Bridge for several years before going into Crediton in a cottage near the church.

8

Was There a Ghost at Dowrich?

The first I heard about any sinister happenings in the district was when I met the girls from the Turner family at school. Speaking from memory after all this time, I think the eldest girl was Lloydie and there was a Zoe and there could also have been a Doreen, but it was Lloydie who came to school one morning with a piece of news which set her above all her classmates.

The Turners lived 'over Dowrich way' in a cottage and 'Mum' Turner was friendly with at least one of the servants at the big house. Lloydie passed on the news of unexplained happenings there, rumbles for no reason, and noises which could not be explained, feelings in the staff that they were not alone. In other words, Dowrich House was haunted.

It was probably then that the Connibear boys added to the tale. They knew all about old 'Dan Dowrich' being drowned at Dowrich Bridge and coming back up the hill at a cockstride a year because he had been 'witched' by someone whom he had wronged. 'Don't pass there at night 'cos he still watches 'ee from the water!'

I do remember that the big house had its own water supply produced by means of a pump which went night and day, 'thump, thump, thump' and certainly this added to the uneasy feeling of passers by, for it was sited not far from the river.

It was only when I read Mrs Daphne Munday's book *A Parish Patchwork* that I realised there could have been some truth behind such tales – besides giving quite a full description of the house and surroundings she has a chapter headed 'The Dowrich Ghost', and I think I shall have to quote it all to give you the full picture. She says:

'Dowrich House is said to be haunted by the Ghost of Lewes Dowrich, the last in the line of that ancient family, who died in 1717.

'It was reported that, at Dowrich Bridge, the last of the Dowriches, returning home late one winter's night after a considerable consumption of brandy-punch at the house of a neighbouring squire, fell from his horse and was killed.

'Some say he died of a broken neck and other reports say that he drowned. The bridge itself has a low parapet and when his horse put its foot in a pothole and threw him, he could well have been thrown over the bridge into the water and either drowned, or broken his neck, or maybe both!

'It was alleged that Lewes Dowrich had been cursed by an old woman who he had turned out of her cottage. She told him that he would die by drowning, afterwards returning to the house by "Cock's Steps".

'Cock's Steps meant that he would go up the hill towards Dowrich at the rate of a cock's stride in every moon, i.e., about six inches a month. The road was narrow and if he fell he had to go back to the place of his death and start again. It was calculated that it would take him 256 years to get from the bridge to the house, a distance of about 525 yards. For this reason, successive owners of the house were warned by the country people to keep the bottom step at the entrance to the gatehouse at least 18 inches high to keep him from getting in. The step is still kept high today. The inhabitants of East Village were said to see the "Wicked Dowrich's eyes glaring at them from the brook".

'In 1973, when the house changed hands, a new driveway with a cattle grid was made, not disturbing the steps or the gatehouse in any way but making a new entrance through the wall.'

'On Friday September 7th 1973, the section of wall had been removed but the cattle grid was not yet in place. In broad daylight the ghost was seen by the gardener, Mr F.E. Larner. The following is his story as told to Professor Trease.

' "Whilst cutting the front lawn, I was at the top of the slope facing the gatehouse and with the house on my left, when I saw, or think I saw, the following. A three quarter view of a man sitting

77

on a black horse, possibly a mare, which was short-legged and held its head low as though having ridden hard, or perhaps placid and standing perfectly still. Sitting on the horse was a man in a long black coat, the tail of which was on the back of the horse. The coat had a cape, one side of which was thrown back over the right shoulder.

' "The man sat perfectly still, holding the reins in both hands, but in his right hand he had a hunting crop which appeared to be of silver. He was of stocky build, not tall, not short and not fat but with a more than 36-inch chest.

' "His face was inclined to be on the heavy side rather than thin and the features completely expressionless except for the eyes. They appeared to be alive and the expression from them was a friendly or favourable one. The man's hair was of a fair colour, like pale gold, not short by my standards but not so long as some youths of today, and a lock or locks fell across the right forehead. Neither the man nor the horse moved the whole time that I saw them, which must have been 5 to 8 seconds or a little longer, and at the end just disappeared. Whilst I find it difficult to believe I saw anything other than sunshine and shadows, I cannot ignore that my eyes did see something. The three outstanding things as far as I am concerned were the hunting crop, the eyes and the hair.

' "When further questioned about the hunting crop, the approximate age and the presence of a hat, or even a wig, he replied, 'The shaft as well as the shoulder of the crop was silver; he was middle aged, approximately that of my own which is 48; (Lewis Dowrich was 40) he was not wearing a hat and the hair was too short and carefree to be a wig."

'The observations were made at about 4.15 p.m. in bright sunlight at a distance of about 43 yards. Mr Larner was said to have been a good witness and with acute powers of observation.

'We must assume that Lewis Dowrich saw his opportunity and managed to re-enter his garden via the hole in the wall, with no steep step to hinder him. Another few hours and the cattle grid was in place. Do ghosts travel over cattle grids? The odd thing about this episode is that it actually was 256 years since Lewis was killed and he could have reached the garden in that time in Cock's Steps, provided he had kept going all the time and did not have to retrace his steps. One thing puzzles me, how did the horse get there? Did the horse also travel in Cock's Steps?

'Mr Larner had only been in the district for a week or so and had never heard the story, but the ghost has not, as far as we know, been seen again and so we hope that having arrived home, Lewis is now resting in Peace.'

I am not sure why he had become 'old Dan Dowrich' over the years instead of Lewis; it must be the same man!

9

'Peter' and Family

Now, I must move my story on, for there is much to tell to bring the history of the three dwellings more or less up to the present day so I must go back to the time when Grandpa died and we left the farm, but not the district.

We left Bremridge to go down to The Bungalow ourselves. What else could we do, for Grandpa had given notice to quit, anyway, and by that time Dad had returned to the Midlands after the barney over Annie Furze becoming pregnant and having to return to the 'Institootion'? Years and years later when contact had been re-established with him I was told a little more about it all and learned that he certainly had nothing to do with it – 'It was some fella over Cheriton she used to knock around with'!

I did know that Dad had been very ill after he left Devon, but he was rarely mentioned and I was too young to realise the significance of seeing him leave by the court gate and walk up over Quarry-pit Hill, but I know I watched him until he was out of sight and that he had turned several times and waved. It was a Crediton Fair Day, so I suppose all the harvest would have been in by that time and it would have been the most convenient time for him to leave.

We had Edith Spear with us for seven or eight years, so you can guess that I must have been quite young. I do not think that Lavinia recalls much more than I do, though I can remember some teas with custard down in the end room when there was trouble between Dad and Grandpa in the kitchen!

There had to be a farm sale at Bremridge as we 'came out' and some of the things which we had used were purchased by the new tenant, the young man who had first visited the farm on the hill with his father in the high trap pulled by a strong pony, 'Kit', several months before and soon after Grandpa had given notice.

There was the separator in the back kitchen, the large oak cupboard in the most lived-in room in the house, the kitchen, and many small things as well, and the settle and Grandpa's large kitchen table with the three drawers.

The Williamses were – and still are – a wonderful family. Whereas the Stoyles were quiet and 'just so' this new young man and his young family were full of fun, song and laughter. There were four children, all to take their turn at East Village School, but, later, there were four more, two of them born at Bremridge.

I can remember going to Upton Hellions Church one Sunday afternoon with Mr and Mrs Williams, Lavinia was there too. Mr Williams made a remark about a blue bottle fly which persisted in coming near our pew, which nearly set us all off giggling!

Work, he seemed to be able to work all the hours God provided – and enjoy it! But there was some critic in those far-off days who was not happy that he also worked on a Sunday to get the hay harvest picked up before it rained. The attitude to work on a Sunday, I imagine, had not changed since the days of Richard Melhuish and his Anna Maria!

Although we had left Bremridge – at least in the physical sense – the spirit of the Stoyles hung about the farm and I have photos showing the young family out in the orchard and Grandma near her favourite apple tree enjoying herself talking to the kiddies. If children showed any interest Grandma was only too ready to explain, to help and to encourage.

From the bungalow we walked up between the gorse and Nannypark hedge over the rough track on several evenings because we had been invited to supper, a most enjoyable meal, always, and a very happy one.

It must have been very difficult for the young farmer as it had been for Grandpa because times were hard, I could almost say 'distressed', in the farming industry, but he never seemed to let it get him down. Before long, though, the gorse disappeared and other improvements were made. Then, of course, when the Milk Board encouraged more dairy work by the collecting of milk churns the monthly 'Milk Cheque' made a tremendous difference, so more cows were added.

No, the lorry did not go up the hill to collect the milk – it had to be brought down every day by horse and cart and left on a specially erected concrete platform almost opposite the entrance to The Plot.

Of course, selling the milk like this meant that very little butter would have been made – and what a relief to the farmers' wives that must have been! It also probably meant that there was no skim milk for pigs and the feeding of calves could have been by other than what we call 'ordinary milk', some prepared substance.

Just a little more about the Williams family before I forget it. At Ivy Cottage under the hill at one time there was a family called 'Parker', with several daughters: Maude, Molly and Phyllis who joined our gang going up and down the road to East Village School, while their father worked for Mr Williams. I think it was the first two girls who were perfect 'Ginger Tops', while the youngest was fair. This must have been before Mr Leigh and his daughter with her husband lived there.

The majority of families who had lived in Ivy Cottage seemed to have had several children and, some years later, there was another family where the mother thought she had produced enough children and did not want any more.

Mr Williams told this tale, and laughed heartily! The lady concerned saw an advertisement in a paper or magazine about how to prevent becoming pregnant.

'Foolproof method', it said, 'never fails' and anyone wanting the secret was asked to send a postal order, and I believe the sum mentioned was 5/-d (25p in today's money).

The lady thought about it for a while and decided that the amount asked for would have been a good investment – if it worked – so, in due course, she got her postal order and sent it off.

When, after days of waiting, the postman brought her a letter she opened it eagerly.

The foolproof method said: 'KEEP AWAY FROM MEN!'

In those days, and still, possibly, today in some country districts, when there was illness in a family the neighbours would turn to and help by taking care of the baby of the family, taking it into their own family to live as one of their own. Mrs Miller at Doddridge, well known for her kindness and Christian sympathy,

82

took one of the young Bedfords when their mother was unwell and another time Dora, her daughter, went up to 'Down' to help nurse a lady who was very ill.

So it was all in the order of things that when Mrs Williams was struck down with an illness which was indeed serious Mum and Grandma offered to take the baby down to Rose Cottage where they were living then. There was the pram, the high chair and all the paraphernalia which a toddler needs, and I believe that Mum was delighted to have charge of a 'little one' again – and what a delightful toddler he was.

I can remember how impressed we were when he solemnly and carefully cleared his little plate of all the food which he had been given, there were no long faces or tantrums, he just sat and cleared everything!

Mrs Williams' mother, Mrs Tucker, and 'Auntie Kate' were probably sharing the farmhouse by that time and would have been looking after the three older children, all possibly going to school, and coping with much of the other work beside helping with the invalid.

10

Moving to Exeter

We remained in the Cottage until 1933, but the problem which was looming up had occupied the thoughts of Grandma and Mum for many months. It was, what is the future of the girls or for the girls when it is time to leave school? If we remained in the country it would mean (a) cycling to a job in Crediton every day, (b) for many years working for another farmer, or (c) taking on some interest and working at home, such as art in Lavinia's case, but not in mine because I was no good at it, and really there was not much future in it unless you really were outstanding. So, (c) was out, (b) was not very attractive to either of us, nor was (a), therefore all discarded.

As soon as she left school at East Village, Lavinia cycled into Crediton every day, through Bremridge, and went up to Exeter to St. Wilfrid's School. She did this for nearly a year until it was realised that she had strained her heart. There followed about three weeks in bed to aid recovery, and we knew that the long cycle rides for her, every day, must cease.

By this time, also, I was saying 'Goodbye' to East Village School, so the decision to go to Exeter to live had to be made – Crediton being thought of as only a half-way measure if St. Wilfrid's School was to be reached every day. I left the village school in December, and there followed a period in which Mum and I, particularly, did the active house-hunting in Exeter.

There was one morning I shall never forget. We cycled Broxfords way and encountered thousands of toads all trying to cross Park Hill, normally such a lovely hill to free-wheel down.

Some had already been squashed under the wheels of the few cars which had passed that way – we got off and walked but it was still quite a job to avoid stepping on the hopping toads. With the superstition connected with the poor little creatures we knew our journey that day would be wasted – and so it was, we might as well just have turned around and gone back home!

But another day we collected from Messrs. Mudge & Baxter, Estate Agents and Auctioneers, details of a house which had been empty for several years. It was a large house, with large rooms, on the corner of Jesmine Road and Blackboy Road, often called Bath Road we discovered.

Mum and I looked at this house, in very poor condition and in great need of modernising and redecoration, it was just about within a price which could be afforded and was, therefore, eventually bought. The house next door was also empty and had been for even longer, it was supposed to be haunted we found out after no. 84 had been bought, but we never felt nor saw anything untoward!

We moved into the big city in March and there followed the renovating and modernising, all carried out by a Mr Martin from Wardrew Road, St. Thomas, Exeter, and his workmen. One large room was divided to make a bathroom and an additional area for storage, always known as 'The Vestibule' and here some of the boxes already referred to were stored as well as the big cupboard which was now half the size of the large walk-in 'clothes closet' which had been in the room above the kitchen at Bremridge – still quite a good size!

There was a jumble of furniture in the big front room for days and I can remember going in before any curtains were up, sitting in a big chair and watching the passers by. It was dark, but there was a street light on the other side of the road which shed some illumination right into the room and, although I knew that I could not be seen, I still felt frightened. I saw some men come out of The Ropemaker's Arms just down the road on the other side, not drunk, but definitely merry! What had we done? We had left the security of the country and what had we come to? Still, it was too late to go back, and there would have been no point in doing so.

Lavinia and I went to St. Wilfrid's School together, in the time of Sr. Beatrice, Sr. Edith, Sr. Louise and several others. ('Sr.' is, of course, 'Sister'.) I enjoyed those days, the ladies were so gentle and kind, and very patient! As usual, there was one fly in the ointment and he was in the shape of Major Harvey the retired officer who instructed us in 'Gym' at Thornton Hall!

On Thursday mornings after the early lessons all the senior classes were assembled and we walked 'in crocodile file' from the school round the St. Bartholomew area, crossed the lower end of North Street, up Paul Street, under Northernhay beside the iron railings on one side and two or three small fish ponds on the other where red fish darted about under foliage with big leaves, into the end of New North Road, and up to Thornton Hill where the hall was situated very near the top.

There was Major Harvey waiting to put all of us through the different exercises the wall-bars, the beam, the horse, and the clubs. Oh yes, there were ropes hanging from the ceiling with their big rings and they terrified me! I never reached them, but I did not dislike the clubs too much – swinging exercises to the tune of ''Peek-a-boo, peek-a-boo come from behind the chair, peek-a-boo, peek-a-boo I see you hiding there'. At home, at Bremridge, I thought I could climb a ladder with the best of them, but when it came to the wall-bars, doing it to music, I always seemed to be doing it wrong! The beam was also 'out' as far as I was concerned, so after a few attempts I managed to remain in the background and let all the others who enjoyed the exercises get on with them. The fact that Major Harvey shouted – I suppose he thought he was training the troops again – made it all the worse for me – so, as soon as I possibly could I remained at school and studied commercial work, probably under the kindly eye of Sister Edith, or Sister Ellen.

At exactly noon a bell was rung and the 'Angelus' had to be said. This sounded beautiful when the whole class was there but not so good when one lonely little voice was the only one to accompany that of whichever Sister was present!

I have forgotten how Lavinia enjoyed Major Harvey's lessons, she must have gone to at least some of them. The girls did not come back to school again in the morning but went straight home to dinner.

After a while it was possible to think about letting some of the rooms – there were too many for just four people – as 84 Blackboy Road was expected to provide some of the funds necessary for comfortable living. So the large lower front room was turned into a bed-sitting-room to accommodate Mrs King and her daughter. There is a photo of them among Grandma's papers. Mrs King was an old lady, not bedridden exactly, but quite frail and now and again Miss King would be very puzzled as to what to provide to tempt her mother to eat, or find something for her to enjoy.

Miss King had an impediment in her speech, 'a very thick voice'. One day she bought a rabbit for her mother's dinner and when she was asked whether Mrs King had enjoyed it, she said 'No, she didn't – it smelt something like the cat did on the mat when it was shut in the other day!'

I know they paid a rent of 50p per week.

Then there was Miss Phillips, who had a first floor room. She, again, was elderly and very careful with cash. She used '84' for a holiday, and Mum had to do the cooking for her. One-third of a pint of milk in a small dish was allowed for a rice pudding – I still have that little dish. There would be a gap of several months, and then she would come again.

There was also a very genteel 'Miss Norse', a tall, very thin lady, usually in long black clothes.

The second floor became a small flat, and home to a Mr and Mrs Plant with their young daughter, 'Joan'. I believe that they came from Torquay but when business interests made a move to Exeter necessary they were glad of this accommodation at a rent of £1 per week.

Lavinia and I had the large front attic with the round window, and this gave us a beautiful view of all who were going up and down the road. We were particularly interested in seeing the mounted soldiers early in the morning out at exercise with, probably, thirty or forty horses – all alike from our vantage point. We had to stand on one of the precious family boxes so that we could look out together and not take it in turns to have a view. I do not think that the soldiers ever looked up and saw us – we were only interested in the horses in those days, or, at least, I was.

A very elderly nurse with unusual eyes – blue with a large brown spot – occupied the back attic for a while, another 50p per week. It was this old lady who had to refuse the task – for 12½p a week – of taking little Alec Grezo from his home in Magdalen Street across Exeter to Norwood School in Pennsylvania Hill every morning. I did it until it was no longer necessary and my half-crown per week (as it was then) provided me with a reputation for being 'monied'. The old nurse had been abroad looking after the children of well-to-do English people and was full of all sorts of odd stories!

It was a happy time for Mum and Grandma, glorying in the new-fangled gadgets which electricity provided, particularly the kettle, the electric light and the electric iron replacing the kettle and flat irons on the hob and the oil lamps which had called for so much attention. It certainly was no wonder they were discarded, dumped, or sold as antiques as soon as possible. But there was one little iron lamp kept 'for a keep-sake' and, yes, you know what I am going to say 'I still have it'. It was the one in use which Grandma used to bring up to the bedroom in Bremridge when she came to hear our prayers, so, Marilyn, how could I get rid of that?

There were all sorts of meetings, exhibitions, etc. which Grandma, particularly, attended and enjoyed. I can remember several at the Civic Hall – often of a religious nature, or instructive in some way – there was one with a lady in charge called the 'Marachel' (I am not sure of the spelling now but that is what it sounded like) and another where a gentleman was so skilled in his profession to do with medicine that he could judge a man's occupation just by looking at him and studying his bearing for a few moments. I think I usually went with Grandma, while Mum stayed at home busy with the jobs which all housewives had. Lavinia, I am not sure about, but I do not remember her coming very often.

The fact that we had gone to Exeter did not cut us off from the friendship of the people out in the country, for there were visits at convenient times of the people who had taken Bremridge, the Miller girls, Ivy Heard and the tenants of Rose Cottage – all very welcome. Sometimes the girls would stay with us for a few days, sometimes it would be a short visit, they just had time 'to run up and see us'.

After he left school one of my greatest friends stayed with us during the week while he had a job in Exeter, going home for the weekend. His sister had already been accepted for a nursing career at The Royal Devon and Exeter Hospital – and glad enough she was, too, to come and see us, for she would sit down on the sofa and be fast asleep in no time. She was not too well fed at the Hospital in those days and could rely on 'something' at our place.

I left St. Wilfrid's School at the end of July, 1935, and began work as a shorthand typist in an insurance office in Southernhay East, while Lavinia already had a job in the art world. Things had already moved on a little at '84' for Lyons Tea Houses (I believe that is the right title) sent us four of their young ladies to look after for several months – I do not remember their names now. There had also been a number of students from Exeter University to accommodate. Lavinia had been quite keen on one of them for a while – until she found that he had another young lady and then she took action – she punctured the front wheel of his bicycle with a safetypin twenty-eight times! All he did was to laugh, as he mended one and then another and another puncture; he took it as a compliment that she had thought so much of him to do such a thing.

Everyone knows what happened in 1939! I had just become a Civil Servant and had to work away from Exeter, and I know that this worried 'the Ancestors' as I called them at times. I did come home at weekends, though, and on one visit learned that we were to billet some soldiers. The first one who had been conducted to '84' said that his name was Williams, from South Wales, 'Ithel', the second one said his name was Williams, from North Wales, 'Noel'. The first was tall and very fair, the second shorter and very dark; Christian names had to be used, of course, to identify t'other from which. Both were very nice young men, and we have kept in touch with Noel through all the years, and his wife, too.

For a house in town, '84' had quite a good sized garden and Mr Leigh used to come in from Ivy Cottage and see to it for us – perhaps twice a year. He was the father of Mrs Gardner, retired, and looking for small, odd jobs. Mr Leigh had a full beard and had obviously been a hard-working country man. He was not very used to the ways of town and one day he saw a car – a big green car – stop outside our house and the young man actually ran in – without ringing the bell. Mr Leigh was worried, 'I took the number of his car', he said 'he might have been a burglar'. But he was not, he was Dr Watson who had called to see Grandma who was recovering after a cold.

It was Mr Leigh who had erected a small shed for us in the corner of the garden for about half a dozen hens. He came in with

89

us to help straighten up when we first moved in, and was quite happy to regard his visits to us as a holiday, staying several days at a time.

Siegfried Hettasch was a young German who stayed with us for a month or so during his long college holidays, in 1938, I think. He was studying to become a missionary in the Moravian faith, and was very earnest and sincere. His English was spoken with a decided German accent and feelings at that time were running a little high where the Germans were concerned.

Siegfried needed his hair cut and went to a barber somewhere down in Sidwell Street, and the request he made to that worthy was 'please may I have my hairs cut?' The barber did not say anything, but became busy with his scissors, snipping away here, there and everywhere. The result was about a 2" high growth which stuck up like a black shoe-brush right on top of his head.

Like the good-natured boy he was, Siegfried just laughed. 'It will grow," he said, 'and I'll have moved on before I need it cut again.'

He had a very heavy bicycle, on which he carried a small tent and everything he could need for camping. He had needles and cotton and could make repairs as well as any woman and he was truly self-sufficient.

Many years later he came back to visit us again. By this time he had several children, and a wife who had to stay in her lodgings because she had some illness and could not accompany him. His youngest was a little boy he called 'Peckie, Peckie', but I have forgotten the names of the girls.

Siegfried told us of some of his experiences in Canada where he had been ministering to his 'flock', both as their Pastor and their Doctor. He had once had an urgent call to a lady with appendicitis, and knew that an operation was imperative immediately. The district seems to have been remote, for he had to do the operation himself under the most primitive of conditions, and was extremely glad that he had been given enough medical training to carry out such an operation. The patient recovered.

Siegfried also had a sister, Gerda, staying with friends in Exeter. I can remember that we cycled to Exmouth with them once or twice and enjoyed ourselves on the sand up by the rocks. They could swim in the sea, but Lavinia and I could only paddle.

In those days car traffic on the roads was not heavy as it is now in the 1990s, and there were some early morning rides for us which were very enjoyable. The air was so fresh and clear, the roads comparatively safe, and the world was ours! In terms of miles I do not suppose we had time to go any great distances, for we had to come back and either go to school or get ready for work, but we often took the road towards 'Fairmile' or 'Sowton'. I think it is questionable whether these places would now be recognised by us as the same little villages we knew for certainly they have grown. In fact, I believe that Sowton now has a trading estate and that the West Country Show is held somewhere near.

11

The War

When I was at Salisbury I came home for some weekends, and returned first thing on Monday morning, catching a train from Exeter Central Station at about 6.30 a.m. I saw it gradually get light as the train raced along and I still remember some of the beautiful mornings with the sun rising red over the distant hills. This must have been before the black-out made such a scene only a memory for stations were later raced through, the blinds were firmly pulled down, and a traveller could not really be sure where he was en route!

I can remember one or two journeys where the passengers were jabbering away in some foreign language with very few clues as to their country of origin.

On a journey from Crediton to Exeter many, many years before this time I am writing about, my Mother and her sister, Auntie Alma, were joined in their compartment by two tall darkish gentlemen who were conversing in a foreign language. Again it was wartime, the First World War, and as the girls had no idea of what the German language sounded like, they wondered whether they were spies and perhaps some action should be taken – report them to some authority or other. There was much relief when the gentlemen spoke in English to each other mentioning two or three well-known Welsh towns, with a very pronounced Welsh accent!

I remember the day the Second World War was declared very well. I was living and working in Salisbury and staying at the Princess Christian Hostel in Fisherton Street. I had come to an office in that town about nine months before and accommodation was not by any means luxurious or lavish, it was comfortable. Often I shared a room with my sister, when she also came up from Exeter, sometimes with another girl at the office.

The day war broke out, in September, was just right for a walk after breakfast and two of us walked right up the Devizes Road and further. This lass came from Bath, rather more upper class than the majority of us. She was very dainty with two piercing blue eyes above a long, thin nose; she had very long, thin fingers, fingers which flew over the keys of an old 'Yost' typewriter.

When we returned to the Hostel we heard the news, Marie's pale face went paler still – I thought she was gong to faint. 'Must go back to Bath' she muttered.

Life went on fairly quietly after the first scare, we both had duty turns late at night in the office but no bombs.

A transfer for me to Plymouth as being nearer home in Exeter and to another office was, again, without any terrible incidents.

I have described fairly fully what happened after I returned to work in an office in Exeter and the trouble which Hitler's activities caused us and many other residents as well. War, however, still goes on in many countries and we know so much more about it all now because of the 'media', the television, and even see some of the horrors!

There was one little incident in my 'Salisbury' days which caused some amusement. It was in an evening session and I was in the 'Typists' Hut' on my own as the other girl had gone over to the main building.

One of the officers came with some work which was 'Urgent'. In those days there was much which was treated as 'Urgent' and to be sure that I understood what he wanted or how it should be set out – or something – Major Edwards read through his draft with me. I spotted a mistake – and said so – to which I was told I was wrong; could not be, never was and never would be right to have three vowels together.

I still said that I was sure I was right and added 'I'll bet you' only in a manner of speaking, while the matter could be settled, I knew, if we consulted the dictionary which was in a drawer.

'Right,' said Major Edwards, 'I'll have sixpence on that.' I won and he paid up. Next morning one of the civilian staff, Quantity Surveyor, I believe, came in with a long draft to be typed. He had rather an unfortunate impediment in his speech, not a stammer but a very thick way of saying anything. He came over to my desk and, again, we went through his writing and figures. As he went out and was about to close the door behind him I am sure I heard him say, 'I can spell agreeable'!

I made several friends from the 'Pool of Typists', one of whom died only last year and I still write to the husband of another and receive a long account of events in his family circle – all very interesting.

I started my last job on the 1st April, 1940, in Exeter. What a lifetime ago!

But while I was in Plymouth, staying with a very dear friend and her husband in Greenbank, there was one happening which caused some excitement – the *EXETER* came in from her successful engagement with the *GRAF SPEE,* leaving the latter lying on the ocean floor. The staff in the Sorting Office went up to Plymouth Hoe, by van or by bus, and I was there!

It was a grey day, a misty wettish morning and in the far distance a large grey shape gradually became clear. It was an emotional moment with the band on board playing, all in their uniforms and big grey coats, coming into the safety of Plymouth Sound. I think we had waited quite a while, as I know that I was 'perished' with the cold, but no one thought of going away until the *EXETER* had really come home.

Next day there was a parade of the lads in uniform and I think I am right in saying that they were treated to a Civic Luncheon with the Mayor as host.

There was that well known text from Philippians, chapter 4, verse 8, beginning 'Whatsoever things, etc.' hanging on the wall of the little office where I had to take dictation and the owner often looked at it, as I did, too, but it must have been very hard for him to abide by its teachings and edicts since he had then very recently lost his own son when the Germans sank one of our famous ships in Scapa Flow.

It took me about twenty minutes to walk to the office. Now I only have a vague recollection of the names of the streets I passed but Greenbank is on a hill and I know I walked over the ridge and used a short cut to reach the level road which was parallel to the railway. Normally this was quite a pleasant walk.

I think I told you I stayed in Plymouth from early December to the end of March and one morning it was very frosty There had

94

been a light covering of powdery snow and the roads were very slippery. Motorists found it was not difficult to spin round the wrong way and as I walked along the flat area not too far from the Sorting Office I saw a car begin to slide. The driver could not control it and it was coming broadside on, nearer to me. To say I was frightened is an understatement; the dark monster had a will of its own and no amount of turning the steering wheel had any effect for it still slid on, my way.

God must have been looking after me again for the car went bang into a tree which had been set into the pavement probably a few years before, missing me by two or three feet.

You may wonder what I did in the war, what little part I could play to help the war effort, so I will tell you.

Everybody had to register at the Labour Exchange within a certain period. This was not compulsory until I had returned to Exeter and, of course, I registered. In due time I was told by one of those little beige forms that I must do fire-watching duty – night time included.

That instruction did not fit in with looking after Grandma at night as Mum could not count on any other help. True, our sitting-room had been strengthened by the fitting of strong wooden supports, making a frame substantial enough to ensure some, however little, protection unless there was a direct hit! So I objected within the period allowed for such objections and had to attend a tribunal at the Civic Hall.

There were three 'Officials' or 'Judges', two men and one elderly lady. Indeed, she could almost have been a sister to Grandma and was wearing a black velour hat just like one in our wardrobe at '84', and a long black coat. But there the similarity ended for she was grim-faced and stern. One of the men asked questions as to Grandma's condition and general health, what my work was during the day, etc. and the other two took notes. I was asked to wait outside for a few minutes and was then re-called and told that I must do fire-watching during the day at my place of employment but that I would be excused the night time duty.

It was all I could hope for, but as I walked home I prayed there would never be a fire emergency for me to deal with, as it would be a case of 'England's last hope'!

I can remember the Saturday afternoon sessions back at the office when I was on duty, alone for a while, at the top of the building, and when there were footsteps on the stairs you can imagine my feeling of relief when the person who was expected came into view.

Oh yes, there was one other thing I did – I gave blood – and I did not tell 'The Ancestors' as they did not think I was really strong enough! Because of the poor start I had in life and the continual colds for many years I think they worried over me too much.

But one night I had to go to Dr Fayle-Seale's surgery for medicine for Grandma and I told him that I had been thinking of becoming a donor. He agreed that I could and, after all, blood was badly needed. So I gave blood, but I had not bargained for the terrific dark bruise which developed from the bend of my arm to my wrist. Although it was summer I had to wear a long sleeved blouse to hide it, and the ancestors did not find out.

Food was mighty tight as the rations were so small, but we were luckier than many people. Because I worked for the Forestry Commission back in Exeter there was the chance of a rabbit once a week and Mum knew how to cook it to perfection – she had had plenty of practice at Bremridge! The nearest Forester would bring in some for the office staff, I believe at 1/6d each, and would pay for the empty skin at the rate of 1/-d next week! I kept in touch with this Forester and his family for many years; it was a very happy relationship.

Even in a serious situation like the threat of war becoming a reality some 'wag' will invent something of a comic nature to lighten the gloom, and when I turned out some old papers dealing with what to do in the event of war (Grandma's papers, of course) I came across the following instructions carefully folded up with the serious rules:

Fire Watchers Act 1941

Equipment to be carried by all Fire Watchers:
1. Respirator.
2. Belt for waist with 10 hooks to carry 6 buckets of water and 4 sandbags.
3. 1 Axe in belt. 4. 1 Stirrup Pump to be carried over left shoulder.
5. 1 Extending ladder over right shoulder.

Douglas and me.

Mum, Jeyne and Andy Moss, 1946.

Me, Dorinda. Wish I still looked like that!

Dad, Nancy and me at Hedgecourt Pond.
Our nearest seaside!

Robert Sparkes relaxing at The Bungalow, 1967.

Douglas, John, me, Janet and Dad.

6. 1 long handled shovel to be tucked under left arm.
7. 2 Wet Blankets to be slung around neck.
8. 1 Tin Helmet with turned up brim to carry spare water.
9. Spare sand to be carried in all pockets.
10. 1 Box of matches to light incendiary bombs which fail to ignite.
11. 1 Whistle in mouth (Complete with pea).
12. 1 Dust Bin lid under right arm for use as a shield or gong.
13. 1 Roll of toilet paper slung at back ready for a log book or other immediate use.

I am sure that there was another 'Instruction', something about children being billeted with a family, and all the food necessary to be bought in – stocks which were completely unobtainable then – so many lbs of rice, sugar, butter, cheese, tea, meat, etc.

All nonsense, of course.

If we had thought that the war had passed us by we were to be rudely awakened, for one night a house in Blackboy Road received a direct hit, not very far up the road from us. We were having supper at the time – about 9.30 – when the terrific thud startled everybody. Within minutes a policeman appeared with the instruction that everyone was to leave immediately and go to one of the halls already earmarked as an emergency centre. Now, pronto, get going, there may be unexploded bombs.

Arrangements were made for an ambulance to come for Grandma. When it did she was amazed – a Military Ambulance driven by a girl! She was helped in and the girl drove off – but not to the hall where Mum and I were directed to – and I had Grandma's slippers in my hand. In fact, they became a pillow for me while Mum used her handbag for the same purpose. Four upright wooden chairs were put together and it just made a bed.

I do not know what he saw, but the little man who worked in French's where we bought our poultry meal must have seen something which amused him for every time we saw him afterwards his face registered amusement.

Grandma had been well looked after in her hall, and next day we were allowed to return – and there was the half-eaten supper still as it had been left!

Life went on fairly normally for us for a while. There was a succession of visitors to stay at 84, Blackboy Road; college boys

e

and more soldiers. The top flat had recently been let to a Mr and Mrs Stephens. He was a blind man, I suppose about 50 years old, and with the aid of his white stick – and his wife – he could manage most things very well.

Grandma became less able to get about and much against her will was persuaded to make use of a wheelchair! She often caught colds and needed the attention of a doctor, but Dr Watson lost his position as her medical man because he prescribed something which made whatever illness she had worse instead of better 'and he never came near to see how I was'. He lived and had his surgery very near, only over the brow of the hill.

Lavinia had gone to Salisbury – not exactly in my place but I had heard of a vacancy in another branch just before I left, and she was successful in filling it. She also became an A.R.P. Warden. A.R.P? Yes, Air Raid Precaution, out on the streets checking particularly to see that no lights were showing, for the black-out had to be total. I have a photo of a group of Wardens, Lavinia more or less in the middle, with only two or three other ladies present.

No one thought that Hitler would bother too much about Exeter, but we often heard a flock of bombers going over, to Bristol we thought, or South Wales; and, of course, the siren always gave forth its mournful sound; even if nothing happened locally it was always a relief to hear the 'All Clear'.

One night in May, 1942, the bombers did not pass over Exeter. They circled and wheeled and for several hours dropped their ghastly cargoes all over the city. Our three soldiers, Palfrey, Thompson and Bulley, all went to do what they could – as he passed the landing window Thompson got some minor cuts from shattered glass, but he still went out.

We had been advised to get under the table in the sitting-room if we were raided, and Mr and Mrs Stephens and Mum did that. But, of course, Grandma had no hope of getting down under anything like a table, so we pulled the piano out from the wall and she and I stayed huddled behind it for hours. We had one tin hat – perhaps I should say 'Protective Helmet' – between the lot of us, and Grandma was persuaded to wear it.

It seemed a very long night indeed, and several times the wall beside us shuddered. There was no means of telling how near or how far off the next bomb would be, the 'thuds' were very close.

Mr Stephens under the table was the only one who could give any idea of the time – he had his Braille watch. Eventually, the raid did end, and when we looked out of the hole in the wall which had been a proper window until the glass shattered, it seemed that the whole of the City to the south of us was on fire. Speaking from memory after all this time, I am not sure which mains services we were left with, I know it was pretty grim, I do not remember how we spent the rest of that night, but next day we decided to evacuate ourselves out to The Bungalow at Heath Bridge.

The Stephens and the soldiers went their separate ways. I never saw any of them again.

The morning revealed how near some of the bombs had been for there was just one house standing across the road on the corner of Elmside. Everywhere there were piles of rubble. The Allens' house was no more, the house beside it was also gone. The next dwelling had had a lamp post right outside on the edge of the pavement and here the daughter of the dentist who lived there said 'Good night' to her young man friend. She had been very elegant in a check costume and a fancy blouse and with very high heeled shoes, a really striking girl, she usually stayed on the pavement looking after his smart sports car as it disappeared down the road out of sight. I do not know what the family had for protection from the raid – there was no sign of life where those houses had been.

But there was an unusual sight walking up the steep part of Elmside – Mr Burton had seven hats perched on his head one on top of the other. This gentleman I knew from my Salisbury days where I think I was known as 'Blondie' or 'The little Missey from Exeter'. A civilian now, Mr Burton had spent many years in the Army and he had a nick-name, too. He was known as 'Ackemma, or Pip Emma' after his way of telling the time. Perhaps it was just as well that he was not young and had seen much in his Army days for he found a human arm, a woman's arm with a wedding ring still on her finger, in the garden of a house just up around the corner. I heard of this many months later!

12

The Bungalow Again

With Grandma in her wheelchair, a case on her lap, another underneath the frame of the chair, and still another wedged up behind somehow, me with my bicycle and Andy Mose on his lead, we set off to go as far as the bus station, but there were no buses running into Exeter at all from Crediton. The nearest they would come was Cowley Bridge, quite a way out of town. So we walked, over the piles of rubble or in the road, marvelling at the amount of destruction all around. The smell of gas was heavy in the air. I had the three gas-mask cases on the handlebars of my bicycle and quite a heavy bag on the carrier.

There, at Cowley Bridge, was the most welcome sight of the day, when the conductor helped Grandma, the wheelchair, the cases and Mum all on the Devon General, while I had to cycle and Andy Mose had to use his own transport. In Crediton, near Vigars Garage, we caught up with the wheelchair party, all waiting to be taken by car, to Heath Bridge. Andy Mose and I made our own way out round Broxfords, so naturally the car reached there first.

Mr and Mrs Hammett had watched the bombing of Exeter the night before from the Brake, and Mrs Hammett had said to Frank, 'They'll be out, they can't stay there', so she had aired the feather bed, lighted the fire and made The Bungalow as comfortable as she could. We had enough furniture in the little building, as for some time we had been using it as a weekend retreat. Although Mum had remained in Exeter, it was a change for Grandma to go out with me and my friend, often away in the Army.

100

I have been concentrating on our life in Exeter from 1933 until the blitz and have not mentioned anything to do with the tenants of Rose Cottage. When we left there it was occupied by Mr and Mrs Hammett. Mr Hammett, Frank, was a brother of Mrs Heard over at Preston, and I believe there was another sister in Sandford, Mrs Discombe. They were all hard working, honest, country people, and over the years we became the best of friends.

It is a great pity that when people write notes, even drafts of agreements, they are not dated, for I have such an agreement with Mrs Hammett to allow her to use the back bedroom of The Bungalow for her family when necessary as there were several girls and boys and only two bedrooms in the cottage. I think it must have related to a later time than when we returned, as her family were then comparatively young.

So, we returned to the peace of the country, to what we hoped would be the safety of a retreat, but for how long?

We slept that night, the sleep of exhaustion and next day began by the fetching of water up from the well, getting organised, etc. Lavinia and Doug arrived somehow or other – taxi from Crediton I believe – they could only stay a day or so, and they had been very worried when they heard of the damage caused by the raid.

What about my job in Exeter? The cat and the fowls in their little house in the corner of the garden?

Well, I had my bicycle so obviously I was the best person to go back. I had to go to work anyway.

It was a beautiful morning when I set out, about two days later. Some mornings in May have to be 'lived through' to be appreciated to the full and this was just such a one. I wondered what I would find at '84', what about the office, was it still there? It was, and so were the fowls in their corner – Mum had managed to leave them with food and water before she left, but the poor cat was starving! I attended to all their needs in the lunch hour and locked everything up carefully before going back to the office, and home again by bicycle at night, all through the Broxfords wood!

When I heard that the Devon General was able to get into the city again, to Paul Street, it was much better for me, for I only needed then to cycle to Crediton.

Another beautiful morning I started out and walked up the hills, nearly to the top, and then I heard something 'orrible, I could scarcely believe it, but he was running behind me as fast as his little legs would take him – Andy Mose!

Andy Mose was an unusual dog, certainly a mongrel, with his grey hairy body, hefty on his little stumpy legs. One of the Heinz 57 tribe, he had two fixations, a dislike of people in long, flowing garments – say, a Nun, or Catholic Priest in his gown, and I have often crossed the street to avoid the confrontation with either which might ensue; the other was a fondness for travelling on a bus. He also objected to people who smelt of 'drink'.

Lavinia had discovered Andy Mose in Salisbury when his owner was looking for a home for him since she had married a publican and Andy did not like him! At about that time I had just lost my own little black-spotted terrier 'Punch', but was not looking too hard for somebody to fill his place. Lavinia arranged to bring Andy Mose home with her, particularly when she saw what was happening to him up there in Salisbury. Apparently he was left to roam the streets a good deal and it was then that he became hooked on bus travel. If he could not get on board at one stop he would run to the next! Lavinia said that she knew he had been kicked off more than once!

Oh dear! If I took him back I would certainly miss the bus. If I took him on it was quite a run for him, particularly down Bradley Hill and Park Hill, where, normally, a cyclist could really enjoy a good spin. I decided he had better come with me, and so he did.

'Is that dog yours, Miss?' asked the conductor when he came to me, I had shuffled Andy Mose under the seat, but he was not hidden. 'You'll have to pay his fare.' I had no choice.

It was not the only morning that he managed to catch up with me, nose to the ground. He did it several times, and I had to tie him to the leg of my table in the Forestry Commission Offices and explain to Major Broadwood (my Boss) the circumstances. He was somewhat stern normally, only had one arm after the First World War, but that did not stop him driving his car, and even lighting a pipe when driving, making any passengers 'see stars' until all was satisfactorily completed.

It was on the 1st April, 1940, when I started my new job that I first met Major Broadwood and I wondered how anyone with one arm could cope with so many things, big and small. For instance, try tying your shoe-laces with one hand, how do you make a tie look 'natty'? There were photographs to be taken of some forest areas and products; and, most difficult of all, how on earth do you manage to fold and unfold the large 25" maps? For the latter task Major Broadwood often brought his shoulder into use, his camera could be mounted on a tripod; and his car, with a very distinctive whine which always advertised its presence, had 'fixed' steering.

The simple task of signing letters could have been very difficult, but was accomplished by a heavy paperweight holding the papers still. This heavy-weight was the brass nose (if that is the right word) of a shell which had landed too near to him and caused all his injuries. In addition to the loss of his arm, he once told me that he had exposed nerves all down one side, which meant that he was never really free from pain.

One morning in the summer I entered his little office to find that he had just taken his coat off and the sleeve of his shirt was completely empty right up to the shoulder. Normally his jacket sleeve was tucked discreetly into his jacket pocket and you became so familiar with his appearance that it was quite a shock to see him as he really was.

Apparently he had been studying to be a surgeon before the shell which had caused his injury had landed near him. Of course, that career was finished.

When he recovered sufficiently he had taken up the study of trees and entered the Forestry Commission.

I discovered in time that this man with the steel blue eyes and abrupt manner had a very soft spot for animals, so we had something in common.

News came one morning that he had been ordered to take up duties in London in Head Office, I think, and I was indeed sorry to see him leave. He was replaced by a tall, youngish man with a disfiguring birthmark of the red strawberry kind stretching from his hair-line right down one side of his face.

He had a redeeming feature – he had a beautiful speaking voice. I could listen to him talking and dictating for hours!

Now comes a little item under the heading of 'ordination' again. Years after I had left the office in Exeter I was treated to an outing – not an ordinary outing, but a visit to the Windsor Horse Show. We had to go by underground for part of the way and who should get on at one of the stops but Major Broadwood! We recognised each other immediately and managed to exchange some West Country news for a little outline of his present existence.

That meeting made my day – to think of all the travellers in London he happened to be on the same underground train – and in the same carriage – with us was a most remarkable co-incidence.

On one of the days I did escape without 'nose-to-the-ground-Andy Mose' he disgraced himself in another way. He followed a couple of girls who were walking past Heath Bridge and was still with them when they neared Crediton.

The girls must have taken him to the Police Station, and he spent the night there. I am not sure how the information was communicated to Mum and Grandma of his whereabouts, but Mum had to go to Crediton next day to collect him – and pay for his board and lodgings! If she had to walk, I'll bet she was pleased, though somehow I fancy she must have had a lift otherwise I should have heard much more about it!

We remained at Heath Bridge from May until some time in August and I had really started to enjoy my cycle rides morning and evening, even the somewhat lonely journey through Broxfords. The fowls and the cat were always pleased to see me at lunch time, with or without Andy Mose! It was thought that the winter out there would be too much for Grandma and that we ought to return to Exeter.

Perhaps some things are meant to happen, perhaps it is not just circumstances but some greater power guiding and controlling our lives. Our sojourn at The Bungalow is one instance of what I mean.

Mrs Hammett was expecting her baby at any time, the last of several, and the labour had been very difficult. The District Nurse came across to ask if by any chance Grandma had such a thing as a drop of brandy. The nurse considered the baby needed it imme-diately, so it was fortunate the little bottle could be handed over for such a purpose – and the baby lived!

13

A New House

Surprise, surprise, and horror! On one of my visits to '84' there was a large notice nailed to the door of the conservatory, the main entrance to the house. It gave the information: 'This property has been requisitioned by the Exeter City Council'.

There had been so many people bombed out, homes were in short supply, in extremely short supply, and any standing property which could be repaired without too much difficulty and which did not seem to be lived in was fair game for the officials. I think we must have been given some time to clear all furniture and personal belongings, but where to?

48, Old Tiverton Road, had just come on the market and it became our next home, although it was even larger than '84' and quite different in layout, again Mr Leigh from Ivy Cottage came in and helped with the move. As usual, he stayed several nights, regarding his visits to us as a holiday.

It was difficult to get anyone to help to move the coal which had been delivered to the cellar of '84' shortly before the blitz – elderly Mr Kitson living almost opposite had a pony and cart but was so busy helping others he could not consider our 'bagging and humping'. So, Mum managed to borrow some bags from the coalman and a girl at the office, Joan Wood, and I worked at night each managing to put a half filled sack on the frame of our bicycles – ladies bicycles were quite convenient, with their curve of frame, for holding the sacks – and we walked up over Elmside, down over May Street and up Old Tiverton Road, where we were more than pleased to dump the load in the little coalhouse under the front steps. We worked night after night doing our coal run – I do not think that we had realised what a job we had taken on but we did shift about three quarters of a ton. The coalman then took pity on us and cleared up the fine coal which remained, glad to recover the bags which he had lent us.

Our new house had fourteen rooms, some of them quite large, but we really only needed the ground floor and the basement. In due course, the first floor was let – to a Mrs Halfyard and her sister, Miss Catlin.

Fortunately, Hitler did not pay much more attention to Exeter although with the bombers going over quite often and the siren sounding its dreadful warning we were all very much aware of what might happen again. I can remember walking round to the office through Pennsylvania Crescent when the siren sounded, and running like a frightened rabbit to get into the shelter. In fact, everybody did the same.

It is no wonder that many of us older folk still cannot hear Vera Lynn sing the old songs without becoming quite emotional. There were Churchill's speeches, particularly the 'some neck, some chicken' one, Murgatroyd and Winterbottom, Dr Hill, (the Radio Doctor) and several others all in that period, never to be forgotten.

Because of what I must tell you about later, here I am going to tell you that I got married on 30th June, 1941. He had volunteered for the Army and with the prospect of his going to foreign parts we had decided that it was the best course to take.

We married in St. James Church, Exeter, and Mr Williams came in from Bremridge to 'give me away'. Grandma could not actually go to the ceremony which was an exceedingly quiet one – well, it had to be, in wartime, didn't it? Hitler razed this church to the ground on that terrible blitz night nearly one year later and I am sure the kindly priest who had conducted our little ceremony had been killed! But on 'our' day the sun shone in through the windows, all was quiet, all was peace.

There was as big a spread as one of our hens from the bottom of the garden and plenty of vegetables could provide and, yes, there was a cake made with sugar rations saved by several people and hoarded over several long weeks – I found too I could drink tea without sugar!

We went off on honeymoon by train at about 2.30 p.m. to North Devon, afterwards I heard from Mrs Williams how they had to hurry home, take off their finery and get on with making hay. I'll bet they said something about me getting married in hay-making time!

Lavinia got married in Salisbury in the following year. By another occurrence 'ordained' to happen, as Grandpa would have said, their 'best man' was killed the day after. Two R.A.F. boys had been offered a flight, tossed for the spare seat, gladly accepted by the 'best man', it became his last outing, for the plane crashed.

After we had settled in at the new premises Mr Leigh came in again to do the garden for us. He stayed, as usual, and one evening he and I arranged to go to the pictures at the 'Odeon'. It must have been a popular picture for there were queues of people lined up waiting to go in. 'What be they 'keeying' up there for'? he asked me and I told him that it was for seats at a different price. On this night, as it was my treat to him, we had seats which were a little more expensive! It turned out that he had been to the pictures only about once in his whole life and I knew by the way he had smartened himself up, brushing his beard as well as his boots, that he was looking forward to tonight.

We were nicely settled and enjoyed the first picture, after which Mr Leigh said, 'We'd better go now, that's it'. I told him to sit still. Then came 'The News', after which again he thought we ought to be off. His watch came out after 'Next Week's Trailer' had advertised the film for the coming week – he could not comprehend that there was even more to be seen.

Then the siren went! Everybody rose and began to make their way out, fairly orderly, and we had nearly reached the street when the 'All Clear' sounded. Thank goodness there had been no raid! So we turned round and went back to our seats, upstairs, and Mr Leigh really did enjoy the rest of his time in the cinema. On the way back home he confessed that was the first siren he had heard 'close to' – and he did not like it!

It was quite a privilege to know Mr Leigh, he was just like a Grandfather!

I expect you are wondering how it was The Bungalow was available to us at the time of the blitz or whether we had kept it empty all through those years from 1933 to when we needed to return to Heath Bridge.

As a matter of fact there had been quite a succession of tenants, and one or two names I can remember and tell you a little about. There was a Mr Harvey who had several big white dogs – I don't know what the breed really was, but they were nearly as big as 'Huskies' but not quite so thickly coated. He seemed to be living there on his own, and housed the dogs in one of the bedrooms. Where or whether he took them out for exercise I have no idea. I think Mrs Hammett told us how he was becoming an unsatisfactory tenant and Mum went out to Heath Bridge to investigate. Soon, he 'walked it'.

Mrs Merrygold and her daughter lived there for a short time. They were Grandma's friends in Exeter, pushed for accommodation, and glad enough to take advantage of the empty little bungalow. Mrs Merrygold looked as if she had spent years abroad in a hot country, dark haired, darkish wrinkled skin, and becoming quite frail. Her daughter appeared to be approaching fifty, a big, strong woman. They must have had access to the furniture stored in the 'hut' – the old furniture van which had been brought down from Bremridge and normally kept locked. They certainly had none of their own.

Mrs Merrygold died, but I think they had moved across the fields over to Pacombe a month or so before. Miss Merrygold did not stay in Devon very long after and went back to London, in spite of the risk from Hitler. Grandma did not hear from her again.

Dan Greenslade asked if he could rent The Bungalow. From what I remember of him I think he took a keen interest in the garden, specialising in vegetables. I should imagine that he and Frank Hammett next door in Rose Cottage were 'very good buddies'!

I may not be putting these tenants into the proper order or sequence and I do not think I have the means of finding out now. Mrs Discombe from Sandford was a tenant for a while, and there was an evacuee family with several girls, named 'Wire' or 'Wear'. I never met them, nor did Mum or Grandma. They were no trouble. The children must have been of school age, and I expect that they went to East Village School. I wonder how they looked back on that period in their lives, so different from the town conditions to which they had been accustomed. No electricity, no indoor toilet, no bathroom, and, I think I am right in saying, no drinking water except from the well down in the field. All rainwater was caught from the gutterings, no one talked much about pollution in those days, it seems to be a 'modern' hazard and I suppose the car must bear some responsibility for it now.

While they had been at Heath Bridge during that summer of 1942 Mum and Grandma received some very welcome visitors. Mrs Heard, Ivy and May often walked across the fields from Preston to call on Mr and Mrs Hammett and to look in and see Mrs Stoyle and Mrs Jeynes. Sometimes there would be a little gift, a precious bit of cream, something from the garden, or a pot of jam, homemade, naturally. People in those days did much in the way of preserving fruit, not only by making jam but also using the Kilner jars for bottling. It was considered to be 'a poor toad of a housewife' who had no interest in providing a good store cupboard.

I have come across some wartime recipes and I think these were broadcast on the wireless in the early morning, possibly giving ideas for dinner.

I know that there was a great economy drive as far as fuel was concerned and no longer was it 'the thing to do' to cook one dish at a time – you filled the oven. Different cooking times for different dishes did not seem to matter too much. You just opened the oven door and extracted what was 'done'.

Wartime Recipes

Boil six potatoes in their skins in the usual way, dry them, skin them if preferred, and cut in half lengthways. Put in a greased tin and pour over one tablespoon of melted margarine. Sprinkle with two tablespoons grated cheese mixed with two tablespoons breadcrumbs. Bake in a hot oven until brown (about a quarter of an hour).

Put a slice of bread and margarine in the bottom of a pie dish and then a layer of chopped cooked vegetables. Add another layer of bread and margarine, with marge side up, and sprinkle with grated cheese. Beat an egg with half a pint of milk, pepper and salt and pour in the dish. Let it stand for at least half an hour. Bake in a moderate oven for half an hour to 40 minutes until the top is brown and crisp. Serve hot.

Two large cups of wheatmeal flour, one small cup of milk, two tablespoons sugar, one tablespoon margarine, three teaspoons baking powder, one egg, salt. Mix flour, sugar, salt and baking powder together in a basin. Beat egg and milk and add to the mixture. Melt marge and put in last. Put all in a cake tin and bake in a moderate oven for about three quarters of an hour. No fruit for this cake, but I suggest that sliced apples could be used when 'fallen downs' are plentiful, in which case it may be advisable to use a little more sugar if the apples are very 'tart'.

It was the same way with clothes, the coupons to buy garments were hoarded. In fact they could be a form of currency if not needed by the rightful owner in too much of a hurry. People with the skill Mum had of turning materials were always busy, indeed she 'turned' a tweed coat for me which I wore to the office! It was a quite dark reddish colour with an inside that was completely different. I wore it for years!

With all the wartime 'rooles and reggilations' in force for farmers, there would be an occasional visit form some 'man from the Ministry' and no one knew when he might pay his surprise visit.

Mrs Heard or Ivy told a tale of nearly getting caught. When they had some cream for tea, no doubt going with fruit which was not much more than half-sweetened, the dish of cream had pride of place on the kitchen table – if a visitor was seen coming across the little court and it was a stranger, it always caused a flutter of excitement in case he should turn out to be one of 'they Ministry chaps'.

This time it was, and he had come to check something, so naturally he wanted to come in and see the records.

Now where were they going to hide the cream? The brainwave of putting it down inside the fender by the fireplace certainly hid it from sight until someone suggested that he should sit down a minute or so while the paper work was produced. He walked over to the only other empty chair in the room and sat down beside the fire!

They never knew whether he actually saw the cream, but he accepted the cup of tea offered and a piece of cake, and kept his thoughts to himself. When he was satisfied that the paper work was in order, that the Ministry's directions were being obeyed, he left. After thanking all for their hospitality he was heard to say 'They certainly have a job to starve a farmer'.

Now, what was the meaning of that remark? Had he seen what he 'shouldn't have' or would they hear more about it later? Thankfully, they did not!

The tragedies endured and the victories enlightening the gloom of the war years are so well known that I am only going to mention the general feelings of pride in the efforts made by 'the little ships' in rescuing the troops stranded with their backs to the sea surrounded by the enemy at Dunkirk. As the stories unfolded even we land-lubbers became emotional, marvelling at the risks taken and when somebody at home started reciting 'Drake's Drum' – you know the poem 'Take my Drum to England, Hang it by the shore, Strike it when the powder is running low', etc. – I noticed both Mum and Grandma fumbling for hankies and the tears were running down my face.

On the way home from the office I had walked, as usual, round by St. James' Football Ground, and there, sitting on a boundary wall in the sun of a very hot afternoon were many of the boys saved from the beaches and the sea. Some were French, I think, with their unfamiliar uniforms – all somewhat dishevelled – but mighty glad to be here.

Of course we did not know anything about the preparations for 'D' Day – the day of the landing on the Normandy Beaches. That was the 6th June, 1944, and before the end of that month my little Jeyne was born – at Woodhayes Nursing Home, St. Leonards, Exeter. How proud of her Grandma was when we were allowed to go back to '48' after the usual fortnight of rest and help at the Home. (No one seems to have such a long period off today.)

It had been quite a struggle to get everything together for the baby – the pram, perhaps, worst of all. About a month before it was expected to be needed Mum saw an advertisement in the local paper 'Pram for Sale, poor condition, 35/-d.' The address was given as St. Thomas, so she took a bus, (no, the bus took her) down through the High Street, down Fore Street, across Exe Bridge and up through Cowick Street, where she got off and had to find the address shown.

Oh, what a pram! Her heart sank, the inside was ragged, the hood and apron completely ineffective and ragged too. But the wheels were good, the springing sound, and after a very careful examination Mum handed over the money and started her long walk home to 48, Old Tiverton Road, almost ashamed to be seen with the 'vehicle', having already decided that she could re-line it herself and have the hood recovered professionally and a new apron made. These alterations were done well in time and with a pot of black enamel paint, the outside was made to look quite all right. Renovated, it became a pram to be proud of and I have no doubt but that the beautiful baby enjoyed her rides when mother went shopping.

Grandma became quite ill that winter, but she loved to have Jeyne placed on her bed and the two of them would be talking together as well as the difference in age would allow. In fact, Jeyne grabbed Grandma's nearest arm one day and bit it. Grandma was almost as proud of that bite as if it had been a medal won in the war!

About this time we received a consignment of furniture which belonged to my husband's family and had been stored at Lee Mill on Dartmoor since Plymouth had received too much attention from Hitler. Many of the streets there had been obliterated, as also the little home which originally housed these belongings. Fortunately by that time the lady of the house had to receive constant care and attention and had been moved elsewhere.

The large top room was empty, so we stored everything there, making many trips for airing, cleaning and getting rid of all the lime or chalk dust which had collected. I do not think that the storage could have been very good, nor the transportation of the items. There were also a number of books to be dried out and photographs to be 'reclaimed'. After looking at them and the rest once or twice all had to remain upstairs while nursing attention was given to Grandma.

Dr Fayle-Seale called several times making examinations and prescribing the strongest medicine, but with all the help possible, all the love and attention we could give her, I am afraid that she slipped quietly away.

So ended the life of one of the kindest, most gentle people I have ever known. She was one of the most learned, too. Lavinia and I were indeed fortunate to have had such an 'Ancestor' with us for so long.

The date was the 19th January, 1945. It was a very cold period with a covering of snow on the ground when I trudged with the Death Certificate to the Registration Office, then at one of the

112

large houses towards the Heavitree District, while Mum had plenty to do at home with Jeyne — it was not fit weather to take a baby out.

I suppose life on earth is a matter of 'time' for us all. Some people have little control over how they use, or spend, or, in fact, misuse the time they have but Grandma had been very active both physically and intellectually all her early life and I have many books and records to prove it. I even have the longhand copies she made of the Reports given by the 'School Dignitaries' and the Scripture Inspector of her work at East Village School. They are all praiseworthy, from when she was still Miss Slade!

To milk four or five cows every morning before she went to school from Bremridge must have taken some doing, especially in the early mornings of winter, with the primitive conditions which existed then, not only at this particular farm, but generally. The swinging lantern, the heavy wet boots, the long skirts, all must have combined to produce a heavy work load.

I think the cows would have been chained in their stalls and for certain there was someone who would do the routine work — Bennett in his time, but there must have been somebody before that — otherwise even she could never have managed, anyway, it was hard labour!

I knew that I was going to be the owner of the Heath Bridge properties when Grandma died and that Lavinia would have the house in Bristol which Auntie Alma had bought when she worked at the Hospital there as a teacher to the sick or recuperating children.

There have been times when Grandma had wondered whether any property was worth keeping as the rents then were so low and sometimes the expenses quite heavy. I know she used to be concerned about the Bristol house when she received letters from the house agents, Huntleys, saying that there were more repairs needed. The tenant seems to have been fairly elderly and unable to do much, or, indeed, anything! Because it had been Auntie Alma's house and she had had thoughts of going to retire up there Grandma had kept it.

Mr and Mrs Hammett and family had been at Heath Bridge since 1933 and were still there in 1945. I did not think that there would be any difficulty about our relationship — and there was not

113

– though they probably wondered whether I would consider selling the property. What, sell Heath Bridge properties, which Grandma had recreated from ruins? No, of course not.

From a letter I found with Grandma's papers, it would appear that about 1933 she contacted Sir William Davie's Agent, Mr Pitts Tucker, regarding the possibility of renting the Brake – I think on account of the tenant of Rose Cottage desiring to use the land. Anyway, gorse, brambles, and the small amount of bracken down over the slope towards the river were all cleared and a small shed was put up for the housing of two or three animals, I can remember seeing some good Red Devon cows with their offspring up in what had become quite a good field.

The far hedge is the boundary on the other side of which is a large field belonging to Hill Farm.

As with everything it seems there comes a time to buy and a time to sell and so it was with the owners of the Creedy Estate after the elders of the family had 'passed on' and Death Duties bore heavily on remaining relatives.

For this reason – so I was told – the sale on the 19th June, 1953 at the Rougemont Hotel in Exeter, sold eleven Good Mixed Farms, totalling 1,520 acres. I believe woodland of 56 acres with a good cottage must have related to Broxfords. The properties returned a rent, then, of £2,611 per annum.

I have been looking through the sale particulars; there are various things marked ('T'), indicating that whatever it was, it was supplied by the tenant. Invariably included were items of bathroom equipment, airing cupboards, solid fuel cookers and water heaters all things which made for much more comfortable living in the country.

There are often two cottages advertised with each farm or holding, and the workers and their families had only bucket closets, and not always water indoors.

All this was less than fifty years ago, but now many properties, even cottages, are connected to the mains. Washing machines have replaced the hard work of washing by hand, copper or fairly simple equipment filled by buckets, with the result in the last few years that there is concern about water levels but not just in Devon – in all parts of the country.

This is how the Brake was listed:

LOT 16
(Coloured Yellow on Plan)

Area 3 acres   1 rood   22 perches

LAND AT HEATH BRIDGE

The land has a good road frontage to Broxford Hill
and is well watered by Holly Water

SCHEDULE – LOT 16

C.S. No.	Description	Area
	Shobrooke	
754	Rough Pasture	3.203
	Sandford	
788	Garden	.187
	Total:	3.390 acres

OUTGOINGS:

Tithe Redemption Annuity 5s.6d.
Let to Mr F. Hammett at a ground rent of
£4.15s.0d. per annum.

It was arranged with Mr and Mrs Hammett that they would attend the sale and purchase the Brake on my behalf since I had little chance of going there myself. This was, in fact, what did happen and perhaps I ought to mention here that Lot No. 2, Bremridge Farm, was sold subject to a condition that water was allowed to be drawn from the well in O.S.789 in favour of Lot No. 16. This was the 'Right' allowed by Mr Pitts Tucker to my Grandmother, dated the 19th March, 1923.

Bremridge itself, described as having 137 acres 2 roods 3 perches, with a Tithe Redemption Annuity of £17.18/4d, and a rent of £227.10/-d, was bought by the family who were the sitting tenants – the Thornes. It is well known that prices paid by such sitting tenants bear little relation to the actual values, but then, that is life, that is the way of things!

Over a period of many years I came to know Mr and Mrs Thorne very well and was always made welcome, both at Bremridge Farm and Bremvilla – The Bungalow which Mr Thorne built very near to the Higher Orchard gate. What a view they have from their windows high up on the hill! It is a view which takes in East Village, and the many outlying properties back towards the next ridge of hills and the villages of Poughill and Pennymoor – up towards the North Devon country. Bremvilla was the retirement home for Mr and Mrs Thorne, Senior, when their son grew from a boy into a man and needed the farmhouse for himself and his growing family.

14

Leaving Exeter

I must now make a leap in time and circumstances – to the move we made from Exeter to an outlying suburb of London, to Worcester Park. My family now numbered two children, Jeyne and her fair haired little brother, John, and we still had Mum with us. When one's work moved to London, in those days the family went too – none of this commuting business!

48, Old Tiverton Road, was put on the market, but it did not sell. Perhaps the House Agents were asking too much, perhaps large houses like '48' put people off – too much for the youngsters with growing families to undertake, too much also for the seniors about to retire. But there was a coincidence in that there were three prospective buyers with the same surname, and they were not related! They were all called Williams!

Never a family to sit down and say 'You can't do it', Mum and I set about furnishing each flat and letting through the house agents, furnished.

It worked all right for a while, but then one 'party' got into arrears and did what is known as a 'midnight flit', this one took him and his family right across the border into Scotland. The law there is not the same as in England so nothing claimed or paid! They took the furniture, too, but I believe that when he did cross the border back into England he was apprehended and served some time as a guest of His or Her Majesty!

After that, as the other flats became empty they were let unfurnished, too much bother to refurnish!

By the time my third baby was born, a little girl with darkish

117

hair which turned quite fair later on, I am afraid that we were on our own as the disease which claims so many women had finally claimed my mother. She had endured an operation in Exeter about four years before – and had gone over to Whiterose, Preston, to Mrs Heard and family to recuperate, very much enjoying their hospitality.

The year she had with us in Worcester Park was probably the easiest of her life – no butter to make, no water to fetch, no cooking for the lodgers or students, and the wartime conditions had been relaxed so that everything generally was a little easier. Mum did what she really enjoyed doing, a little dressmaking for herself and a few things for the kiddies.

We still had Andy Mose. Quite suddenly he developed an attack of rheumatism or something which meant he padded round the sitting-room in a completely dejected manner, then stopped. Mum and I would put his blanket under him and carry him up to the garage at the side of the house, quite expecting that he would not respond to the treatment advised – Shirley's Tablets for rheumatoid conditions, or aspirins. Before long there would be a scraping at the back door and he asked to come in, apparently better. This was repeated many times and he did recover, running around and becoming amorous! But he went out one day, at his insistence, never to return and we could not find out what had become of him in spite of many inquiries. Perhaps he had a heart attack, perhaps someone took him in a car – he was still rather partial to car travel. We just don't know.

I think it was Her Majesty's Coronation Year when we first had a holiday in Devon, staying at Starcross with Mrs Williams and her family. I know we went to a Coronation Tea in a hall of some description in the road which comes out opposite the 'Courteney Arms', and watched much of the ceremony on Mrs Williams' television set. It certainly was a very impressive ceremony with the clergy, the fine robes, the grand music. 'Long Live the Queen'.

The ferry from Starcross to Exmouth was our means of getting to the seaside where some very happy days had been spent in my youth! The sea wall was still there to slide down, as soon as possible and as many times as possible, always with the little thud on contact with the sand. Paddling, picking up seaweed, looking for shells of different shapes – all things children have ever done and all things they will for ever do for a day's enjoyment at the seaside.

Somehow I think we visited the country, Heath Bridge, on this trip, though I do not quite remember how for in those days we did not possess a car. Our house in Worcester Park was not far from the Station for daily journeys to London for the breadwinner, or the bus for us to visit Kingston or Sutton for major shopping, so a car was not really necessary.

15

Our Greatest Loss

It was on a Sunday evening when Mum was writing a letter to Lavinia and Derek in Salisbury that she felt something unusual, a lump near her left breast. Next day she visited Dr Watson and he advised hospital investigation immediately; this resulted in an operation as soon as it could be arranged.

Later, visits to the hospital in Exeter for checks revealed secondaries and an appointment was made for the necessary treatment. Mum went on the appointed day but very soon returned – there had been an accident involving a bus or coach and the emergency meant that her treatment had to be postponed.

Another appointment and fate again was against her. She went to answer the door bell at '48', slipped on the lino, fell and broke her left arm above her elbow. The caller had been an old man selling combs and, of course, he was shocked at the consternation he had caused. The hospital doctors had to plaster her arm at a difficult angle, so the secondaries still could not be removed.

She had seemed fairly well when we left Exeter for Worcester Park in Surrey, but by the end of the next year she became poorly and was ultimately admitted to a hospital some distance away. The date was the 4th November 1949.

Unfortunately Mum was not well treated at this hospital, but there is no point in detailing just what went wrong more than to say her Ward thought more about Christmas and decorations than they did about looking after really sick patients. She asked us to bring in some 'Harlene' hair tonic, she said she could not rest for it itching so. On examination the Sister told her she was not the first patient to need 'de-lousing' treatment!

There were wreaths at the end of beds where the patients were really ill, Mum's included. She knew.

'Enough is enough' Lavinia said and she asked to see the Doctor. We heard what the Sister said to the person at the other end of the 'phone, 'These relatives are insisting on seeing a doctor,' in a very disparaging manner.

When he appeared after a long wait – a very lame young man – he was blunt and unsympathetic. 'There is nothing we can do for your mother, the sooner she goes the better'.

She died on the last day of the year.

Together Lavinia and I saw our Doctor and told him of the treatment Mum had received, asking his advice about taking the matter further.

'Whatever you do, you will never bring your mother back. Besides, what proof have you?'

This was after the funeral, and Mum was laid to rest in the grave beside Grandma. Lavinia and her husband Derek and Douglas and I were the only mourners. We could not expect visitors from the country and I believe we came straight home!

My two infants and Lavinia's Marilyn had been cared for at home by Lavinia's Derek's Mum so we knew that they would be all right. Visits to the hospital had presented difficulties until the next door neighbours catered for the hours when we were not able to be home. At such times anyone is very grateful for good neighbours, such as we had.

So, here we were, now orphans, completely, no Grandparents, no parents, it was just Lavinia and me. She had always been very protective of 'Little Sister', possibly because I became ill so often when we were young. At that time she and Derek did not live very far off – a bus ride along the Tolworth road past 'The Toby Jug' and change to another bus which would pass at the end of our road. Lavinia came over as often as she could.

Her attitude to life was 'You must stand up for yourself' and she did! There were no half measures with Lavinia. When time and opportunity allowed she developed her artistic talent and I still have two pictures in the sitting-room which were her productions. One is a harvest scene with three horses in the binder and the other is a Tor and Stream on Dartmoor.

She was very good at sewing, too, and altered several garments

121

f

to fit properly for herself and for me. In fact she made my blue coat, which became a great favourite and I wore it for years.

Then Derek's Civil Service Department moved to Southampton and visits could only be occasional.

16
The Letter

One day I received a letter, a letter postmarked 'Brierley Hill' which caused me to sit and think for a while. It was from a firm of solicitors enquiring the whereabouts of the wife of one of their clients – Mrs Jeynes – and if she was deceased, the date and place of that event.

I replied that I was very surprised and pleased to realise that I still had a father, considering the circumstances of illness and the war years, and could they put me in touch with him, please. I gave them the information they were seeking.

About ten days later the solicitors wrote again giving me the address of a Mr Jeynes. Obviously they had been in touch with him and asked whether he would wish to communicate with me. Of course he did, and so we began writing. After all these years, 'the years in the wilderness' to have found my Father – and a Grandfather for the children – was little less than a miracle.

I felt that I could not rush up there to see him, partly in view of my commitments here, partly from – what, I don't know, perhaps a feeling from the past that there had been difficulties between him and Grandpa at Bremridge. Mum rarely spoke of him after he had left, but, never, I remember, in any bitter or disparaging way.

A sentence should never begin with 'But' I was always taught. However, that is the word which exactly fits the circumstances I am now going to describe. But Jeyne who had now left school, had a friend with whom she went youth-hostelling and also much to my regret 'hitch-hiking'. One day, they found themselves in

Enville, roughly between Stourbridge and Bridgnorth, all planned, no doubt, by Jeyne.

In a quiet road off the main thoroughfare she said she saw an elderly gentleman in front of his house attending to the garden and she said to him that she thought he was her Grandfather! He dropped his gardening equipment as if they were red hot coals – and then ushered the two girls into the house.

I do not know exactly what followed. Certainly they were introduced to Dad's housekeeper, Nancy. She was a little lady, very Irish/Scots, very dainty. Mrs Nancy Wilson was a widow and had been extremely happy to have found a post which suited her so well. She had relatives in America and a niece, Julie, wife of an officer serving in Germany. Dad and Nancy had received visits on several occasions from 'these foreigners' and he had survived on his own when Nancy had family business in America.

There was an invitation to me to visit as soon as I could manage it – and a £5 note for Jeyne for going up there and 'finding him'.

Jeyne had obtained a job in London and trained as a Shorthand Typist. One morning I went with her, complete with a packed case, and she saw me off on a coach which would take me right up to Stourbridge, via Cheltenham, where I would have to change to the 'Black & White' coaches. There was another change at Stourbridge to the little country service which would put me down beside 'The Cat' if I asked for that stop!

Of course there was someone to meet me and take me 'home'. All the way up I had wondered about so many things – maybe I should be a disappointment to him, maybe it would be the other way around, how would I feel about Nancy? So I tried to concentrate on the scenery, the little villages, the fruit farms and cottage gardens.

It was late Spring, early Summer time – one of those years when the seasons seem to run into one another – but there seemed to be much order everywhere (not nearly as much litter as is evident today) and I took it all as a hopeful sign that my visit would be a happy one.

A nervous Nancy, a diffident Dorinda, and Dad – what a trio, I thought! But in the evening Dad and I had a good talk about the Bremridge days and he asked, 'Why didn't your Grandmother and Mum send for me when the old man died – I'd have run the farm for them without any trouble,' and I am sure he would have since he had been in agricultural work for many years. He still was, though he had never learned to drive a 'dractor'!

Whatever he may have done could not have helped because Grandpa had already 'given notice' to come out at the following Lady-Day, and young Williams was already being considered for the tenancy, and obtained it.

Dad took from the chest pocket of his coat a photo, a photo of Mum as a fairly young lady. I have a duplicate among my papers. He said 'I've never looked at another woman, and I've always carried this one, too, a photo of you and Lavinia as youngsters'. I believed him. I believed the relationship between him and Nancy was exactly as he told me, she was his Housekeeper, but she did have one unusual idea. 'Never', she said, 'let anyone round here know that your Dad was married before, never call him 'Dad' in front of anyone, just say that you are a relative of Mr Jeynes, only visiting'. She honestly thought it would cause a scandal!

I asked Dad why he had wanted to find out what had happened to Mum. 'I had to,' he said, 'because of my Old Age Pension and what I was entitled to, and "they" said they had to know and told me to go to a solicitor.' Apparently a letter addressed to 'The Occupier' of Bremridge Farm had produced the information which enabled the solicitors to write to me. Therefore he would have been just about 65 years old, another indication that he had 'put his age on' when he had volunteered for the Army in the First World War – so he had been little more than a boy when invalided out.

Well, I stayed with them in Enville for several days. Dad still went to work for a local farmer and also found time to see to his garden. He was very proud of his vegetables and I was given as much as I could carry of whatever was plentiful and in season. He also had a wonderful apple tree at the top of the plot, near where the pig-house had been in wartime, plus a rhubarb bed which had to be seen to be believed!

The next visit I made at least a year later was much easier for the journey up, as it was by car. Two very good friends were driving up in that direction and gave me a lift as far as Worcester (I think) and I got the bus from there. I cannot remember how I got home!

Nancy did become 'Mrs Jeynes'. Apparently she fell and broke her leg and stayed in hospital for some time. When she came home she had to be nursed by Dad to some extent and her relatives in America tried to get her to cross the Atlantic again as they thought it was not right and proper for her to remain with Dad!

I did not know anything about this until well after the deed had been done, but I received a letter from Dad with the request that I should visit again fairly soon. By this time John had left school and was able to look after what animals we had, and help with the fowls and customers, so getting away was a little easier.

The welcome was as before, Nancy always wore a wedding ring anyway from the days when she was Mrs Willson, so I did not suspect circumstances had altered, she was then heavily dependent on a walking stick. On the second day of my visit Nancy announced that she would take a hot water bottle and go up to have a rest, and 'no doubt you and your Dad will find something to talk about.'

'What would you think, my dear,' he began, 'if I told you that Nancy and I have got married? Because we have, Nancy's people wanted her to go back to America, she did not want to, so we nipped off to Wolverhampton Registry Office as soon as she could do without her crutches – and now nobody can take her. They can't say it is not proper for her to be here with me any more either.'

What could I say? I could never put Nancy in my Mother's place, and it was probably the best thing for them both – she would continue to look after him well – easy going, cheerful Dad!

When she reappeared: 'Has your Dad told you?' she asked. 'I don't want you to call me anything else but "Nancy" – certainly not "Mother"!'

From the big cupboard in the wall Dad produced a bottle of 'Brown Sugar' as he called it, and we drank to the happiness of Mr and Mrs Jeynes!

Dad and Nancy came down together and visited us here and we took them out for drives round the neighbourhood. Dad certainly enjoyed seeing the beauties of Surrey – not unlike some areas in Devon he said. Nancy could manage without her stick now and seemed to be completely restored to health. I think they were both very happy together, so we will leave them for the time being and return to . . .

17

Devon Again and the Diaries

I have just forgotten the circumstances, but when Lavinia and Derek said that they were going on holiday to Devon – or Cornwall – in 1959 it was arranged that I should go down with them and stay with Ivy and May Heard in Crediton.

A very sad piece of news greeted us there – Mr Hammett at Rose Cottage had died and his funeral was to be next day, in Sandford. Would we go? Of course.

A letter I had received from Mrs Hammett some time previously had given the impression that they were thinking of going into Crediton to live – or, at least, somewhere where there was not so much work, where it was not so hilly. They had not given notice exactly, but thought I ought to know in case they did find something suitable in a hurry.

Mr Hammett – Frank to all his friends – had not been ill for any length of time. He had enjoyed a good dinner but before the end of the afternoon he had collapsed, a stroke or heart attack. The result was the same.

As with Grandpa's funeral nearly thirty years before, Sandford Church was nearly full of local people. After all, the Hammetts and the Heards were very well known and many farmers and their families attended, all speaking well of 'Frank'.

Lavinia and Derek also attended but afterwards went where they had planned. I returned to Heath Bridge with Mrs Hammett and stayed with her in Rose Cottage. To my mind, she was a lady of great courage and character and, having accepted the inevitable, knowing there was nothing she could do to bring

127

Frank back to be with her again she did not sit and mope, no she just got on with her work.

A sale of surplus goods had been arranged for the 29th September, 1959, so there was preparation for that.

The Heards, all of them, thought that now I should have to sell the property. May said, 'You'll make on what your Grandmother gave for it – and you'm too far away, anyway, to look after it. Take and sell it, Maid.'

Not for one moment did I seriously consider this suggestion. I know they all meant well and it would certainly have been much less work for me but I had a good agent in Exeter, a good solicitor in Crediton, so I considered I had sufficient help with management. Besides, now that The Bungalow was again a property 'on its own' and not let in conjunction with Rose Cottage, I had an idea that I could let it for holiday visitors.

I expect that I cadged a lift into Crediton and spent another night with the Heards, buying paint and paper for redecorating, and many other items which I felt would be needed to make it comfortable.

True, there was no electricity, no bathroom, no indoor sanitation, and I knew that I could let it only on the basis of a retreat from pressures of town life. The area was still beautiful and unspoiled – not much traffic, in fact, some days there was only farm traffic!

So I stayed for another week with Mrs Hammett. It was during this time that I remember a visit made to one of her daughters, the one who lived half way up towards Poughill, and the mushrooms which we brought back and cooked for breakfast next morning. I never remember enjoying mushrooms like those, and to say that they were delicious is to put it mildly. There was also fresh butter made very quickly from scalded cream to spread on a fresh loaf delivered the day before. What could be nicer?

By the time I returned to Nutfield on the 22nd August, the interior of The Bungalow was looking quite fresh and clean. A gas cooker, with calor gas cylinders, had been provided, and I had bought a Victorian chair upholstered in green velvet, a 'tub' chair covered in red patterned material, a good oak sideboard with a mirror back, and several other items and Mr Connole, my agent, had selected a bed with an interior sprung mattress, which went in the front room. I also went to a sale in Sandford and bought a double bed with a good mattress for the back room.

The first year of letting was in 1960, on the understanding that visitors would bring their own bedding.

It was let for thirteen weeks, though one week was cancelled due to a family bereavement. Our grocer from this village was the first visitor and he was very taken with the peace of the place.

Rose Cottage? It was empty for a little while until Mrs Hammett's eldest son, his wife and two little girls moved in. Since there may be some confusion with Mr and Mrs Hammett, Senior, I will use the Christian names of the younger generation, so they will, from now, become Bill and Amy. I think that Amy quite enjoyed helping the holiday visitors with local information, etc. and people who gave me any report of their holiday always said how helpful the people in the Cottage had been.

I had not been idle during 1960 and on the 7th of March 1961 at about 6.30 p.m. a carrier from Exeter, Pearce, called here with his big red furniture van and collected several big items for The Bungalow and all the pillows and eiderdowns which I had made myself and was very proud of. Young Pearce had an assistant and I went with the two of them, in the van. I remember the journey very well, through Redhill and Reigate, Dorking and Guildford, and all the towns and villages West. I was quite comfortable in my little 'passenger cabin' in the body of the van above the driver and his mate, but felt when they stopped at a café somewhere about midnight that if I got down I might not get back in a dignified way again! Therefore I said I did not want anything, stayed where I was – and went to sleep!

We arrived in Exeter at 1.30 a.m., and young Pearce dropped his mate off near his home just outside the city and took me to his own home, where the spare bedroom had been prepared – and I slept like a log. I also had breakfast there fairly early next morning and set out again when 'mate' arrived. The destination was 'The Bungalow' where the large items were delivered and I soon put the piles of bedding in the back bedroom, I began to redecorate the front bedroom with Magicote.

I did not return home until the 26th March, after one of the longest 'holidays' I have had in Devon. Mind you, it was not all work, for I had been visited by Ivy and May and their brother, Walter, also Ena from up in the village. I had seen Mrs Thorne Senior and she had loaned me a kettle when I told her that I needed a new one at The Bungalow and was managing in the meantime with a saucepan for making a cup of tea.

There was a visit to the Fishers 'Up shop' where I was made very welcome. There were negotiations with Mr Smale for making alterations to The Bungalow windows and putting in two glass windows in the 'double doors' which opened out on to the verandah.

Every weekend there was indeed a holiday for me – for visits to Starcross made periods of light relief. There was always something going on, someone coming in, plenty of fun and chatter – and they were all so good to me. I am indeed lucky to have such friends.

On the 2nd April in the same year Walter Heard had a heart attack and died. I could scarcely believe the news – for only on the 11th of the previous month when he came to Heath Bridge with his sisters he had appeared to be in the best of health – always jolly, but too plump. But then, most of the Heards were a little, shall we say, 'well favoured', full of good humour, Walter particularly so.

1961 brought its crop of visitors and I received several compliments on my handiwork which had produced the eiderdowns and pillows. Well, yes, I was quite proud of them myself and anyone who has wrestled with 'fevvers' everlasting knows that using them is not an easy task. The bedspreads, matching the eiderdowns, were easy, but the stitching seemed to go on for ever.

You may wonder how I can be so definite about the dates I have quoted – and shall quote – but I have kept diaries for years. Beside the files of the houses have sufficient notes to prove accuracy, though the diaries are much more comprehensive. Reading them quite recently I have learned something about myself which Jeyne declared years ago and I did not really believe then. She said 'Mother notices everything', and I see I have several instances of what she means, as when I had to wait at Reading for the Exeter train for over an hour on one of my journeys to Devon. I observed an elderly gentleman doing a crossword puzzle and himself observing with the eye of one in authority, a young Adonis swinging his way up the platform, then a gentleman from a hot country wearing an overcoat over an overcoat – and still shivering with the cold!

Every year while the letting of The Bungalow to summer

visitors continued I found it essential to go there myself, do some redecorating, cleaning and generally making sure as far as I possibly could that everything was in order. It also gave me an opportunity to pick up the threads of the district which I had known so many years ago to see the Millers, the Fishers, the Heards, the people now occupying the farm I loved and knew so much about and I counted it a privilege still to be able to visit there. The tenants of Rose Cottage were not just tenants – I considered them friends, and I hope with them it was the same; it was not 'Just to keep in with the Landlady' for, almost without exception, they did go out of their way to help as much as possible.

It was not until 1964 that electricity came to the area – promised for so many years when I had called at the Electricity Office in Crediton!

It was in 1964, too, that Bill and Amy had considerable difficulty with the generator which brought the water up from the well in Little Hill Field. Bill had been able to service it – maybe kick it or swear at it long enough to get it going again producing the essential liquid into the storage tanks in the top of the Cottage orchard. Come to think of it, I never heard Bill swear, he has a fairly soft voice, with a strong Devon accent, of course, and always seems to be good tempered – 'a son of his Father' as the old expression goes!

Therefore, 1964 was a Red Letter Year for the district generally and for Heath Bridge in particular, for I was able to get in touch with a firm of engineers in Martock, Somerset, to install an electric pump. I stayed at The Bungalow long enough to meet the firm's representative and after he had seen the set-up and done his calculations his estimate was that it would cost £178-odd and, once installed, would ensure I should not need to think or worry about water for the next ten years. So the Sumo Pump was put in the well, land drainage near it was completed, and it did, in fact, last much longer than ten years, though it has now needed replacement.

The South Western Electricity Board estimated for the wiring of both properties, to be re-paid at the rate of 11/-d (55p) per week for the next 'umpteen' years, (ten, I think). They duly carried out the work, re-wiring Rose Cottage which had been wired some time previously by the Hammetts to obtain electricity from the

131

generator I mentioned. I do not think it could have provided a very good supply for them for as with other users in the district 'juice' had to be conserved – too many 'electrical' gadgets could not be used at once. If you needed the kettle to be boiled you could not use the iron at the same time!

With the modern convenience of electricity it was now possible to think about indoor toilets and bathrooms. Not only did I think, I acted. Mr Connole, my agent in Exeter, had been able to help a builder out of some little difficulty – I do not know what – and as one good turn deserves another the builder was called upon to work with all speed possible – and did!

So, with the work being supervised by the Crediton Rural District Council Surveyor, a Mr Pilley, both properties were brought up to date as far as was possible. The Cottage benefited more than its neighbour for it was supplied with a bath, the bathroom being made from a partitioned off section of the 'L' shaped room. An additional window was put in where a window space had been blocked off two or three hundred years before! In my view the new window is far too small and, some day, I do intend to have it altered. Frankly, I was surprised that this small window was 'passed' by the Crediton Rural District Council.

Heavy machinery was brought in to dig the drains and construct the septic tank in the orchard of The Bungalow, so the drainage system passed quite near and The Bungalow waste could be incorporated into it. The toilet here was made by taking a partition off the 'bedroom' side of the kitchen and making a door for entry from the long passage. Had the positioning of the toilet itself been a little more toward one of the walls there would have been room for a shower as well. Whoever decided its position was, I think, shortsighted and only a basin could be provided, though it was supplied with 'ot water from the immersion heater. Since this was a great advance on the nothing which was there before it had to be accepted!

A 'pre-payment' meter was installed in the kitchen and caused considerable trouble when S.W.E.B. realised that visitors would only be there in the summer, so they re-set the meter from the 4d which I had told everyone was the cost of electricity, to 1/-d – one shilling – 5p instead of under 2p. Of course there were complaints and I referred quite quickly to S.W.E.B. I was told that the increased charge was necessary even to meet their costs of collection, but I did get them to agree to revert to the earlier charge on condition that I made up any deficiency at the end of their accounting period. I agreed to this provided they did not alter it again, and had to see several different officials to impress my point!

Before the coming of electricity, Ivy and May Heard had moved from Crediton to 'Snows' at Sandford – (a large house with several acres where, do doubt, the idea was that Walter would have his own farming interests, May could have her poultry, and Ivy would be very near the school where she had been in charge of the infants for many years), and they had more than welcomed me to stay with them at night as I could go out to Heath Bridge by school car every day to work. This arrangement suited me very well – until I missed the school transport one day when I had a heavy load of paint to carry! The evenings were spent very pleasantly – often I would have some sewing to do or a letter to write to them at home. Over the years I found out that they liked plenty of letters and to be kept abreast of what I was doing.

Ivy and May had a black dog, a puppy when I first knew her, but called 'Matthew' until they discovered the pup was not a male, and thereafter named 'Muffie'. She and I were great friends, but I did not get on any too well with the Siamese cat – he (or she) was never friendly!

Most of my weekends were spent at Starcross when members of the family there would come home to visit 'Mother', indeed, there was always something of interest happening or being talked about. There were outings on a Sunday afternoon to various places, and I am going to include one of my diaries more or less just as I wrote it as soon as I have told you about the one weekend I spent in Sandford with the Heards.

I heard the church bell ringing for the Evening Service – just the same as so many years ago when three of us walked from Bremridge up the track along the Downs and on into Hellions Mill, across the river on the wooden footbridge (which never seemed very safe) up the lane and out beside Nortax, up the hill and on into Fanny's Lane and so to Church. Sunday's tea nearly always consisted of apple pie and cream and the feeling of having eaten too much was with us all the way, especially if we had to hurry. But Mum and Lavinia and I felt that we should go at special times, no car was available and it was not thought necessary to use the pony and trap, so we walked it.

Many years before this, there was a succession of Bremridges who used to ride to Sandford Church from the farm and leave their ponies in a rough stable in a corner of the churchyard, so the people of Bremridge have been connected with the church over a very long period, centuries in fact.

I had not thought of going to the service until I heard the bell. I asked Ivy and May if they would like to go, but they said that they did not think they would, so I put on my blue coat and little grey fur hat and went alone.

As I expected, there were not many people at the service and I felt quite glad that I had decided to go if only to make one more person in the congregation.

I had no difficulty in finding the Bremridge pew for it is near a pillar which has a carved 'saucer' with two figures below it. They appear to be naked children, who are fighting. Mystery surrounds the origin, for I was always told that it was probably to commemorate the fight which two men were known to have had in the church when one killed the other, thought by some to have started over a lady, by others that they were workmen who could not agree. Whatever the reason, the church was shut for a number of years – I can remember being told that brambles grew in at the windows – and that it was only opened again because of appeals to King Stephen.

This King, the grandson of William the Conqueror, reigned from 1135 to 1154, but the incident occurred in the reign of his father, Henry 1st, some eleven years earlier.

I have wondered if the fight had anything to do with the people who lived at, or near, Bremridge, and so the 'saucer' was attached to the pillar nearest to the seat allocated to that family. It could have been attached to one of several other pillars, or was it the spot where the fight ended?

The service finished and I am sure there was some curiosity as to who I was, sitting all alone on the other side of the building.

The gentleman who spoke to me as I was leaving walked back with me to 'Snows'. He was a Mr Glass, member of a very well known family.

The 1966 diary gives a very good idea of the kind of 'holiday' every visit to Devon had become – a mixture of pleasure and work, a mixture of work and pleasure. I think I ought to disguise one or two names – just in case I give offence since I have not asked for permission from the people concerned to include them, as they might say, 'in the blooming ole book 'er's writing!'

Diary Extract

My visit to Devon began at 6.55 a.m. on the 14th March, a short journey by car to the station at Nutfield and then a very pleasant ride to Reading. I saw quite a lot of horses and ponies in flat, marshy fields near the railway. In one there were eight animals, which included one donkey who seemed to have a particular friend – a large dark bay animal and the little donkey trailed her (or him) just like our little kitten follows the other cats!

At Dorking station there was an elderly, stiffish man using a tractor with a 'bucket' on the front. The train stopped long enough for me to see his problem – how to get a round length of wood standing on end to remain upright while he brought the bucket down on top. This was perfect 'Laurel and Hardy' and I enjoyed his performance, obviously not the first time he had done it, but the train moved on before success was achieved.

At Reading I got out as did the Superior Young Man talking to another Superior Young Man about the forthcoming General Election and his own more personal problem as to whether it was a boy or a girl to add to his two sons. In fact, I changed trains there to one from Paddington and nearly convinced myself that the train was going the wrong way – back to London. At the beginning of any train journey my sense of direction is suspect! The new carriage was warm and 'Granny' sitting opposite me was knitting a baby's small jacket. We talked a little and she told me that she had made twelve! A farmer and his wife seemed to be having a difference of opinion about everything in general – his monosyllabic replies gave nothing away but she rattled on again, again and yet again!

The Paddington/Exeter train loped along very happily – not even appearing to be out of breath after many, many miles! As we travelled I saw what I thought at first to be stooks of corn left out from the last year's harvest, I now know that they were bundles of withies cut from very flat fields which were separated by dikes and ditches. Withies are used for basket-making I believe.

When Exeter was reached the sun shone and I heard the wonderful Devon voices – slow, full of humour, rich and strong. Two young people came up to me at St. David's Station and asked, without any trace of a Devon accent, 'Excuse me, are you Dr Rossendale?' I told them that I was not and they hurried off on their search among the alighting passengers. Were they students, and was the Doctor a University teacher, I wonder what she taught!

I caught a 'D' bus to Queen Street and was very glad to dump my luggage in my Estate Agent's office. I did some shopping and returned at about 2.30, laden again – and there met a tall, fair young man who was to drive me out to Heath Bridge. I snatched just enough time to scribble a note home to let them know I was there or here (as you will).

We collected the paint from Widgers and he drove me to Crediton where I made a lightning call on Mr Veitch, and gave him his eggs. He was looking very fit and well and referred to my letter describing my visit to the Bank Manager some time before. He said he thought I should have been a writer! I must call again with the insurance documents. He did say that 'the lady' had left her Crawley address and that the case was heard at Horsham and judgement found for me. ('The lady' owed me the money for her stay at The Bungalow, the only 'Bad-Debtor' I had – and I still have not recovered any money, so I have given up hope now!)

On to Heath Bridge, where it looks as if there are a few jobs to be done. Flaming mice have ruined an eiderdown for me and made some holes in two blankets. The tenant at Rose Cottage found the possible culprits – dead – I must make a new eiderdown, or can I mend it, or shall I buy one of the terylene filled creations so popular just now? I must think.

I busied myself till bedtime, then made myself a large dish of tomato soup for supper and soaked my joint of bacon to boil tomorrow. From the Cottage I 'phoned Dora and Stan, inviting them out here, with Ena too if she can manage it. Ivy and May will not be coming as they are not well – 'flu I think.

There is another baby expected in the Cottage in May. A brother or sister for Simon.

This is now the morning of the second day, so I'll write up yesterday's events. It is only 7.30 a.m. but I have breakfasted very well off cold ham, and used some of the slightly salty fat as a spread instead of butter. I hardly think it could be called a slimmer's diet!

Well yesterday was quite a busy day. The night I arrived I felt a little deflated, the bounce had gone, leaving me as flat as a punctured bicycle tyre. The toilet could not be flushed, so I turned the tap on in the kitchen to fill the cistern. There was the sound of water dripping on the floor! I soon saw that the drip had no intention of becoming less and that for as long as the tap was on water would find its last resting place on my kitchen floor, so I turned the tap off and filled the cistern by making two trips with an outsize green plastic jug which once did duty as a bedroom accessory in the days before the coming of electricity and water in plenty. Did I really have the nerve to inflict those conditions on my holiday guests? Needs must when the devil drives and I believe he has been with me for quite a number of years now. Good job he lay dormant until the end of the Hammett era, and I hope that he will be quiet again soon.

The handle is off one of the bedroom doors, the back door drags, the lavatory door will not shut and rain has come in over the front door, staining the wallpaper.

So I went to bed, between 7.30 – 8 p.m. and I slept like a log until just before light. In the morning the sun began to shine, the air was clear, and I began to smile again in spite of discovering even more imperfections. My table top in the living room is badly marked, the braid from two chairs is loose and that cupboard is certainly in the wrong place in the kitchen.

My breakfast was the left-over tomato soup from the night before and I began the day's chores by taking off the pillow cases and cushion covers and washing them. I saw the occupant of the Cottage very briefly as he was just off to Bristol – to return the same day I think – and he seemed very cheerful.

I phoned my Exeter agent about 10.30 a.m. – at his home as he seemed to have retreated there to get some work done and I told him of the water trouble.

Mr Norton arrived at about 3.30 p.m. (What a big man he is, and what a dwarf I feel beside him!) He discovered the cause of the trouble to be frost damage and I had to help him by going into the toilet and either pushing hard against the pipe or pulling it back. To any onlooker we must have presented an amusing appearance – much as the candid camera series on TV a few years ago. Finally, however, it was in order to turn on the tap again – and there was another leaky joint near the basin! This was dealt with and now it is OK. Mr Norton is coming out next Wednesday to 'Aquaseal' the rubberoid on The Bungalow roof, alter the position of the cupboard in the kitchen placed too high on the wall to be of much use to me – without my standing on a chair every time I needed to use it – and he laughed when he saw my difficulty, and bent down and tried to put himself in my position.

I must meet him by the Crown & Sceptre (Iron Bridge) next Wednesday at 9 a.m.

Half the big room ceiling has been done. The border – the pretty border – has been removed and the paint washed. I hope to finish it all today.

But last night I forgot the decorating and entertained my guests, schoolmates and playmates from so long ago – but sadly only three of them could come. Ivy has not been well and May has 'flu – or something very near it and I must write to them – so it was only Dora, Ena and Stanley.

We enjoyed our evening and I hope that they enjoyed their supper. Hot ham, savoury rice, mashed potato, followed by fruit salad and sweet rice, and of course, cups of tea. It made a meal which I could provide without too much preparation because I had no stocks of this and that and all sorts in the larder as I would have had at home. They understood, and we exchanged news of our families and, indeed, spoke of many things. They were nice – are nice – and ever will be to me. I gave Ena her last year's Christmas present – always the same soap, she can use no other!

And so to bed, but not to sleep. I kept thinking I heard something or someone and I began to wonder whether there was anybody lurking about outside on the verandah. An individual had only to break the front door window glass to be able to put his hand in and undo the door and, oh dear, I'd left my pair of big sharp scissors on the dressing table and if I shouted no one could hear and the tenant of the Cottage would not be back that night anyway!

I knew there was someone there, I could feel it, and again I heard a slight rustle of vegetation. Someone walking along the verandah perhaps and just touching against the shrub at the door! I could not shut my eyes, my mouth was dry and I wished I could get a drink but I could not turn on the light. I scarcely dared breathe, let alone get out of bed. Had I not asked the gypsy woman months ago in the security by my own warm kitchen, 'What is there to be afraid of?' – adding, 'all you have to do is say your prayers and march on.' Oh, you hypocrite you, you humbug you, you're just as scared as the rest of 'em. One of my three hot water bottles was beginning to 'bite', but I scarcely dared move it.

What was that? A cough – a deep throated bovine cough? I laughed and I slept until it was light. The bullocks had prowled around the brake unaware of the fright they had given me or, perhaps, of the lesson they had taught me – not to be so silly in future!

And so now to work, for there is much to be done and only me to do it.

Lord, for tomorrow and its needs I do not pray. Give me, O Lord, strength for today – just for today.

Those were the words running through my mind as I awoke for the second time today – about 6.45-ish. The first time was about 3 a.m. when I got up, had a drink and padded round for five minutes or so. I really thought it was a little too early to start work, so I returned to bed and soon slept. I know I had retired at 9.30 the night before but, Boy, oh Boy, did I need it!

The day had been spent in dealing with ceilings and walls and ceilings and ceilings everlasting. The large room ceiling now meets with my approval. The front bedroom ceiling likewise, but the one in the lavatory, mercifully small, must be done again. The kitchen ceiling really should be coloured too.

I now know a little more about Magicote than I did before. I know that pots can vary considerably – the palest of pale pink for the ceilings is comparatively easy to use. The blue in its pot is a devil! It drags. It does not flow. It is thick and it drags. It clings to the brush and it drags. It needs considerable strength to spread it over the walls evenly and firmly and last night my arms ached, my feet ached with going up and down those steps which I borrowed from 'next door'. True, they make the job a lot easier, but I always had trouble with my feet when working on steps. My shoulders ached, but my head was all right!

Yesterday was a good day for weather so 'Mrs Next Door' walked to Cheriton Fitzpaine and back with her little boy in the pram – (which meant she had to stick to the roads) what a walk! She goes there to see her doctor regarding the coming of the next little one. She says he is quite pleased with her progress. Good.

No extra visitors yesterday but I did see the Thornes' truck dashing up round the corner more than once. When you are working near the ceiling it is easy to observe life going by. I am sure one car I saw belonged to an A.I. man – just like the new ones our own Surrey men have. Only the driver, up and back in less than ten minutes and, no doubt, another little life started in the interior of a cow.

When I awoke with the words of the Sunday School Chorus running through what must serve me as a brain, however inferior, I felt happy. I said them aloud. I sang them, no one there to laugh or criticise. I tried the modern style of swinging them and still the words are with me. 'Lord, for tomorrow and its needs I do not pray'. No, we should only live one day at a time, and yet one has to make provision for all the mundane business of the world – paying the rent, paying the poultry food bills, getting bookings for The Bungalow months ahead, ordering new batches of chicks, trying to get the water system at home efficient so as not to have to carry water all round. Like cooking the dinner, too, I suppose. And yet, 'Lord, for tomorrow and its needs I do not pray' – I know that you are with me today. 'Silly, soppy old Mummy' I can almost hear someone saying and I suppose I am. I'll continue my diary tomorrow morning.

Friday. Yesterday I worked very hard in the morning finishing the large room. A great piece of luck was the arrival of Todd's Van, full of merchandise, towels, needles, cottons, lengths of material, made up garments (shirts, nightdresses of brushed nylon), wool, etc. even blankets, and I bought one much like the four heathery mixture ones already here, for 18/11d. I also bought some needles and mending wool for the blankets the mouse had made a hole in!

In the afternoon I went visiting at Bremvilla. What a wonderful view they have to be sure! Wonderful, wonderful, beautiful. Norman and his father were just finishing dinner, and I was welcomed to a cup of tea.

Apparently, Mrs Thorne had asked her son to bring up from the farm some poultry crumbs for baby chicks, only a fortnight old. He had brought a bag all right, but it was Pauls Calf Starter. I

140

recognised the bag immediately as being one like our own. There was, of course, some leg-pulling.

Also, his bullocks from the Brake were in Mr Sturgess's field enjoying a lovely bit of fresh grass on Hill Farm. He did not seem worried, but I noticed he soon had them out all the same.

There was a W.I. dinner in Sandford last night and the Thornes were going.

I lighted my fire again last night and sewed the upholstery braid back on the chairs. I suppose some child had pulled it off. It was not an easy job to repair but I did manage it with some of Todds' 'Terylene' cotton!

To bed fairly early (I believe) and to sleep like a log. Perhaps 'wooden head' would describe me quite accurately at times. Now, to work, again.

On Saturday I made the journey from Heath Bridge to Starcross by three stages. Stage One was walking up to the top of Broxfords, so that I could call in and give Mrs Thorne the dairy detergent for egg washing which I had promised. She was very pleased. I walked on, pausing in each gateway for a few moments, enjoying the beautiful, wonderful fresh morning, and the views. That I had seen it all before made no difference, it was still beautiful.

In about the lowest and loneliest part of the lane I met a man, a young man, carrying a puppy on a towel. Of course we spoke. He said that he had walked out from Crediton and was going to the bottom of the hill. Could be a sheepdog pup – some largish breed anyway.

I passed Broxford's Cottage – a property almost unrecognisable now to what it was in the days of Jim Bedell when he used to come in and help with the hay or kill the pigs for Grandpa at Bremridge. There was a lady sitting on a log in the morning sunshine having a drink. Naturally I spoke to her, and her husband soon rolled up. He said 'Ya' frequently and I discovered that he was a Dutchman. His wife was English but had lived in Holland for over 20 years. We talked about the water problem, electricity, properties in general and several other matters.

Stage two was the arrival of Rose Cottage tenants in their mini-van. I got in the back (quite comfortable) thinking I was on the way to Crediton only. They announced that Exeter was their destination, so I stayed put as they made their one call on a shop in Crediton.

Exeter at 11.30 was quite good going, I did a little window shopping and I met two old friends – first Mr Kevern who lived quite near us in Old Tiverton Road, Exeter and a girl who went to St. Wilfrid's School when I was there, Joy Newman, now a Mrs Mitchell. We talked a little of the girls we used to know and Joy said that there were some plans for forming an Old Girl Association, old girls as old as 50! Before my time I'm glad to say.

A little to eat and a little shopping and Stage Three – the bus to Starcross and the walk up the lane to Staplake Farm.

Now there is far too much activity for me to describe it all in detail. They are still lovely, lively Williamses, full of noise, full of work, full of chatter and still the centre of life is the large kitchen with its stone floor and long table, long forms, and the old oak cupboard which had been in the Bremridge kitchen for so many years and was purchased at our farm sale!

There are always people coming and going at Staplake. Yesterday, Sunday, Yvonne and Lenore and Lesley came home with their huge bunches of flowers for Mothering Sunday. Dennis and Philip came to dinner and Leslie and Phil with two of their daughters came at night.

There were also two unexpected visitors at night – Bill Lee and his wife. Bill Lee is the grandson of old Mr Lee who used to ride his horse up from 'Land' to see Grandpa at Bremridge. This Mr Lee is much like his father, whom I remember quite well. Now these Lees are grandparents themselves and are living out at Thorverton next door to Vera Kemp, a girl at East Village School in our time. I should very much like to see Vera again and if I stay with Ivy and May Heard in Crediton I might, just might, be able to get a visit in.

Sunday afternoon was a treat indeed. Dennis took Mrs Williams and me and Philip out up over Haldon in his Rover 2,000 car. The men explored some of the Racecourse jumps and we wound around and along so many of the small roads that I was completely lost in no time. We passed Harcombe House – a gentleman's residence – and we drove through parkland up to Whiteway House. This is a truly beautiful spacious residence – and I am not using estate agents' phrasing as I am not trying to sell it!

142

There were a number of cars and sitting in the sun beside their cars many people who had the same idea, apparently, that is, to go for a drive and have tea beside the road.

There had been a surprise for me at Starcross on the Saturday which I have not yet mentioned – a Mothering Sunday card from Jeynie-Jayne, Janet and John. Thank you all, my dears!

Monday, still at Starcross, was a day of rest for me. When I say 'rest' I don't mean sitting still or lying in bed. But it was a day of ease with no decorating and I saw Peter's wife, Jeanette, and Carol (a friend) and went out to Crediton with Mrs Williams, Peter and his wife, out to Yvonne's hair dressing establishment, where the ladies had their 'wigs' done. I went to see Ivy and May Heard who had left Sandford and were living in People's Park, Crediton.

Truth to tell, I felt a little out of tune with some of their suggestions or hints. I hope I did not show it. Of course I'm not going to sell Heath Bridge properties, even if May thought I ought to be tempted by what they may fetch. 'Oh well,' she said at last, 'Her've made up her mind and nothing us says is going to change her – even if her is a stupid little toad.'

I knew they meant well and thought they were giving me good advice. I soldier on.

Back at Starcross, and to bed after midnight (and more) but still not to sleep for some while, so I had a rush to be ready at 9.00 a.m. next morning – case packed and all – ready for my journey to Exeter with Peter.

My first call on that morning (Tuesday) was at the office of the Forestry Commission at 22, Southernhay West, where I intended to enquire the address of Forester Carnell. District Officer Carnell was in the office and was delighted to see me. He said that he had recognised me immediately which is more than I can say about him. I believe I must have expected a young man in a khaki uniform, dark and tall, as when I also worked for the 'Forestry' in wartime! Instead, the softly spoken grey haired gentleman wore a fawn tweed suit, sported a grey moustache and his hair was very thin on top. However, it soon became clear that he was the same Mr Carnell I used to know. He told me the news of his family, gave me his address as Kitts Close, Chudleigh, and an invitation to visit them there if ever I could do so. (My brief call was a very happy one – and I did go to see Mr & Mrs and daughter, Mary, one year, but not this one!)

Leaving Southernhay, I began shopping for The Bungalow, kitchen gadgets, shelf material and more Magicote and, yes, a pair of black shoes for myself. I dumped my case and big shopping bag at my agents and wandered round doing more shopping. I took my old shoes to Waltons who do a repair job while you wait and while I waited I watched several young girls bring in spike heeled shoes needing the attention of the shoe doctor. There were two 'doctors' using power drills and other fast whirling machinery and they very soon did the jobs. Quick, simple, sure and '7/6d please', and that was another straight haired young lady disposed of.

I got back to Mr Connole's office a little early but waited only a few minutes before he came with his driver, Mr Dodd. We loaded my luggage into a little white mini and went out first to see a large fridge in Fore Street, Heavitree, which the owner wanted to sell, but I am sure it is much too big for The Bungalow kitchen.

48, Old Tiverton Road, Exeter, was next visited. The flats were looking well but the stairs must be seen to immediately as I consider that they could be dangerous. The outside of '48' has been painted black and after the initial surprise of seeing the woodwork that colour I began to feel that it was very nice – at least it made a change!

The next journey was out to Heath Bridge and Mr Dodd knew the way on his own without direction. No, that fridge would not have fitted in The Bungalow kitchen.

While I made a cup of tea Mr Connole went next door to have a few words with the tenant of Rose Cottage.

Left alone again, I began to get on with the work I had to do. The weather was not as good now as it had been the previous week. I shivered and shivered at night and I began to wonder if 'flu was catching up with me. What would happen if it did? Of course I'd stay on at Heath Bridge and look after myself.

Thursday morning I 'phoned Mrs Miller at Doddridge and had a good natter. This saved me the journey up there.

I also 'phoned Mrs Thorne at Bremridge and arranged to go into Crediton with her in the afternoon as there are still some odds and ends to buy.

Young Mrs Thorne is a very pleasant girl, perhaps I ought to

My daughter Jeyne.

Upton Hellions Church.
Drawing by my sister Lavinia.

The Bungalow, Heath Bridge. After extension and reconstruction.

The garden is mine — so saith the one above all!

Me, May, Ivy and Jeyne, March 1967.

Douglas, me and Jeyne, with Girlie the greyhound, May 1999.

say 'lady', and I quite enjoyed my trip. I saw Mr Veitch for a few minutes.

It began to snow and rarely have I had to face a more biting perishing wind. 'Enough to freeze a brass monkey' as they used to say at Bremridge.

Friday, and Mr Dodd is collecting me at 4 p.m. so I am up early and went across the valley to see Mrs Yeandle. The walk over Pakeham fields was fresh and cold, and I looked across at the lower reaches of the Brake but not for too long as the ground became 'stuggy' and I had to watch where I was going! In fact I thought one spot was going to stop me as I began to sink nearly up to the top of my white plastic boots before I could find a firm footing! But I did get through and met Mrs Greenslade in the court at Pakeham – and there was the puppy again, the one being carried on a towel, waiter style, by the young man who walked from Crediton. Mystery therefore solved.

Mrs Yeandle was delighted to see me – all in broad Devon. She still flatters my abilities and almost makes me feel I have only to wave a magic wand, write a letter or two, and it'll be all right. Poor girl, she has heart trouble and is rather poorly some of the time I gather. I had a cup of coffee.

Back over the mud and stug of Pakeham and I worked all day as I had rarely worked before. I painted two little tables, the gilt picture framed mirrors, the second bedroom ceiling again and the lavatory walls. The kitchen ceiling, too, seemed a little patchy, so had to be done again. I finished hanging curtains and replaced cleaned pictures. I borrowed the carpet sweeper – more properly the Electrolux Vacuum cleaner from 'next door' – and thoroughly 'did' the floors. I collected all the rubbish to dump and cleaned up the grate.

About 2.30 p.m. Mrs Yeandle came to 'inspeck'. She approved, and washed up the oddments while I changed. Time was so fast running out, I was afraid I would not get packed and ready for Mr Dodd who was to take me back to Exeter. I still had all the blankets to fold up and leave 'just so', the steps to put out and a chair which makes a bed to be shifted into 'my' bedroom. I introduced Mrs Yeandle to the tenant of Rose Cottage and I think they will become good friends – at any rate I hope so.

Eventually Mrs Yeandle departed in her van and I put my things in my case. Perhaps it was as well that I was in such a rush

145

– certainly there was no time for sentimental thoughts because I was leaving Heath Bridge again. When Mr Dodd came I got him to shove my (cleaned) white boots full of small oddments into my bag while I struggled with the case. He said we would be lucky if we saw Mr Connole who had an appointment away from the office at 5.00 p.m.

I settled up for the telephone calls I had made from the Cottage and left money for the postage of the parcel containing the eiderdown, said 'Goodbye' and we were off.

Mr Dodd was very quiet. Depressed, gloomy almost. Can't imagine it is because it is the last time he'll be giving me a lift to or from Exeter! That marvellous infectious laugh was completely gone, so we drove into town almost in silence, each busy I suppose with his or her own thoughts.

Exeter in the sun, but today it was Exeter in the cold and I shivered – or was it just me? Mr Dodd turned the car heater on and we made for the bus station where I intended to leave my cases.

'Closed in half an hour,' said the counter man, so I carried my cases back to the car and we set off for Mr Connole's office. He had gone and left a message that he would see me on Monday morning.

Now my wits began to work again and I asked Mr Dodd if I could use the 'phone. I knew someone in another Estate Agent's Office who came from and went home to, Starcross, even to the farm at Staplake. (This is what my husband calls 'my low cunning' working.) I felt I could not traipse all the way back to the bus station and scarcely had nerve enough to suggest that Mr Dodd took me again. I was fortunate for the gentleman in question was just leaving and, being such a gentleman, of course, he took me.

In fact, he gave me several lifts up and down, Starcross to Exeter, Exeter to Starcross and I was very grateful to him.

Saturday I went to the Higher Cemetery in Exeter with two bunches of pheasant eye narcissus flowers and two bunches of anemones. Grandma and Mum used so much to enjoy the narcissus clumps in Bremridge orchard, and they therefore seemed more appropriate than daffodils. It was with something of a shock that I discovered that the graves had been levelled. Now it all seemed so modern, no familiar 'humps'. I found the right

146

grave with some difficulty as all the numbers had been removed too. But the large granite flower pot with its cavity for a vase marked the spot – beside 'Chamberlain' and in front of a young girl called 'Poole'. There's a 'Taverner' quite near too, and a tree, a holly tree with a white-ish stem. It had been quite a small tree when our first funeral had taken place, now, after all this time *quite* a tree. I suppose the Graves Department of the Council call it progress – easier to keep the grass looking tidy – but I do not like the unfamiliar appearance.

I did what was necessary for water and flowers and when I turned from the path to look back the beautiful white and coloured heads were waving gently in what wind there was – saying 'Goodbye' to me – but soon I could not see them for my eyes were full of tears.

I am afraid this always happens to me when I visit 'Mum and Grandma'. I am afraid I presented a face to the world which was for a while a complete wreck. Fortunately, there was a wait for the bus back into town and this gave me a few minutes to recover.

Back in the city, I thought I would next visit my husband's cousin, Barbara, at 44, Powderham Crescent. I bought her a box of Black Magic chocolates and found my way round by St. James' Football Ground, the same route I had used four times a day years before when I had lived in Exeter and worked for the Forestry Commission. Seems quite different now for there is a big school where there was a bombed site. A sight too much bombing we had in Exeter, too, and yet out of it I suppose something good has arisen.

A little schoolgirl in a navy mack had obviously been sent shopping and was reckoning aloud the cost of her purchases. '1/6d and 7d – that's 2/3d. 2/3d am, no, 1/6d (very slowly) and 7d. 1/6d and 6d, that's 2/-d and 1d – 2/1d.' Skip, skip, basket swinging. What it is to be 8 or 9 years old!

Barbara was just recovering from a bilious attack and while she said that she was very glad to see me I am quite sure she found my visit an added burden. She insisted on making tea and getting some biscuits, while she gave me news of her brother, Alan Stevens at Bognor Regis. Apparently she rather envies my girls for their hitch-hiking exploits. As children of somewhat Victorian parents, she said, they were not encouraged to take any risks, and consequently she and Alan 'did nothing'. As my girls

147

are contemplating yet another trip in the near future I feel that there is quite a lot to be said for the Victorian attitude. I am sure that there must be a Guardian Angel somewhere watching over them or they would have been in grave trouble long before this. I only hope he continues to keep looking in their direction.

I left Barbara and walked up Longbrook Street to the shops and the Post Office where I bought two Premium Bonds for the gentlemen at home, and, from Waltons, skirt material for the two girls. My walk to the Remnant Shop at the bottom of South Street was not very agreeable for now it was raining, quite hard, but I wanted some curtain material for large windows at home – and if you want something you just have to go and get it. I did, and also cotton for sheeting and pillow cases, and vinyl for chair covering and fawn downproof material because of the Heath Bridge mouse's meal!

I had time to go back to Crediton and see Mrs Hammett and Ann and her baby, Shaun Leslie, a big fat bouncing boy in blue. I am afraid that Mrs Hammett is getting a little frail and she looks very tired but is that to be wondered at for she must now be over 70? She was, as always, delighted to see me and asked all about the alterations at Heath Bridge.

I have rarely seen such a queer conductor as the one on the bus back to Exeter. His peaked cap was set well over the front of his head and showed a fringe of hair at the back. He wore glasses and peered rather closely at tickets and money after the manner of short-sighted people. His eyes were, anyway, shaded by his cap and he had a shaggy 'moleish' kind of look. He wore shoes with quite high heels and bounced along, sometimes whistling quietly.

A young man walked quickly to the front of the bus. He was looking at the racing results in a newspaper and said aloud in an educated voice (if there is such a thing) '50 to 1. By Jove, 50 to 1'. Must have been the Grand National winner by the name of 'Anglo' (I believe). I had heard that result on somebody's transistor at the Remnant Shop.

There was nearly an hour to wait for the bus to Starcross. I watched the world going by again and I saw a young man have a most vigorous collision with a lamp post. It is nearly always a mistake to walk one way and look another! Poor nose and forehead!

I saw many young ladies with long straight hair and very short skirts meeting their boy-friends. Those skirts really are becoming ridiculous! Are the makers economising on material or are the skirts getting shorter and shorter to please the boys and, of course, the men? One very, very, skimpy skirted young lady met an 'It' – a boy with shoulder length hair and a 'pretty' face. They walked hand in hand and out of sight, as ships that pass in the night!

Leather-jacketed young men seem to be putting their decorations on their backs – decorated in reverse! Is there competition as to who can sport the most, with swinging chains and brass studs and different designs? Some of the girls wear trousers which are much more suitable with a biting wind like this than the skimpy skirt. More than once I wished I was wearing my wellingtons – my farm boots I mean, not my white town plastic ones. Legs would at least have been more comfortable.

Starcross again at last.

Mrs Williams and Oriel are up at her son's farm and Oriel's two little girls are quietly playing by the fire. These children are always quiet, they are always well behaved. Miss Booth is there, in charge until Mrs Williams and her daughter return, but she has a headache and is not feeling very bright. She has had several lately and they are beginning to worry her so she leaves as soon as the ladies return.

We go to bed late, again.

A drive is planned for Sunday afternoon. Peter and Jeanette and Mrs Williams take a route which will take them to Heath Bridge and an inspection of The Bungalow. I am pleased about this for I know that Mrs Williams would point out anything she thought could be improved since she had much experience of catering for summer visitors.

We had a most enjoyable drive round Stockleigh Pomeroy and Bickleigh and arrived at Oriel's home in Pinhoe after we passed through Stoke Canon and Rewe. What memories it brought back of walks with 'Punch' or 'Andy-Mose' and a certain young man! It had taken us a whole afternoon to get to both villages and back and I also remembered that Lavinia and I had walked to Stoke Canon to a church service when the Preacher had been a distant relative, a Rev. Cheriton.

Nothing is ever too much trouble for Mrs Williams' beautiful daughters and it made no difference now that tea at Oriel's had already been cleared for the table was very soon made ready again and tea and chatter were most enjoyable.

Oriel had married the brother of a girl with whom I went to school at St. Wilfrids so I learned the fate of several old friends.

We made an early return to Starcross where I had packed some of my goods up into a parcel and loaded my shopping bag with the apples we had fetched from the loft earlier in the day. We went to bed – eventually – after standing in the kitchen by the 'Aga' for some time, talking.

Monday morning, I knew, would be the worst time for me of the whole fortnight. To say 'goodbye' to Mrs Williams is never easy; to realise that it will probably be a whole year before I see any of them again; to know that the 'holiday' is well and truly over and that there are all sorts of responsibilities lying in wait for me at home suddenly seems too much – and the tears come easily. Perhaps I am just feeling sorry for myself, perhaps I am feeling sorry for everybody else whose life I shall probably make uneasy.

My good friend from the estate agent's office allowed me to leave my cases there until I was ready to collect them en route for the train at St. Davids.

I went to Mr Connole's office, to see him for the second and last time of this visit to the West Country. We discussed the matters of importance at '48', particularly, and touched on affairs at Heath Bridge.

The journey home was quite pleasant. The carriage was warm, but the young student sitting opposite me with a somewhat haughty expression, had some coffee cups tucked away by his feet and they rattled and they rattled. His displeasure became more and more obvious and he almost sighed with relief when, eventually, they were collected.

At Reading it rained, heavily. A slow train to Nuffield, but at Reigate I was joined by Janet. She entered my compartment and it made her day that we had a taxi from Redhill – home.

I am not going to copy out any more complete diaries. For nearly ten years my interest in letting The Bungalow for holiday visitors necessitated about a fortnight in Devon, with every weekend the break which my friends at Starcross were able to allow me to enjoy, and the days in between were very busy ones, getting the place as ship-shape as possible.

150

I think, maybe, I could mention one or two things of interest without becoming too boring and the first one concerns the road men who came to do a little patching somewhere down by the bridge. They left their van right in the gateway of 'The Plot' and I was a little concerned that Bill Hammett would come home in his own vehicle and have to leave it in the road so, at about 4.30 p.m. I wandered down to have a word with them and ask them to shift it.

What did I see? A whole brazier full of burning coke – and I was getting a little short of fuel for my grate. Amy had ordered a hundredweight for me and I had stretched it with sticks but found stick-gathering to be more time consuming than I could really afford. I said, 'You are not going to leave that alight are you?' 'No, Missus, we'll throw it out and you can have it if you like.'

Of course, I 'liked'. I took my black 'helmet' coal scuttle down and filled it after they had gone and the coke was cold. In fact, I made two journeys and it lasted out for the rest of the week. I certainly regarded that as a miracle – and thanked God for providing it!

A smaller miracle, but just as much appreciated, was the large swede dropped in the gutter just above the Cottage – a welcome addition to my dinner!

I see from a long letter I wrote to them at home on the 9th February 1964 that I was unlucky with lifts from the School Car 'I have had to puff all the way up over Priorton Hill three times. The second and third times I went right to the top without stopping once at the spanking pace of a five-year-old! The country is beautiful, the air is fresh, my shoes are comfortable and though I seem to have debts of hundreds of pounds piling up, who can worry in such conditions?' This was when electricity was being put in and I was staying at night with my friends in Sandford – in fact, I stayed a few days longer in Devon because of this work as Amy was away from Heath Bridge looking after a sick relative in another village and could not be there to let the electricians in!

The same letter says: 'My slimming effort is getting me nowhere. May gives me sandwiches to take for lunch, and one day the bones of a chicken to pick. The same day I had a colossal cold lunch at the Thornes (Bremvilla) and at night there was another cooked dinner followed by apple pie and cream! I regret to say that I enjoyed and devoured the lot.

'I met Mr Hall, the ex-school Attendance Officer, in Crediton, and remembered how he used to create fear and trembling in the hearts of the children who "mitchied" in my school days. He knew me, but not my name. He said he remembered Grandma very well and spoke kindly of her. Apparently he is now a widower and talks to the television for company. He said, "Only thing is, 'ee never answers back!"

'A Wayleave Officer for the Electricity Board was a Mr Ken Triggs, an extremely pleasant West Country gentleman. He appeared at The Bungalow door with a large meat chopper on the end of an axe handle and I began to wonder what was happening – or going to happen. But it was only to take the marks of 'F' off the apple trees which they thought would need to be felled but, apparently, have been reprieved. It seems that the trouble was from Mr Thorne who had not welcomed the idea of the trees blocking his road out to the milk lorry, but he had also to lose several trees, and when I went up there on Thursday just after dinner (I thought) he was most co-operative and helpful. He used a phrase worth noting: "It was a pity you could not foresee backwards!" I said, "I thought it was after dinner," because Mrs Thorne insisted that I had two warm Cornish pasties and a large plate of gooseberry pie with cream, and two cups of tea! I have an invitation to dinner again this week if I'm around here!

'Norman Thorne drives his truck into Sandford some mornings and collects several women for work out in Nanny Park, the swede field. They'm cleaning and bagging all day and were sitting on a bale of straw by the roadside drinking tea when I puffed up the road. I know they were exceedingly curious about me because the day before Mr Connole and Mr Hilton (his driver) and I walked up to the little gateway just below the entrance to Hill Farm from where we could look across the valley and see where Mrs Ridge's cottage was in relation to the Brake as she was thinking of renting it for keeping ponies. There were some wolf whistles and strange noises from the field but I can assure you that everything was entirely above board and in the open – no funny business!'

How the times have changed from the days of my visits for work in the little country village and, later, pleasure at Starcross. One entry in my 1967 diary illustrates this.

Apparently I had walked up the hill behind Rose Cottage and The Bungalow to see Mrs Thorne at Bremvilla. On the way, just by Mr Sturgess's farm gateway there was a man sitting in a cream Ford van. He waited for me to come up, and shouted, 'Did I know if Mr Sturgess was in yet – back from the hunt?' Of course I did not know but it gave him a chance to open the conversation. I soon learned that he was a farmer/dealer/Covent Garden lorry dispatcher who was trying to buy some hay which Mr Sturgess had for sale. We talked of income tax and hitch-hikers and doing deals. What an expressive face he had – long and very 'elastic' with a quick changing meaning smile. Blue eyes. When he talked about some of his deals he would almost screw his mouth into a little round and suck in his breath. His tweed hat – cousin to a 'pork-pie' sat squarely on his head. I judged him to be a man of about 45 or so, and it seemed perfectly natural to be talking to him there in the empty lane – with the patchwork of fields stretching away to distant villages.

A young man on a motorbike, a Mr Leach, came out of Mr Sturgess's lane and spoke to 'him'. The stranger gave me a lift up to Mrs Thorne's bungalow and said he would go into Crediton for something to eat. Mr and Mrs Thorne were very pleased to see me. I had a cup of tea and some biscuits!

'Don't accept lifts from strangers' is more important now than in those days!

153

18

The Accident

Most of my journeys down to Devon and back again by rail were uneventful, but there was one which had a horrible incident connected with it.

On Tuesday, the 6th June 1978, I returned from Dawlish to Redhill by the 3.40 p.m. train from Exeter, St. David's. This was on a monthly return ticket purchased from Redhill about a fortnight before; the route was via Reading, where I would change trains to the Guildford/Tonbridge line.

My daughter Jeyne, her husband John and their baby Kathy joined the train at St. David's station and we travelled up together, enjoying the journey until there was a horrible jolt between Westbury and Newbury and the train came to a standstill – and remained at a standstill for a very long time, nearly two hours I believe.

John had jumped down on the line to investigate and found that an elderly man walking near had been struck by the train before it could stop. He was not dead but was certainly injured. Railway staff collected white tablecloths form the Buffet Car and a doctor, a passenger, gave what aid he could.

Very soon police were running along the rails; firemen called to bring a stretcher could not arrive for some time since one had to be brought from the nearest station, apparently stretchers are not carried on trains. I realised that my husband would be at Redhill to meet me and before long would be most concerned, especially if he had heard that there had been an accident. If only I could let him know somehow, but how?

Jeyne had a brainwave. 'Write a note, Mum,' she said, 'and

throw it down to one of the police and ask if they would ring our Nutfield number and explain about the accident delaying our train.'

I fumbled in my handbag and found an envelope on which I wrote the telephone number and my husband's name and address. The young policeman who picked it up would not promise that anything could be done about it but that he would, at least, try.

Apparently he was able to contact them at home, and I do not know who was most worried when they heard it was a call from the Police and that there had been an accident, and a delay of about two hours.

Instead of changing trains at Reading I went on to Paddington and down to Redhill by a faster train than I would have been able to catch at the former station. Travelling by that route with Jeyne and John and little Kathy was much easier than if I had been on my own.

I learned from John later – he was working on the railway at the time – that the elderly gentleman on the line was a patient at a mental institution and was not really responsible for his actions. Surely someone, somewhere, should have been in charge of such a man and made sure that an accident like that could not happen.

19

The Visitors

Now I had better tell you a little about the people who did go to The Bungalow at Heath Bridge on holiday. The first thing to do was to advertise – no one would have a holiday there if they did not know the place existed, so I had to type some cards for display in shop windows, get an entry into one of the 'Holiday' papers and put my board out. 'HOLIDAY ACCOMMODATION IN DEVON' it said, and I did get a number of enquiries from local people who later stayed there. The 'feed back', to use a very modern expression, was generally very favourable – until S.W.E.B. put the price of electricity so high, as I have already mentioned. Almost without exception, the visitors remarked on the peace surrounding Heath Bridge, the views and the walks up the hills, the fact that they could get either to the South Devon coast or to the North Devon Moors for a day's outing – by car, of course – to Dartmoor, to Plymouth, to Exeter, to that queer little town of Crediton, which is not so little after all this time for Crediton has certainly expanded – in fact, anywhere their fancy took them or the weather allowed!

There were several families who went to Heath Bridge little Bungalow for more than one holiday, but people do not always play fair and I heard afterwards that ten individuals crammed themselves in though it was advertised as accommodating six people, since there were two double beds, a chair bed (usually for a child) and a single put-u-up in the living room. The cushions were pillow sized and shaped and only needed the outside covers removed and white covers slipped on to be adapted for use at night.

One family went on the Saturday morning leaving much clearing up for the tenant of the Cottage. Whoever the tenant was, Amy, first and others later, all kept an eye on things for me and all did everything within their power to ensure all information needed by the visitors was available for them. Some people did get lost, and some drivers were not very happy about the narrow lanes for the first two or three journeys.

One Spring I found that the garden in front of The Bungalow had been neglected and the grass was almost as long as if it had been grown in a meadow. I could not expect any children to play in there! The tenant of Rose Cottage had little idea of gardening and although they all promised to do what they could to keep things tidy I found very little had been done most years. In this particular year I walked up to East Village, borrowed a hook from Doddridge and set to work myself, mainly early in the mornings when the air was so beautiful. It is not a small garden by any means and 'I worked myself into the ground' (to use an old expression). But I did it, and had just finished before I was collected by car to return home. It was a journey which I scarcely remember at all for I slept most of the way!

20

Longer Lettings and Rose Cottage

After the summer visitors of 1968 The Bungalow became home to a local family who had a little boy. When the second baby was expected they gave me notice that they would be leaving for larger accommodation, towards the end of the 1970 holiday season. They had used and looked after my furniture well.

The lady once wrote to me that she had been approached by a secondhand dealer to sell the little Victorian chair covered in green velvet – for £30. The dealer would have taken the red tub chair for a good price too. Naturally, she had refused but she thought I ought to know.

There was time only for two or three visitors in 1970, but my agent in Exeter thought he had a 'long let' tenant who would be suitable.

It was a long let all right, from 1970 to 1986, but not a happy one. I had been warned that the gentleman was of an odd appearance, tall, thin, with a beard, somewhat asthmatic or with chest trouble – and always wearing wellington boots. He had a wife and I believe that any children were not his for it seems that his wife had been married before. I can remember meeting a good sized girl during one of my visits.

It is a fact that both Mr and Mrs were too fond of the bottle, but more about that later.

My first visit after they became tenants revealed evidence that there had been neglect of elementary principles of tidiness. When I pointed this out to them both the gentleman made some excuse – he had a number of small jobs which gave him some sort of income but not enough time, apparently, to do what was so obvious around his own home.

'Mrs' said that she did not like Heath Bridge at all and was going to ask the Doctor for certificates which she hoped would enable them to have other accommodation – probably from the Council. However, they did promise to do what they could.

On my next visit – about a year later – Mr and Mrs were out – they had an urgent appointment in Exeter. They were very sorry not to have seen me but hoped to see me next year.

I could see that there was little, if any, improvement. Empty crates of bottles advertised their weakness! I say 'crates' instead of describing the miscellaneous containers in detail, for empty bottles seemed to be everywhere.

There were visits at varied intervals to the Heath Bridge area by my agent in Exeter who would report to me that either he had been unable to see our tenant or that he had seen him and under threat of notice there had been the usual promise to clear up or do the small repairs necessary. I think there was quite an attempt at gardening, vegetables, of course.

Down in the Plot the weeds grew apace. That little area also seemed to grow van bodies or car bodies which remained undisturbed for years. In spite of requests for their removal and promises that they 'were going' after some gadget or part had been removed it seemed to me that the same wrecks were still in situ at my next visit about another year hence! I do admit that makes of car or van are about alike to me and I had never been able to pick out the different ones unless the name was written somewhere. I could easily be confused that the old 'Ford' of this year was not the same make as the one there last year, especially if the vehicle had been shifted round a little!

To be sure of seeing these untidy tenants as usual I wrote and told them the day and time of my next visit and expected to see them. Came the day – a Friday – and they were not there and would not be back until late at night. The tenant of Rose Cottage had the message for me.

They did pay their rent, little enough in those days, so they could not be given notice on that account.

My 'holiday home' was the same as always – Starcross. When I told my friends of my problems we discussed plans. One of the girls had a little car and we arranged that on Sunday we would

159

have a drive around, calling at The Bungalow about four o'clock which we judged to be well after closing time. So we went from Starcross to Exeter; to Crediton and around the Broxfords way. We stopped the car at nearly every gateway and 'gawked' over for a few minutes. The view was very interesting to both of us, for her childhood had also been spent at Bremridge. She knew all about East Village, the school, and all the neighbours I knew and have mentioned.

When we knocked at the door of The Bungalow we realised that we had picked the right time for our visit. The smell of cooking beef was very strong. It is very difficult to disguise the smell of a Sunday dinner, and when the door was opened by 'the lady', to give her a title she did not deserve, she was not pleased, not pleased at all. She said she thought it was a dirty trick to arrive on a Sunday afternoon. To put it mildly, we had words. Eventually, again, I received the promise from 'Mr' to clear up and clean up, remove the untidy clutter near the back door, etc.

That was the last time I saw 'Mrs'. Some months later I was sent a small cutting from the local paper, with an account of a fire at Heath Bridge. An oil stove was being lit when the fumes overcame the lady. She died, drowned in her own vomit! The fire brigade had been called out, no doubt, and there was consternation all round.

There was not much damage to The Bungalow – the glass of the window broken, the carpet burnt, and some furniture severely damaged, in addition the ceiling of the living room where this tragedy happened, was as black as 'the ace of spades'.

No, I did not write to offer sympathy as I did not feel that would be appropriate after our last encounter.

I was disgusted to find on my next visit that after yet another year had passed the ceiling still had not been cleaned, or coloured, and was still as the fire had left it! Although the old man was at home he said that he had a bitch, Sheila, shut in the passage and she was fierce and he would be afraid to open the door. I told him that I was not afraid, usually I got on well with dogs, so I would risk it.

Sheila came up to me, gave one little bark, and her tail began to wag. I spoke softly to her, stroked her head, and we were friends.

I wondered why I had bothered to look in the bedroom – there

160

was the biggest shambles you could imagine. Heaps of clothes everywhere – too much for me to describe – but on one bed there was a pile of egg trays nursing dirty eggs! The curtains at the bedroom windows were the same ones I had hung with such pride when summer visitors were expected, almost ten years ago! I scarcely dared to open the door of the toilet but I did look in – it was no better than the other places.

Of course the green chair had disappeared, and the tub chair and also the picture on the wall which had been painted by my Great Grandfather. It had shown all the flags of the different ships and countries with which he had been connected. 'Mr' said he could not remember it at all!

I asked the tall man in the wellington boots what his plans were now that he was living on his own and suggested that he might be much better off living with relatives. I already knew that he had some sort of connection with Bristol, though exactly what that was I did not know. No, he did not want to move and he assured me that he liked it at The Bungalow and was only waiting for good weather before he could concentrate on the outside jobs and he promised, again, to do what he could.

Since it was furnished accommodation which this problem family had rented I had paid the rates for several years after they came to live at Heath Bridge, but I jibbed when I realised they were not short of cash and were rather foolishly spending it 'by the bottleful!'

For reasons best known to himself – or, perhaps because he had the beds so laden with clothes and clutter that it took him so long to shift it all – he chose to put a mattress down on the floor of the living room and sleep there. He stood it on its side and pushed it back behind the table against the wall in the daytime.

When he could see by the movement of the leaves of the rose bushes on the verandah that it was windy out of doors, he told me, he did not get up. He had an idea that his poorly chest could be made much worse if he had to go out and face the elements! Was that yet another excuse for doing nothing? He always seemed able to drive the van to Sandford or Crediton, returning hours later.

After my memorable Sunday visit he still managed to wriggle out of meeting me if he possibly could. There was a note pinned to the back door which read: 'Have got to have the van MOT'd, hope to be back to see you.'

Of course he was not.

I caught him on my next visit – for a few minutes only – he had to drive into Sandford to collect his pension 'and do a little job for someone' after, so he would not be back for some time. I could feel what that would mean, therefore the brief look indoors where little, if any, improvement had taken place was about all I could manage.

If only the rent had not been paid regularly the problem of getting the old man to leave could have been solved long ago. However, everything must end sometime and it was in 1986 that all his earthly troubles were over, and the muddles which he had created and allowed to increase were open for inspection. He was found dead in the passage near the toilet on the 1st of July.

The tenant of Rose Cottage must have had the task of getting in touch with someone who could decide something and help. I was told that there was a relative up in this part of the world who had 'phoned him frequently about lunch time on Sundays at one of his favourite drinking places in Crediton. Obviously she cared what happened to the old man. Eventually I did contact her myself and she said she remembered how attractive The Bungalow had been when she had seen it, somewhere about 1971 or 72, she thought.

In time other relatives went to Heath Bridge and removed some of the old man's things – and I was left, as I knew I would be, with a very big problem. For a while I did nothing. I always find that 'to do nothing' when difficult circumstances arise is often the best policy. The solution may take a little time. Opportunities may present themselves quite unexpectedly but in the meantime I was left with a place so overgrown there was some surprise expressed by passers by who had not travelled that road for some time that a bungalow was still there! Everything about it was bad, poor, neglected or just did not exist. I did not go down to Devon again for several years.

I must bring you up to date with the affairs of Rose Cottage. When Bill and Amy left to go into Crediton to be nearer his work the next tenants had one little boy and expected another baby. They were followed by a local lassie and her family. She was extremely good at making soft toys for sale and on one of my tours of inspection there were several bears and rabbits sitting up neatly in the corner of the big room on some article of furniture. I remembered the toys but I have forgotten what the article of furniture was. I believe her husband had the daily journey to Crediton to work.

Then there was a young couple – from London I think. Again, one baby, and some cats. It seemed that Mr stayed home, looked after baby and cats and followed his calling as a wedding photographer when opportunity presented itself. Mrs had a job in Exeter helping the financial position along. I never knew her mode of transport, or, if I did, I have forgotten!

I was fortunate with the next tenants for they remained at Rose Cottage for a number of years. Much of the work of tidying up outside The Bungalow in the first instance fell upon them and I am sure they had some good bonfires.

I always had rather a soft spot for 'Mrs'. She was fond of animals and had two dogs. They were both mongrels I think and I know that she told me she had rescued one as a puppy when she lived in London – yes, she was a Londoner. Someone had tried to put it down a toilet!

21

Back to Enville

My Dad and Nancy lived very happily together in Enville, a country village not too far from the Midland town of Stourbridge, until Nancy became ill.

Over the years they had received visits from as many members of the family as possible – those owning cars finding the journey long enough, but possible. I think that Janet and Jack were, perhaps, the most frequent visitors, in fact they took me up to Enville several times.

One day there was a letter from Dad saying that Nancy had gone into hospital. She remained there for a while but was eventually sent home and Dad had to do much nursing. She died on 16th December 1979; we were informed by a telephone call from one of the neighbours, Mrs Wentworth.

Who could go to the funeral? At that time Janet was driving an ex-telephone van, bright yellow, so with a full tank and determination we set off from Brookside at 6.30 a.m. on 20th December 1979 to reach Enville Church by 12.15 p.m., we hoped. Good progress was made until we were held up by road works in Worcester and then we had to belt along! We missed the service at the church but were in time for the internment of the coffin in the churchyard on the hill. Dad was so pleased to see us.

There was his nephew, Nevil, several of Dad's relatives, and Mrs Jones from next door, and it was after we returned to Dad's house that she said, 'You are Fred's daughters, aren't you?' I was only too pleased to confirm that I was!

I don't know why my Dad had been called 'Fred' locally, for

his name was Dorrel Nelson Jeynes, but he said that he had some very good friends in the area and did not plan to leave his home. Nevil did not live too far off and would do what he could to help. The other relatives, particularly his sister-in-law, Winnie, now a widow, said that she would come over – from Worcester, I think, now and again. Dad said that he had some friends 'Up at the Hall', the establishment of the local gentry, I gathered.

So Janet and I set off again, about 4 o'clock, in the gathering dusk of the chill December day, got slightly lost which cost us a detour of a few miles, but eventually reached home very tired. We had one stop on the way, somewhere near Oxford, I believe, when Janet felt she needed a rest from driving in the dark.

It was on this journey home that we talked about much of the family history and of our life at Bremridge with my Dad being there. As with many young people she found it difficult to imagine life as we had known it, the primitive conditions, the horse and cart transport, the old fashioned values which had existed. 'Why,' she asked, 'did people visiting the farm always refer to your Grandfather as 'Maister' or 'Sir'?

I now know that this must have been common in the days of the apprentice, when the servants certainly were not treated as equals – they had to 'know their place' and show respect, at least publicly. What they said behind the 'Maister's' back was anybody's guess!

I had the chance to go to Yorkshire on the 11th September 1982. Our son John, and his young family were living in Boroughbridge and when a great friend offered me a lift – she was going with a neighbour to the North Yorkshire Moors on holiday – of course I took it. I stayed with John and Sue for several days, until I caught a bus and journeyed to Leeds and through to Stourbridge. The local bus deposited me beside 'The Cat', where Dad was waiting for me.

I was extremely glad the journey had finished for I was beginning to feel quite ill. I thought a cup of tea at Dad's home would be all that was needed to restore my usual good health, but it was not, and the whole evening I spent feeling very sorry for myself.

This was very unfortunate, as Dad had asked a friend round and thought that we could have all gone to the 'Cat' together. I persuaded Dad and his friend that I would be all right on my own

– I certainly did not want to spoil their enjoyment.

Months before, on the 23rd April, to be exact, I had spoken to Dad's friend on the telephone since I was more than a little anxious about a cattle problem and Dad said that this young fellow 'up at the Hall' was very good with cattle and that he would advise me about what to do. We had quite a discussion about cows and calves and their ills, and he recommended liquid treacle!

I did not know it then but this young man and his family certainly come into the story of 'Under the Hills of Bremridge'.

Beside Janet and Jack visiting Dad my sister Lavinia and her husband Derek made several trips up to Enville. With 'Meals-on-Wheels' and the cooking he could manage for himself, his visits to 'The Cat', exchange of garden produce with Mr & Mrs Jones – both Dad and Mr Jones were very keen gardeners and each one seemed to have a surplus of something – he did not do too badly. There was a little shop on the corner of the road where papers and a few groceries could be bought, stamps, too, and when I went there during one of my visits the lady behind the counter said, 'I know who you are, I recognise your Dad's little shopping bag!'

Dad had two or three periods in hospital after Nancy died, chest trouble and 'tests' though he never said what they were for, but always the nurses gave him a very fond farewell – he was very popular.

He was in hospital again, in January 1986, when he died. Lavinia and Derek and I went to the funeral, by train from Winchester as they thought the weather was likely to turn to snow and driving could be difficult. Yes, it snowed and was extremely cold, so we had made the right choice and were lucky to get a taxi from Stourbridge to Enville.

Again we met relatives and neighbours – and the young man from 'The Hall'. Nevil had been with Dad to the solicitors and he said he would see to everything.

I understood that Dad's young friend was shortly off to Scotland to work and I remember saying, 'Keep in touch – you know our address.'

22

The Brake

Many years ago when Mr and Mrs Hammett left there was the problem of what to do about the Brake across the road. Who would want it? Bill and Amy certainly had no need of it, but there was a lady 'across the valley' who had some ponies – I do not know how many. This was in 1963 or 1964 and I think that she used it only for a short while. Her intention, I was told, was to establish a small riding school but I am afraid that because of matrimonial difficulties her plans came to nothing. It all fell flat!

When I was visiting Devon so many years ago to do the work ready for the next season's visitors beside going up to Broxfords Hill to Mrs Thorne, Senior, I made a few visits to Bremridge. It was on one of these trips up to the farm that I had a conversation with Mr Norman Thorne which resulted in him becoming the tenant of the Brake. He said that he could do with it for wintering his cattle and I could see that there would be no other applicant from either The Bungalow or Rose Cottage.

I advised him to contact my agent in Exeter and in time Mr Connole wrote to me that he had negotiated an agreement with Mr N. Thorne which apparently did not restrict him to cattle wintering only, but the tenant made it clear that he did not intend to remove gorse and bramble which were beginning to encroach. He was obliged to do the fencing himself if he wanted to keep cattle there.

For a number of years the hedges around Broxfords bordering Bremridge Farm had been trimmed in accordance with good husbandry, so it was little trouble to Mr Thorne to run his machinery down over my adjoining hedges, which he did and for which I was grateful.

I had first met young Norman when he was a boy at school and still wearing short trousers, so I was quite happy to receive a low rent if the land would be used and looked after.

There were big lorries which used the Broxfords Lane when they came from the Tiverton direction and turned up round the corner of The Bungalow garden. The snag was the lorries were big enough to be a problem to get round the corner and into the Bremridge track.

Negotiations again took place and Mr Thorne bought a little of the corner of The Bungalow garden, for £50, removed the earth and improved the access to Bremridge.

It was quite a surprise to me when a friend in Devon sent me a newspaper cutting that there was to be a sale at Bremridge and that this would be followed a few days later by the sale of the farm itself. The actual dates were the 7th May 1985 and the 21st of the same month. I thought that Mr Thorne was probably going to retire although he was young enough to carry on for some years before old age and weariness would normally be expected to catch up with him.

I went to Devon at the beginning of November that year and was collected from Starcross on Tuesday, the 5th, to go out to East Village and yet again try to have a talk with The Bungalow tenant and to introduce my new agent to him. New agent? Yes, I am very sorry to say that Mr Connole had been ill for some time and that he had died. His business had been taken over by a very old, established firm.

We did see the occupant of The Bungalow and I was very ashamed of the state of the place with the garden a wilderness, with the interior a shambles and a large collection of bottles which had contained 'something to drink' – I would not know what! We received the usual excuse that his health was not good enough to allow him to work out of doors, especially in bad or windy weather.

There seemed to be many relics of farming activities up in the Brake – parts of machinery and drainpipes and pallets to mention only a few, so we decided to go to Bremridge to see Mr Thorne as he was said to be still there.

The journey up in the car took only a few minutes. In the 'dip' by Nannypark gateway I saw a parked van but I was more interested in the view across the fields and the new 'fishpond' which had been made at the top of 'Little Hill' field not too far from the oak tree which we always knew in our schooldays as 'Grandma's armchair' because it was possible to sit in a space between the exposed roots and rest awhile. It was too far from East Village to see much activity there but any vehicle crawling up or down Cross Hill would lead to a guess as to who was going home or 'up Poughill'. Of course the lane was not rough now – it was a good hard road fit for any car!

Near the court gate there had been alterations. Accommodation for cars had been built – I am not sure whether it was one single large garage or two small ones and I do not remember seeing the court gate at all.

Perhaps you can call this a 'flash-back' of memory, but it is still very clear to me and returned when I saw all the alterations which had been made to accommodate the modern car:

Two children were riding up and down the courtyard on scooters, up and down beside the wall of the front lawn, past the trap-house and nearly up to the stable. Lavinia was one, I was the other! Her scooter had been bought from Woolworths when the store advertised boldly 'Nothing Over 6d.', but what they did not say was where it was possible to sell something in two parts each part would cost 6d. Thus it was that Grandma had been persuaded by Lavinia on a shopping trip to Exeter to buy it. Lavinia did enjoy that scooter and the faster she could go the better she was pleased. 'Out of the way, ducks' I heard her shout one day when they waddled out of the pond – and I do not believe that exists now, either.

My scooter was a home-made affair – by Henry, I expect. It was larger than the one sold by Woolworths, with wheels from a push-chair I think. The handlebars were bigger than the shop one and they did not have any means of turning – you just went straight. I did not mind that and many were the races we enjoyed together.

Our footwear on fine days had been what we called 'daps', more properly plimsolls. I can also recall a pair of lace-up boots I wore. They had leather laces, leather soles and when they were worn at the heel Mum mended them herself with a bit of leather cut from some discarded piece of harness.

169

h

There by the front door I saw an old friend – the Japonica bush! It was said to be the presence of this bush which had attracted a swam of bees to make their home in the porch above the door with its two panes of glass which were liable to break if the other door at the end of the passage was left open and there was much of a wind!

The front door was now open and a black and white sheepdog came from somewhere. He barked and Mr Thorne appeared from the direction of the sitting-room.

I had noticed that there was a car in the yard and a young man had papers spread out on the large table. At Mr Thorne's invitation we sat in the same room and it was only a matter of a few minutes before he was able to give us his full attention.

The studded door at the back stairs was still there with its brass handle. That was the door which had always creaked so loudly that anyone intending to conceal the time of going to bed would need great care in closing it. I also saw the door to the cupboard under the stairs which had housed all sorts of odds and ends in our time.

After the introductory pleasantries I told the farmer the purpose of our journey to find out if he still wished to rent the Brake for the time being. As I had no need of it then it was agreed that he would continue renting it for another year. Since he had so many things there, so much equipment, there seemed no alternative anyway.

There were a few references to the tenant of The Bungalow – apparently the van we had passed on the way up belonged to him, parked there to avoid congestion at the bottom of the hill.

Mr Thorne provided us with a cup of tea and a little further news of happenings in the district and we soon left.

Back on the road to Crediton around East Village and Sandford my new agent was obviously very unhappy about the state of the property at the foot of the hill. He asked whether I had it insured against fire. Yes, of course.

I am convinced that this agent thought it was not worth trying to do anything with a building in such a sorry state and that the best thing would be to remove it and sell the land as a building plot, but, of course, it was still occupied. Nothing could be done until the tenant left and he certainly did not appear keen to vacate.

So Mr Thorne would still use the Brake for another year, the tenant in Rose Cottage was apparently quite happy. He and Mrs had had various agricultural enterprises – kept some pigs for a while and I think they had poultry for several years. Certainly they planted some fruit trees up in their garden. They also made an entrance from the road so that their car could be taken into a safe area at night, more convenient than leaving it at the bottom of the hill in the Plot.

When Mr Thorne received a letter from my agent in due course asking him to vacate the Brake he took no notice. He did not reply to further letters and the information that we were taking possession merely brought a letter from some solicitors to the effect that Mr Thorne regarded himself as a full Agricultural Tenant and did not wish to leave. He paid the rent again for several years, and grew mangolds or cabbages or potatoes.

The weeds still grew strong and tall where no disturbance had taken place. They were said to be the best weeds in the district but, worse even than the weeds, were rabbits and rats which had started to invade. Where two or three of either of these species exist there will very soon be many more!

From the gate in Broxfords Hill there were very deep ruts – made by the farm vehicles which were employed to do some cultivations no doubt. But the old apple tree was still there on top of the slope, showing signs of age, I knew that this may have been the clue to the use of part of the area – it was an orchard in the time when cider houses were common for there was the 'New Inn' in the village of Heath Bridge in 1790 and at least until 1800.

In a local Devon newspaper there appeared a small notice – the kind of notice that every farmer in financial difficulties must dread – the Official Receiver was in charge and in due course the matter of the renting of the Brake was brought to his notice. Early in 1993 I received an official 'Disclaimer' from the Exeter office, but as far as I was concerned 'What did it mean?'

There are times when I have been told by someone who knows me very well that I 'have the luck of Old Nick' and it happened at about this time that I met a gentleman who was a retired Official Receiver – I met him in Chandlers Ford near Southampton. He was one of my sister's friends and had been known to her family for years.

Naturally I asked him just what a 'Disclaimer' meant and he gave me the assurance that the tenant of my land had no further claim to it and that I could now do just what I liked with it. It had reverted to me completely.

I thought of the weeds and the rabbits and the rats, the overgrown hedges which had not been trimmed for a number of years, in fact some of the branches of a roadside tree were becoming a danger to big lorries which used that road to reach Bremridge. If he had been allowed to remain how much longer would I have such a wilderness there? Beside that, in the wooded area around the quarries were a number of good trees which now had ivy growing up their trunks enough to spoil them, it should be removed. In time Mr Thorne did vacate.

23
'To Be, or Not to Be?'

'That bungalow has had it' – that was the opinion of more than one person! The place was empty and an empty house soon begins to look forlorn and neglected – not that it could be said to be anything but that for the few years when failing health, breaking his arm and being 'full of asthma' meant that no outdoor work could be done by my tenant. That he was full of good intentions I have no doubt, especially when he was talking to me! On the few occasions when he could not escape there were always the promises for improvement in the future – I must say that he did make some attempts to grow a few vegetables – and seemed quite pleased with the results. I do not think there were any flowers and the few bushes which existed seemed to be completely overgrown.

Therefore, what was I going to do? As I have said, nothing in a hurry, so I waited for inspiration or opportunity, or something.

Then I received a letter from the young man who had been such a friend to my father. He had gone to Scotland but did not really like it – nor did his dog, he said.

His next letter said that he was thinking of returning to England and was looking round for somewhere in the country, possibly near some relatives up in the Midlands.

I wrote to him telling him all about the little property I had under the hills of Bremridge. I think I described it accurately – there was no point in doing otherwise. Small, run down, no bathroom, but there was ground, gardens and orchard and land down by the river. There was indoor sanitation and electric light.

I think I probably 'phoned the tenant of Rose Cottage and told him of the possibility that there may be someone to look at it. He recommended a firm who would be prepared to do the essential repairs now that the place was empty and, as he was well known in Crediton and seemed to have several contacts, if one firm – or individual could not help then there may be another who could. Electricity was 'seen to', the very obvious repairs carried out, so there was nothing more for me to do than write to my Dad's friend with full instructions as to how to reach The Bungalow at the bottom of Broxfords Hill – hoping that he would not get lost, turn tail, and even go home before he had at least seen it.

Oh yes, he got lost – as nearly all the holiday visitors had done – and went miles and miles out of his way. The trouble seems to be at the top of Park Hill, or just over the brow, where there is a signpost pointing down the side road to 'Stockleigh English' and if anyone intending to go to Heath Bridge missed that they went on to Stockleigh Pomeroy! Cheriton Fitzpaine was also often visited by the holidaymaker before he could return. At the next turning 'our way' there is a signpost to Heath Bridge, put there at my request by the Council of the day – Crediton Rural District I believe. That points to an even smaller, quieter road, through the woods, the little cottage where Jim Bedell had lived with his wife – a very straight faced lady – and grown up daughter, May. She died when she became consumptive and would not consider going away to a sanatorium on Dartmoor where she would have had a chance to be cured. I believe she was between 20 and 30 years old, but her father had already passed on and perhaps she felt that she could not face life without him.

From that cottage the lane turns down into a steep little 'dip' with a stream at the bottom, then there is a climb up quite a long slope until the top of the hill begins to slope down again over the ridge. In fact, it does not slope, it descends fairly rapidly, and if any driver is tempted to 'gawk' about him and admire the view instead of keeping his eyes firmly on where he is going he will very soon find himself in the hedge!

There are a few farm gateways along the way, and they provide the only passing places. There was only a very little traffic years ago but once or twice on that route home – whether at Bremridge or when we lived at Heath Bridge – one or other of the travellers would have had to make full use of the extra width of a gateway.

174

Our pony and trap had to 'back' a long way when a loaded wagon pulled by two big horses was coming towards us. Then, too, in our day you could almost describe the surface of the lane as 'corrugated' because of the ridges and wheel tracks – if you rode a bicycle it was important not to try to change from one to the other; the middle track was always where the horses walked and sometimes contained more than mud. That seemed to remain there.

I waited for news. What would the result of the visit of inspection be?

I had not told the agent in Exeter very much about the prospects for The Bungalow since I already knew his views that it should not exist any longer. He must, I think, have been in communication with someone at Heath Bridge for within a day or so I received a letter from Exeter saying that he knew my friends had visited The Bungalow and that they did not stay very long! The inference, of course, being that the property could not hold any interest for them. True, he refrained from saying, 'I told you so!' I am sure that the thought was there.

It is fortunate for me that my Dad's friend and his family were young enough to accept a challenge – the challenge of tackling the garden, and of trying to make something of the place, for they accepted the tenancy and in due course came to live there.

I am sure there were several factors which appealed to them – one of the most important being the view from the windows of the front room – the view over the river and beyond, the one large tree on the high part of the field belonging to Doddridge, a farm in East Village. That tree has been a landmark for years – under its branches there must be a view for miles. The river itself, so quiet and peaceful, but which, by now, they must have realised has quite another mood after heavy rain. I am sure it still comes out over the road by the bridge – it always did, particularly up towards Dira Cottages. I think that also accounts for the tale that some pigs had to be taken upstairs 'to save their bacon' when the cottages existed along the lane!

As soon as they were settled in at The Bungalow the tenant set about clearing the garden, to get some order out of the chaos and 'Mr' in particular must have cut and slashed and had some good bonfires. Before long a passer-by remarked that he was surprised that there was still a bungalow there!

There was nothing to suggest what was going to happen on the night of the 15th October 1987 – in fact the whole country went to rest happy in the knowledge that the autumn was passing normally – even the weather forecast did not foretell what a terrible night it was going to be. I slept through it all and only became aware that there was something odd happening to our trap door into the attic at about 6.00 a.m., banging with all the force it could muster. Branches of trees were down across the road and the news reports told of the terrible damage right across the country, so I was nearly afraid to ring up my contacts in Devon to find out what was blown away. According to all reports Devon had not fared any better than anywhere else. It would be the last straw if there was much damage – too much to repair – but could the little building exist against such force?

I had forgotten that the properties were right under the hill, and therefore somewhat sheltered. The Cottage next door was untouched by the gales but The Bungalow's verandah had been ripped from the front – needed a completely new one. There was also some damage to the roof, but nothing that could not be repaired or replaced. Perhaps The Bungalow is like a cat – it has so many lives and it certainly lost one of them thanks to the tall man in wellington boots. However, the new tenant has worked hard there and now the garden is something worth looking at and admiring.

Many years ago it was Grandpa who planted two bushes either side of the front door. I do not think he knew the proper name for them, but they were always referred to as the 'you-nonomous' shrubs. Along with the rails – or railings – around the verandah, they disappeared and the front became 'open', and completely re-designed. All this I saw on my next visit with my agent from Exeter.

There was one great drawback, however – there was no bathroom – and for someone engaged in gardening or farm work it is not regarded as a luxury these days. It is essential and the builder who repaired some of the October storm damage, seemed very reliable and said that he could undertake such a job if there was room and if it was all passed properly by the local Council. He also knew someone who could draw up the plans.

Since there was room to expand where the old horse drawn furniture van had existed it was decided that an extension would be possible and that the bathroom could be where the present kitchen exists.

The plans were sent to me in due course — all such alterations take some time before they can even be decided, let alone completed. The extension would be the new kitchen. The Mid Devon Council were able to give me a grant and after all the preliminaries were completed, the conversion was started, and finished!

24

Officials, Dogs and the M23

I could not possibly repeat what Grandpa used to say about 'Officials', whether from the Councils, the Tax Authorities or the church, but I never heard him decry the role of the police.

There was one official from the Council I could very well have done without many years ago. He – a young middle-aged man – arrived here early one morning. I think it must have been when the children were all at school – certainly I was on my own, washing up in the kitchen, having already seen to the baby chicks in the big house down the path.

This individual said he had come to look for mice in the bedrooms! He wanted to go upstairs immediately.

I saw red, what, take a stranger up into our bedrooms, not likely! How would anyone start to look for mice, anyway – stand in the middle of the room and squeak! If he called 'puss' any mice would take fright and hide even if they were not aware of footsteps coming up the stairs. No, I thought he would need to pull all the furniture from the walls and I would not have anyone defiling the camphor-wood box in such a way. No one from the Council, so I assured him that we did not have mice upstairs, to which he replied that he had to go to look for them!

Brainwave: 'This is not my house,' I said, 'and I am certainly not letting you go upstairs without the owner's permission.' An argument followed – both of us were cross, to put it mildly. Man suggested I 'phone the owner – I knew only too well what the response would be from that quarter, 'What a cheek – no go!'

'I've got to investigate,' said several times.

'Who said?' said I. Then I 'phoned the Council and asked them to 'call their dog off'. They did.

Another Official

When all eggs were supposed to be stamped before sale to shops with the little British lion or with the place of origin, I did get into trouble with the Egg Board.

One morning towards the end of a week a tall man dressed in a smart dark overcoat and wearing a black felt hat called here. He asked where a certain lady lived and as I knew of course I directed him correctly. I did notice that he took quite an interest in the lady who was just leaving with a couple of egg boxes in her hands but thought nothing of it.

About ten days later this same tall man called here again, dressed in the same manner — shall we say, 'impressive'. He asked if I remembered him. I did, and then he introduced himself as an Inspector for the Egg Board and said that he had information that I had supplied 27½ dozen eggs to a shop, unstamped, and did I know that I should have paid a levy to the Egg Board, etc? Also, where did my husband work?

This last question worried me — and he knew it — for I thought 'What have I done, maybe jeopardised his position, or something?'

His original enquiry as to the lady's address ensured that I knew her and he had been to see her in connection with his enquiries as to our 'crime' for she had allowed her assistant to 'dress' their premises with a barrel filled with nothing more incriminating than straw, but on top of that straw there were eggs, good brown eggs, which had come from my fowls! Unstamped eggs, so Inspector had asked the assistant if the eggs had been 'home produced' or bought in. 'Ours,' she said, 'were not laying enough so we got some from a neighbour.' That did it, so his enquiries led to me. Providing I would register, keep records of numbers of dozens sold for re-sale and make the appropriate returns to the Egg Board he felt I could be 'let off with a caution'.

As it happened there were about 30 dozen eggs in our little shed from which all selling took place, and I asked him if I could grade them while we were talking. He agreed, as I picked up egg after egg my hand was not behaving itself, it was shaking like a

179

jelly!

A customer saved me from further embarrassment that day by arriving just then, and the Inspector said, 'I'll come back on Friday and finish sorting you out!'

So, every big white car which stopped outside was suspect until the occupant was known. He did not come that Friday, but on the one after, with his long form of registration, and Egg Board literature. We had to have our own 'production number' and distinctive symbol, for which we had to pay £1.1/- or 105p. A blessed old lot of rigmarole, I thought it.

Once caught by an Inspector you were not completely let off the hook, for he would call at odd times, perhaps at 8.00 a.m. or late at night in the hope of catching you out again. But the last time I saw him I shall never forget. He was still somewhat pompous, still full of self-importance and said that there were to be new regulations introduced by the Egg Board which would be 'Citty prevere' instead of 'Pretty severe'. I laughed so much I certainly could not talk to him. He just said, 'I've got my wrong teeth in today,' but ex-C.I.D. Inspector's dignity was permanently punctured as far as I was concerned!

In addition to my little skirmish with Mr Elliott of the Egg Board there was another rather peculiar encounter which I am sure would have led in the direction of trouble with a capital 'T'!

After we were involved in producing milk for sale to the Milk Marketing Board, one Saturday morning when I was up in the Egg Shed busily grading eggs, for Saturdays were very busy with people who came both from London and locally for their weekly supply, I saw a smallish red car pass our gateway and stop out of sight though still visible through the hedge.

I thought nothing unusual in that. I do not remember the exact features of the young man who walked past the house and up to me in the Egg Shed, only that he was dressed in what I would term 'a town suit', quite a smart town suit.

The following conversation took place.

'Morning,' said I.

'Good morning,' said he, 'I don't suppose you could sell me a pint of milk, could you?'

'Milk,' I said, 'we don't sell milk, but if you want eggs – '

He said, 'Well, it is for a baby, we've run out.'

I thought for a moment as to whether I had enough to *give* him

180

sufficient for an infant, and then I thought again and I think that a sixth sense must have come to my aid.

I said, 'There are shops which sell milk – '

He became a little worried (or appeared to), 'Shall I have time to reach a shop before it shuts?'

It was getting on towards mid-day but a car could get him to Redhill quite soon. Certainly I heard no baby crying and could not even see if the young man was accompanied by baby's Mum, or baby's Gran, or even if the infant was there at all.

He still persisted. 'Won't you consider giving a baby enough for a feed?'

'No,' I said. 'In any case I am not allowed to sell milk.'

By this time I was convinced he was not 'on the level' and I considered that he was one of the inspectors sent out by the Milk Marketing Board to catch the unwary being either generous or forgetful of the contract signed by them that no milk was to be sold while they bought the farmer's full production – apart from what he needed for himself, of course.

After he had gone I thought of all the people who came to Bremridge with any request for aid of whatever kind and how Grandpa would always have done his best with the big machinery – very small by the present day's standards – to accommodate a neighbour. I remember that he loaned a horse to one farmer in difficulty – Henry took his bicycle and led Smart all the way up to Down and then cycled home again. She worked there for some time.

The women folk were always eager to assist anyone in trouble – and a pint of milk would have been considered as nothing. This feeling of helpfulness was common all through the district – Mrs Miller at Doddridge seemed to me to be a general benefactor and many people in trouble turned to her for help and advice if not actually assistance with goods or services.

A pint of milk was nothing – 'just nort' to use a Devon expression – and I had refused it for a baby but the more I thought about it afterwards the more I was convinced the polite young man was not what he had seemed.

Within days there would have been a sinister communication from the Milk Marketing Board outlining my 'sin'.

I am going to include just a few words about the dogs we have owned during all these years – not strictly necessary, of course,

181

but there are many people who find dogs have many things to recommend them – they bring companionship if nothing else!

Well, the first one we took over from the previous owner here, a large brown animal, though I am not sure of the breed now for we only had him 'George' – for one day. We had taken the children to their various schools in the early morning and had returned to straighten up what we could. I was actually upstairs making the beds when I heard a squeal of brakes and as I looked out of the window the driver of the Jersey Milk lorry shouted 'I've killed your dog!' Oh dear. Yes, George was dead. Apparently he had tried to rush across the road to investigate some noise, and that was that. The children were very upset.

Many years later, during which time there had been umpteen cats but never such a thief as we had possessed at Bremridge, a neighbour gave Janet a black and white cross bred dog – Tom. He became a very much loved friend and we nearly made a mistake with his training, training to be a cow dog. We were encouraging him to sit and keep the cows from turning the wrong way up – or down – the road when we realised that he might sit in the road and get knocked over. True, there were not nearly so many cars in those days, but enough, if a driver was going too fast, to cause a fatality. So we kept him on a long lead for cow work and stood beside him.

That same neighbour had another pup to find a home for about two years later, and he came my way. 'Little Ben'. He had a golden coat, some white about the face, but was a little weak on his hind legs – wobble, wobble, down, when he should have been able at least to walk.

The vet needed to come to the cattle and before he got back in his car and drove out of the yard I asked him to look at the pup. He did and felt him all over and his pronouncement was somewhat gloomy. 'He'll never be a mucher,' he said, 'but I'll send you over some calcium for him'.

Poor man must have been very busy, for he forgot to send it. I thought if calcium was what was necessary to produce strong bones perhaps I could obtain it from another source. 'What would they have done at Bremridge?' I know, eggshells are the next best available supply, even if a homely recipe, so 'Little Ben' had raw eggs, with the shells, cooked eggs complete with shells and shells from eggs which everyone else had!

182

It worked, and the pup's little legs became very much stronger, normal, in fact. When the vet next came, and he was shown the lively little dog, he seemed quite impressed – the eggshells had worked wonders.

There was, however, a side effect. 'Little Ben' created the most obnoxious smells which could ever assail one's nostrils!

The driver who brought the Brewers' Grains that year needed to wait for John's assistance before discharging his load. As usual he was offered a cup of tea in the kitchen and gratefully accepted. There were no prizes for guessing why he suddenly decided to finish his drink in double quick time and to go out to his cab and wait for John there!

For years we had Tom and Ben together, very good friends. Tom's name was often upgraded to 'Thomas' while Ben became 'Bengymealo', and then 'Mealo'.

Unfortunately there was a slight accident with a car in which Ben had a knock near one of his eyes and this in time, we noticed, caused him to bump into things and, years later, he was completely blind. He was still able to go for walks and the word 'Mind' would control his direction and he rarely bumped into anything!

Eventually, of course, we lost both of them. In time they were replaced by Big Ben, Janet's dog, who was young and needed a home in the country for his owners were out at work all day and when they returned to their home, Ben had been busy, chewing and knocking things over, so he had to go. In fact, his original home had been a very unfortunate one for him as there were children who must have been cruel in the extreme for even the sound of children – even after years away from them – created fear in him and he would bark furiously. The R.S.P.C.A. had removed him from that home but the house in the town was not the answer. When Janet saw him, she said it was love at first sight, and often he would accompany her in whatever vehicle she was driving.

Big Ben became the father of eight pups, the mother being a Golden Retriever who lived quite near. Janet was convinced that we should have one of the pups, and chose a black fat little animal who immediately adopted me.

All this was years ago and, sadly, Big Ben now rests at the bottom of the lawn, in a garden created as a memorial to him, while his son, Jake, is at this very moment of typing, snoring on the floor, although he, too, is quite elderly!

I know you are going to laugh at this and probably say to yourselves 'How daft can anyone get?' The truth is that Ben and Jake had their own dressing gowns! I don't know what else you could call them, but they were garments spread over the double bed when 'The boys' came up to say 'Good morning' to me before I had a chance to get down. Ben's was of fur-like material, had been an orange and white cape garment for a good sized child, and Jake was quite content with a towelling dressing gown. Each had their particular spot and kept to it, above their dressing gowns – Jake's by my feet and Ben well away on the other side of the bed.

Jake is now getting on in years. He has adopted a method of sleeping in a chair which is unique to him – I have never seen another dog in such a position.

'His chair' is now quite an old one, though still very comfortable and should go on for years yet. He sits in it just like a person, with his back fitted neatly into where the arm joins. Often he lifts his front legs so that they are not resting on anything, just hanging over his tum. When he is really asleep his mouth drops open and he shows his top row of teeth – everyone who sees it has to laugh. He never seems to dribble or to make any mess.

I have looked at him sometimes and wondered if I should give him a little apron for the sake of his modesty, but he never seems to worry, so why should I? In any case, from being fast asleep one moment, he can be up and wide awake the next – and he would probably trip over his apron anyway.

For some time in the 1960s there had been whisperings and rumours that there was going to be a big road built in this district. In my 1971 Diary I have a note in June which says 'T.H. Contractors start constructing sewer' the prelude to all the work in this area for the benefit of the M23 which is now taking much traffic. It does not come across our own land but did affect land which we were renting and this had to be given up. It meant that the dairy work was curtailed and many of the cows had to be sold, though I did retain some animals in calf which could be entered in a market at the appropriate time.

The 'living' left was not sufficient for a young man, and John therefore left home making his way to Devon and working for a short time on road construction there until he took Relief Milking. He worked in the Sandford area for a short while, visiting other farms on his bicycle, Prouse among them (and I believe he met Mary, Peter Stoyle's wife), exploring Heath Bridge and district. John is a quiet person and did not say very much more than that the countryside was quiet and very hilly.

Then came other farm work, harvesting, etc. and he eventually settled in Yorkshire where he now has a very nice family.

The M23 went through all the stages of construction from the whine of the chain-saw cutting down some trees, 'ploughing through hedges', building up a heap of earth which resembled a mountain, laying foundations, doing everything necessary to produce the monster which is now our near neighbour. At times it is very noisy, particularly in wet or frosty weather and on Sunday nights in summer. Then normal talk means shouting at your companion! Sometimes there is a police siren, soft in the far distance but harsh and strident close to this area and dying away up over the slope. I have also seen a Police Helicopter shadowing the motorway more than once. There have been at least two heli-copter crashes which have just missed the M23 and only by a matter of yards!

We kept our poultry and the sale of eggs to many customers continued, and I still used my £8 egg shed. One night we were visited by a fox when there were some good young pullets which had just started to produce. This was in a big double house which had a concrete passage. No doors had been left open, no windows wide, the blighter had somehow scrambled up on to the roof and had entered, to kill everything that was alive.

I have no sympathy for foxes, they have none for poultry, they are ruthless killers and somehow or other ultimately they win.

One cow, one pony, one tom cat still exist here – like me, all elderly. We do have help in the garden, every night little paws dig holes – rabbits – but they do not plant anything!

I have not been down to Devon for several years but that does not mean that I am unaware of all that has been happening. I keep in touch by means of the telephone and Sunday evenings are the most convenient or favourite times both for me and for the tenant of The Bungalow. Of course there are letters as well and I have received many photos of the Brake which has been back in agricultural use for some time. The grassy area now resembles a

185

field. No one can say the best weeds in the district thrive on 'The Hump' now.

Rose Cottage also has a very good tenant and I am not going to end the story of the properties Under the Hills of Bremridge without paying tribute to all the help and assistance I have received from so many people in the district. I would like to name them all but feel I just might leave someone very important out — builders, farmers, friends — they have all helped me to make it possible to continue the existence of this little part of Devon which was 'home' for so many years.

Yes, I have known 'Bremridge, Sandford and Other Places' very well indeed, and been very happy in them.

Some day I shall return.

CW00456659

A Field of Tents
and
Waving Colours

A Field of Tents
and
Waving Colours

NEVILLE CARDUS
writing on Cricket

With an introduction by
Gideon Haigh

SAFE**H**AVEN

*The publisher gratefully acknowledges the
assistance of Fiona Hertford-Hughes, copyright
holder of the Estate of Neville Cardus, in putting
this selection of his work together.*

First published 2019 by
Safe Haven Books Ltd
12 Chinnocks Wharf
42 Narrow Street
London E14 8DJ
www.safehavenbooks.co.uk

A catalogue record for this book
is available from the British Library.

ISBN 978 1 9160453 0 9

1 3 5 7 9 10 8 6 4 2

2019 2021 2023 2022 2020

Typeset in Filosofia by M Rules

Printed and bound in Great Britain
by Clays Ltd, Elcograf S. p. A.

Contents

Introduction

by Gideon Haigh

For a long time, Sir Neville Cardus was regarded as cricket's greatest writer; then he wasn't. The two perspectives
may be related. What one generation exalts, the next is
almost bound to despise. But there is something odd about
his fall from grace, because it often feels more concerned
with whether it is 'OK' to like Cardus, and to arise from
assumptions about Cardus rather than involving the effort
of actually reading him.

To be fair, Cardus's canonical status was never univer-
sally agreed. 'Ah don't like thy writing, Mester Cardus,'
Yorkshire's Arthur Mitchell purportedly reproached him.
'It's too fancy.' But he is especially ill-suited to these aggres-
sively neophilial and levelling times. *Sir* Neville Cardus:
why, the very name is anachronistic. He must have been a
posh boy, mustn't he? Didn't he throw in allusions to classical music? Didn't he use fancy metaphors? Ignoring that

classical music was in Cardus's time perfectly popular culture, not least in the Manchester of his boyhood. Ignoring that in reaching outside the sporting vernacular for a fresh perspective on participants and feats, Cardus was arguably more in tune with the sportswriting of today than his own.

Ah, but he was a snob, wasn't he? Now, there *is* something to this. Cardus was dedicated to the memory of the cricket and the cricketers of his pre-World War I youth, with a partiality to the pedigree amateur batsmen who defined it – or indeed, it should be said, who he helped define it, for it was Cardus who pressed into common coinage the notion of an Edwardian 'Golden Age of Cricket'. Likewise could he be nostalgically deprecating of what came after, a lamentation of 'the nation's lost peace and plenty'. He could be glib, facile. He was assuredly no historian – you would no sooner rely on factual actuality in a piece of Cardus's than in a Trump tweet.

But show me a sports writer not occasionally star-struck, not periodically jaded, who does not have favourites and harbour prejudices. At least Cardus's were sincere rather than sycophantic. When he derided Bloggs of Blankshire, furthermore, he was making a point every cricket watcher can understand – that there are players who hold, for all sorts of reasons, greater personal and aesthetic appeal than others. The scoreboard, he maintained, 'will not get anywhere near the secret of Woolley. It can only tell us about Bloggs.' Those greats, too, have better days than others: 'Only mediocrity is always at its best.'

2

Nowadays it is a term of approbation to refer to a sports writer as possessing the 'enthusiasm of the fan'. Cardus was here a pioneer. Few cricket writers have so often mentioned the perspective of an everyday spectator, for a simple reason: being not an ex-player, he was well acquainted with the cheap seats by the time he gravitated to journalism in his early thirties. So when he described the post-1947 Denis Compton, for example, he saw it from the terraces: 'In a world tired, disillusioned and bare, heavy with age and deprivation, this happy cricketer spread his favours everywhere, and thousands of us, young and old, ran his runs with him. Here at any rate was something unrationed. There were no coupons in an innings by Compton.'

Oh yes, one last thing: the parrot cry that Cardus 'made things up'. Some of his stories were too good to be true because they weren't. But literary licence, as Cardus's first biographer Christopher Brookes observed, is nothing so new: 'After all, Shakespeare missed Agincourt.' It's also worth considering the factual economy of Cardus's era, unassisted by the real-time stat and the media soundbite, based on the unaided eye versus the unyielding distance. Writing fifty years ago, Cardus had this to say about his starting out as a reporter of county cricket:

Silence reigned supreme. There was no specialist statistician to inform us that so-and-so had bowled so many overs, or that so-and-so had completed his 50 in two and a half hours. We had to make our *own* statistical recordings. Jimmy Catton, of the now defunct *Manchester Evening Chronicle*, himself wrote down a ball-by-ball analysis of each bowler, also detailing the value and direction of every stroke. So did all the other cricket reporters.

It was Cardus, in fact, who became the first correspondent to liberate cricket journalism from the menial transcription of action, who discerned in the game the scope for a literary imagination. Cardus is not, then, to be understood merely by his own writing, but from cricket in newspapers before and after him. Never before had press box journalism been worth reading for its own sake: as John Arlott put it, Cardus 'forced cricket into a position where the literate had to notice it, and, in doing so, compelled an improvement in the general standard of writing about the game'. He provided word pictures where there were as yet no serious photographs. He offered reflections on cricket's place in public affection where there was so far scant thought. And if this involved the occasional tactful fiction, then so did his life.

His real name was John Frederick Newsham. He was born illegitimate in 1888. He never knew his father, a smith, who left Manchester for America days after marrying his mother; he knew his mother, a prostitute, perhaps too well to write about her. He was haphazardly raised in a crowded semi by an extended family of launderers, minimally educated in a board school to the age of ten. It's a modern affectation of the successful to embroider their early CVs with mundane jobs because they pulled some call centre shifts and worked a night or two as a dish pig. Long before he started journalism as a penny-a-liner for Manchester's left-wing *Daily Citizen*, Fred Newsham was a jack-of-all-trades: he delivered washing from the family laundry, worked as a pavement artist, drove a joiners' handcart, boiled type in a printer's works, sold flowers on the street, confectionery in a theatre and funeral insurance door-to-door.

How did such a leisured and picturesque style emerge from such a hardscrabble existence? The question may answer itself – the writing constituted an act of self-creation. Fred Newsham belongs in the tradition of autodidacticism, culturally conservative but insatiably curious, described by Jonathan Rose in his *The Intellectual Life of the British Working Classes*. Manchester had a huge university, great law courts. It was a musical city – the home of Sir Thomas Beecham, the headquarters of the Hallé and numerous smaller orchestras, of pantomimes that cannibalised opera, of pubs that nourished music hall. Its local authority had acquired an extensive gallery with a superb fine arts collection, the Manchester City Art Gallery, and been the first in Britain to endow public lending and reference libraries.

The Manchester Free Library's opening was attended by Charles Dickens. So was Fred Newsham's intellectual awakening. He 'went crazy' on discovering the novelist in Harmsworth shilling editions:

> It was scarcely a case of reading at all; it was almost an experience of a world more alive and dimensional than this world, heightened and set free in every impulse of nature; not subtle and abnormal impulses but such as even a more or less illiterate youth could at once share.

Dickens was then out of highbrow literary fashion – plots too sentimental, characters too caricatured. Youthful Newsham dared think otherwise: 'He [Dickens] simply let me see them more than life-size. David Copperfield so often behaved and thought as I behaved and thought that I frequently lost my own sense of identity in him.'

Fred Newsham allocated his new identity a new name. The Cardus scholar Christopher O'Brien reports that 'Neville Cardus' appeared for the first time in print in a journal called *Musical Opinion*: a December 1916 critique of the composer Granville Bantock appears under the byline 'J. F. Neville Cardus'. Cardus was his mother's surname; Neville was inspired, O'Brien conjectures, by the all-rounder John Neville Crawford, whose virtues the writer often later extolled. Arlott observed that Cardus understood the impression left by 'Neville' as distinct from 'Fred' – in the same way, perhaps, as 'Cyril James' understood himself better off as 'C. L. R'.

In that same month, Cardus applied successfully to C.

P. Scott for a job at the *Manchester Guardian*. He started in the reporters' room in March 1917, a spare pair of hands. Though Cardus loved cricket – in his mid-twenties, he had spent four summers as an assistant coach at Shrewsbury – there was none for him to report. It was after a 'breakdown' he suffered two years into his career that Scott's sympathetic lieutenant W. P. Crozier decided Cardus 'might recuperate myself by sitting in the air one or two days at Old Trafford' for the first county match since 1914.

'It was indeed easy to feel the sentimental aspect of the occasion,' the apprentice cricket writer began. 'One came into the enclosure from the dusty town, and there were for many an old cricket lover strong tugs on the heart as they saw again the soft green splashed with the spring sun and the red pavilion and the county flag streaming in the wind.' The sense of occasion; the sensitivity to the palette; the kinship with the crowd; the sense of what has gone before: these features of Cardus's writing were present from the very first. Also the attachment to the local, for he would remain a man of the north:

> In most matches the critic endeavours to be impartial; he sits aloft in the press-box, like an impersonal god, seeing all things moving, towards their predestined end. The Lancashire and Yorkshire match is an exception; I step down from the pedestal of impartiality . . . I have found that a partnership can often be broken by leaving the

press box and retiring for a moment (usefully) behind the scene. I have this way taken a hundred wickets for Lancashire in twenty-one successive seasons.

After a year, Cardus was allocated a pen name: he was christened 'Cricketer' by Crozier's redoubtable secretary Madeline Linford, the *Guardian's* only female member of staff, shortly to become its first women's page editor. Was it used advisedly? Because the whole point of 'Cricketer' was that he was not, or barely. He had ceased to play even humbly; he would lead instead a movement of journalists distinguished by their professional writing rather than their amateur cricket credentials. Cricket's most popular pre-war bylines had read like the batting order of the Gentlemen: Ranji, Fry, MacLaren, Jessop, Warner. Between the wars would emerge a new mandarinate: the likes of Harry Altham, Beau Vincent, William Pollock, Harry Carson, R. C. Robertson-Glasgow, and the Great Panjandrum himself, E. W. Swanton. None was so well known as Cardus. In the front row at Old Trafford by now, he was regarded reverently by Robertson-Glasgow:

Here sat Neville Cardus, of the *Manchester Guardian*, slim, grey, contained; master of the rhapsodical style, cutting his epigrams from the most amorphous material . . . On the great moments and the top cricketers, he has no equal. He is made for the mountain top, and he ranks among the English essayists.

In this centenary of Cardus's debut as a cricket writer, he still is. For those who have read him before, this book will be a pleasant reminder; for those who have not, it's high time. How to describe Jack Hobbs in the nets? Cardus finds a way, bridging the technical and impressionistic. How to bring alive long-forgotten stumper William Worsley or the batting polymath C. B. Fry? Wodehouse penned nothing funnier. A photograph of Walter Hammond at slip is flavoursome, but Cardus describes *how* he moved.

His shoulders were broad; the physical frame as a whole maybe at first hinted of top-heaviness somewhere, and there seemed a tendency of his legs, as he stood in the slips, to go together at the knees. At the first sight of a snick from the edge of the bat his energy apparently electrified the shape and substance of him, he became light and boneless, and down to the earth he would dive, all curves and balance, and he would catch a ghost of a 'chance' as if by instinct.

Statistics are dandy, but 216 wickets at 24 explains *who* Clarrie Grimmett was far less effectively than this:

He walks about the field on dainty feet which step as though with the soft fastidiousness of a cat treading a wet pavement. He is a master of surreptitious arts ... To play forward to Grimmett, to miss the spin, and then to find yourself stumped by Oldfield – why, it is like an amputation done under an anaesthetic.

Is he the greatest cricket writer of all? That's a call for those who want to turn literature into listicles. What I would propose is that there's scarcely been a cricket writer so influential – in emancipating his trade from the yoke of the action, in breaking the by-line thrall of the ex-player, and in aspiring to craft work *worth reading*, which is, after all, what we in journalism are trying to do.

Gideon Haigh
Melbourne
May 2019

Myself When Young

To this day I can't explain why one morning in June 1899 I went to Old Trafford for the first time to watch Lancashire. I wasn't a cricketer yet, wasn't much advanced beyond my ninth birthday, and my pocket money seldom ran to two-pence a week. It remains, and apparently must remain, a mystery not only what was the attraction that drew me on football that way (and long before the summer holidays had begun); but where did the gate-money come from?

Lancashire were playing Gloucestershire, and as I passed through the turnstiles I heard a terrific roar and didn't know, till I was told by one of the spectators, that Board had just appealed for a catch at the wicket. I am unable to remember if I then knew much about the laws and procedure of the game. I have looked up this match in *Wisden*. Jessop played and made 28 on the day I was present, but he left no indelible impression on this occasion. Why do we retain in memory some things and not others? C.

L. Townsend made 91, and I can vaguely see him now, tall when the ball was coming to him, but he bent gracefully over it as he played forward. F. H. B. Champain drove several fours that made me, with the boy's naïve delight in a play on words, see something very apt in his name.

A year afterwards I was definitely enslaved by cricket for life. On Whit-Monday 1900 I was again at Old Trafford, up at the crack of dawn to get a front seat. For some reason I cannot fathom, Lancashire didn't play Yorkshire that year on Whit Monday; they played Kent. At noon Kent went in first, C. Burnup and Alec Hearne the opening batsmen. I sat facing the pavilion, on the grass in front of the sixpenny seats, which were occupied mainly by men and youths in bowler hats or straw 'cadies'. Moustaches everywhere, and scarcely a girl or woman, though away on the right there was the Ladies' Pavilion, arrayed in long skirts and puffed sleeves. Only women of the middle and upper classes attended cricket matches half a century ago.

From the Stretford end Mold bowled very fast, taking a short run, just three or four strides. At the other end Briggs bowled slow. A fast and a slow bowler to begin, new ball despite. There wouldn't be another new ball during the Kent innings, even if it lasted until tomorrow, which it did. A new ball was available in those times only at the beginning of an innings, as John Gunn once said, 'till t'owd un coom in two'. Mold's speed made sudden havoc of Kent's innings: three wickets went for 11: Hearne, B. D. Bannon, W. H. Patterson. The crowd gloated. I gloated. A marvellous

Bank Holiday morning... J. R. Mason came in third wicket down, and to my dismay he seemed to 'see' Mold's bowling at once, which I thought an impossibility. Meanwhile, at the other end of the wicket was this little Burnup man. I didn't like the look of him, for he played everything in the middle of his bat, and nothing flurried him. Burn-up, I said to myself: a silly name.

Mason, thank goodness, was out soon after lunch; but the 'bad start' had been retrieved, and he made 68. The batsman answered to the name of Perkins – T. N. Perkins – another ridiculous name, I assured myself. He missed his stroke at Mold on the off-side time after time. The crowd laughed derision at his helplessness. I joined it. Again I was cheated and cast down. Perkins began to drive classically through covers, as I see it now, left-leg forward. Such cricket today, against very fast bowling, in a searching situation, would be anachronistic. And the little man, Burnup, stayed there, unobtrusive but not idle, gathering runs by neat cuts.

So the warm afternoon went to cool evening. There was no tea interval: drinks were brought into the field, and the crowd rose and stretched itself. T. N. Perkins was not dismissed until he had scored 88; he and Burnup increased Kent's total from 110 for four to 350 for five. If I am not mistaken, Burnup was caught at the wicket from the last over of the day – Kent 400 for six at 'close', Burnup 'c Smith, b Cuttell, 200'. A report of the match in one of the newspapers next day praised Burnup's innings something like this : '. . . occupied the crease all day . . . punctuated by judicious cutting . . . periods of slow scoring excusable in view of Kent's bad start . . .' A score of 200, after 11 for 3, wouldn't seem inordinately slow nowadays, even with Compton 'occupying' the crease.

I walked home from Old Trafford on the evening of this Whitsun Monday of 1900, a sad cast-down Lancashire boy. Why had Mold allowed that Perkins to survive? All the way from the county ground – planted in the country then, next to the village of Stretford – I walked to Moss Side, down Shrewsbury Street, past Brooks' Bar. Next day I was again at Old Trafford early and I received compensation for the ruined Bank Holiday. I saw Johnny Briggs score 50 – flicking his bat to the off-side in a way which in contemporary circles would quickly bring him to the notice of courts-martial; also he often blocked a ball and dashed out of his ground, pretending to run, 'chancing it', to use the gamester language of the period. He bounced about the wicket as though uncontrolled and uncontrollable.

It was during this summer of 1900, I think, that I saw Johnny Briggs take all ten wickets for Lancashire against Worcestershire at Old Trafford, on a quiet, dull morning. After the fall of the ninth wicket, Arthur Mold pitched his bowling wide, so that Johnny could put the finishing touch to a performance of some distinction half a century ago. For ten minutes he couldn't find any length or direction at all; he was so worked up, so excited, eager, happy, and so afraid this last wicket might elude him after all.

Poor Briggs, it was necessary to send him to an asylum; yet need we be sorry for him? I am assured that during his incarceration he was bowling Australia out every day, and driving four after four through the covers. One of his attendants told me that he'd go into his patient's room to find him beaming, a little exhausted. 'Eight for 52', he would report, recover his breath, 'bring me 'alf a pint, George.'

Briggs wasn't born in Lancashire, he was from Nottinghamshire, and Lockwood too; nor was Arthur Mold a Lancashire man; he belonged to Northamptonshire. But Briggs and Mold became household words in Lancashire, part of the rubric of the day-to-day and evening-by-evening cricket scores:

b Mold
c & b Briggs . . .

and so on through many many innings – 'c & b Briggs' – he was one of the cleverest catchers from his own bowling. I suppose in his dying moments he remembered best of all his comical days in the sun the morning at Sydney in December 1894 when he and Bobby Peel caused an astonishing collapse of Australia and won the most remarkable victory in the annals of Test cricket up to that moment. Australia batted first and amassed – for those days of moderate scores 'amassed' is the word – 586. England responded with 325; the follow-on then was automatic;

the fielding side had no option but to field again. So the Australians, tired from long labours under the sun, naturally waxed and waned in attack; England in their second innings scored 437, leaving Australia 177 to win. At the fall of the fifth afternoon, there was no suggestion that the match wouldn't after all go to its expected end, a heavy defeat of England. The wicket was still excellent and Australia made at close 130 or so for two; only a handful to get in the morning, with an array of superb batsmen in hand.

But there was, in the early hours of 20 December, a violent thunderstorm in Sydney, with torrents of tropical rain. It so happened that neither Johnny Briggs nor Bobby Peel heard the thunder or the bursting of the floodgates. They slept well, having drunk deep. The morning was a blaze of sunshine from a clear sky. The earth sprouted green and was dry, Briggs and Feel went to the ground together, blue serge and watch-chains. They went straight into the 'middle', according to a lifetime's habit, to 'look at pitch'. Bobby bent down, with a curious glint in his eye at Briggs. He pressed the earth, then said, 'Eh, Johnny, but soombody's bin wa-aterin' this wicket in t'neight. Coom on – we'll bowl 'em all out in a jiffy' ('bowl' pronounced to rhyme with howl).

And 'bowl' them out they did: Australia collapsed for 166 and England won by ten runs against Australia's first innings total, a record in 1894, of 586.

Other shadowy pictures from the 1900s chase one

another across the film of my mind, perhaps mingling together and eluding pursuit: I saw Carpenter of Essex, also at Whitsun, caught by Tyldesley at deep long-on in front of the Ladies' Pavilion at Old Trafford, the same gracious, black-and-white gabled Ladies' Pavilion where Kenneth Hutching fielded at third-man, tawny, supple, muscular and leonine, the cynosure of all eyes. Carpenter, entirely forgotten now, was a splendid batsman, equalled in stroke-play by not more than half a dozen players of 1950.

In 1901 the wicket at Old Trafford was a scandal. Fast bowling on it imperilled kneecap, breastbone and Adam's apple alike. Something had gone wrong with the ground staff's cultivation of the turf in the early spring. I have been told – but it is too good to be true—that one of the groundsmen was at work 'in the middle', separating with a riddle the impure from the pure and essential marl; he had almost finished the task, and had made two piles of the stuff – but at this critical juncture it was time for midday refreshment.

As luck would have it, he met an old friend at the adjacent inn, where every day he relished a modest sandwich and a glass of ale; on this occasion a reunion after long separation needed to be celebrated. When the groundsman returned to the 'middle' at Old Trafford he proceeded to sow the wrong pile of marl – containing many rough and foreign bodies – into the wicket, a natural enough error, all things considered. As I say, Old Trafford was indeed unfriendly to batsmen that year and a fast bowler's joy and inspiration. I saw C. J. Kortright knock Johnny Tyldesley out of action for an hour or two; but Johnny returned after lunch, his forehead bandaged, and he counter-attacked the fastest bowler of all time.

I am not sure that wasn't in this same match against Essex, in the early 1900s, that Tyldesley didn't win a match in an over. Seven or eight Lancashire wickets were down and nearly twenty runs still wanted when a storm broke; for an hour black clouds had rumbled up. Suddenly great spots of rain fell; you could hear the smack of them on the grass; then a flash of lightning was seen across the Stretford sky. Tyldesley, quicker than the storm, hit four fours in one over from Buckenham; square-cuts, flicks high over the slips, death-and-glory strokes as forked as the lightning. Before the players could reach the shelter of the pavilion, Trafford was a lake or an archipelago. In this season of dangerous pitches C. B. Fry one day extracted some pebbles or minerals from the wicket, and they were later exhibited in the window of Tyldesley's cricket outfit shop in Deansgate. People would look at them for hours, like students going the rounds of a museum of geology.

This same season, playing half his innings on this nasty, brutish turf, Tyldesley scored more than 3,000 runs, average more than fifty, which must remain one of the wonders of batsmanship. Consider, too, the pleasure he gave while making 3,000, to himself as much as anybody.

By the time 1904 burgeoned for Lancashire cricket, I

was an addict, hanging on to every hour's news from everywhere, Taunton to Trent, Bournemouth to Bradford. In 1904 Lancashire won the county championship and didn't lose a match; and the first three in Lancashire's batting order have never been equalled by any other first three, for mingled majesty, grace, swordlike power and brilliance: Maclaren, Spooner, Tyldesley.

Of Maclaren I can say no more: I have written of him elsewhere. Nobody has occupied a batting crease with his sovereignty, his sense of born prerogative. A youthful impression of him will not fade – yet I can't believe it is a true one. On the other hand, I am not poet enough ever to have 'invented' a picture as evocative and as true to the Maclarenesque manner and atmosphere as this:

On a calm morning at Old Trafford in that distant and indeed lost world of the early 1900s, Maclaren went forth with Albert Ward to open the Lancashire innings against Warwickshire. Hargreave, a clever slow left-hander, began the attack, and in his first over Maclaren played forward with the sweep of grandeur which was for him sign of the blood-royal; but Hargreave's ball, 'coming with the arm', beat Maclaren and bowled him. Only the leg bail fell. And when Maclaren returned to the pavilion the members rose for him in silence, as he passed them up the steps. At least, if they didn't, they should have.

Batsmanship of Manners

In the summer of 1899 a schoolboy walked to the wicket at Lord's to begin a Lancashire innings against Middlesex; with him was Albert Ward. He was a graceful young cricketer, and a little tuft of hair stood up on the crown of his head. His flannels seemed soft and billowy. This boy – his name R. H. Spooner –was making his first appearance in county cricket in his summer holidays, fresh from Marlborough. It would be hard to imagine a severer ordeal for anybody: a trial in the sacrosanct air of Lord's, the searching eyes of the pavilion on you, MacLaren your captain, and one of the bowlers against you Albert Trott at his best, spinning and curving and dipping the ball astonishingly.

R. H. Spooner that day made 83, an innings full of strokes that seemed to ripple over the grass, light and lovely as sunshine. Straight from the playing fields of Marlborough he came and conquered – nay, the word conquered is too hard and aggressive for Spooner: he charmed and won our heart and the hearts of all his opponents. 'It were a pleasure to bowl to Maister Spooner,' said an old player to me the other day; 'his batting were as nice as he were hisself.' Yes, it was nice; it was the batsmanship of manners. Spooner told us in every one of his drives past cover that he did not come from the hinterland of Lancashire, where cobbled streets sound with the noise of clogs and industry; he played always as though on the elegant lawns of Aigburth; his cricket was 'county' in the social sense of the term. This flavour of equability took the grimness out of a Lancashire and Yorkshire match even: I once saw him score 200 against Hirst, Rhodes, and Haigh at Bank Holiday time, and he transformed Old Trafford to Canterbury. I'll swear that on that day long ago there were tents and bunting in the breeze of Manchester while Spooner bat flicked and flashed from morning till evening.

He was the most lyrical of cricketers, and for that reason he had no need to play a long innings to tell us his secret. The only difference between 30 by Spooner and 150 was a matter of external and unessential form or duration; the spirit moved from the very beginning. A rondo by Mozart is just as complete and true as a symphony by him. One daffodil is as precious and delectable as a hundred daffodils. And a single stroke by Spooner was likewise a quality absolute, beyond the need of mensuration or any mathematical means of valuation whatever. If you consider

Spooner's average for the whole of his career it will tell you nothing of consequence about his cricket; as well count the word in a poem or the notes in an allegro.

I must suppose that he hit the ball hard, because I remember seeing fieldsmen blowing their hands after they had stopped a stroke by Spooner. And once I saw on the shilling side when Parker, of Gloucestershire, bowled his first ball in county cricket: Spooner pulled it clean over the rails, and it crashed amongst the dust and cinders like an exploding shell. Yet my impression today is that Spooner's cricket was all bouquet; I think of it I think of a rose, because of the perfume, not because of the substantial stuff which went to its making. Never did I see Spooner strike an ugly position, either at the wicket or in the field, where at cover he was the picture of swift, diving elegance.

If I have called his batsmanship that of manners, I do not mean it was ever affected: every innings by Spooner was natural and modest, like the man himself. The poise was a consequence of an instinctive balance of cultured technical parts. What's bred in the bone comes out in an innings; I never saw Spooner bat without seeing, as a background for his skill and beauty, the fields of Marlborough, and all the quiet summertime amenities of school cricket. He was my favourite player when I was a boy – he and Victor Trumper. And with a boy's illogicality I at one and the same time thought him wonderful and yet always in need of my prayers. All the time I watched him – and often I played truant to do so – I said in my heart, 'Please, Lord, don't let Reggie get out; let him score a century.' Sometimes I was more moderate: 'Please, Lord, let Reggie make 59.' I called him 'Reggie' even in my petitions to Providence. Like every delightful cricketer, he seemed at any moment ready to get out; no great batsman has ever been content to keep strictly within the scope of the things that can be done safely. I remember once seeing Spooner begin an innings against Hirst. All round his legs was the notorious Hirst 'trap' – four fieldsmen holding out avaricious hands. And Hirst swerved the ball terrifically across from Spooner's off-stump. And time after time did Spooner flick the swinging ball at his wrists' end through the leg-trap – each stroke a brave and lovely butterfly going into the flame.

Yet he was a sound as well as a brilliant batsman. There is a stupid legend about the batsmen of old. Because they made runs handsomely it is thought in certain places that they were constantly thrusting out the left leg and leaving their stumps exposed to the breaking ball. Not long ago a cricketer actually said to me, 'Yes, Spooner was splendid to watch, but he couldn't abide the "googly".'

And I said, 'God forgive you for blasphemy.'

In 1912 Spooner made a century against South Africa and amongst the bowlers were Pegler, Faulkner and Schwarz. These men have never had superiors as master of the 'googly': they were as clever at spinning the ball as anybody today. Spooner played them easefully – with his bat, not with his pads. He was superb in his back strokes: he could hit a four from a defensive position. The second line of defence – which is the pads – was known well enough to the batsmen of the Golden Age: Arthur Shrewsbury organised it scientifically. But it was a second and not a first line of defence; Spooner never put his bat ignominiously over his shoulder to any ball and stuck out his legs crudely and ungraciously. The fact that he could achieve a great innings as a boy against Albert Trott is ample retort to the absurd notion that he was ever at a loss against swerve or spin. No bowler who ever lived could give to a cricket ball more than Trott's curve and break.

Spooner and MacLaren – has a county possessed two batsmen who could begin an innings with more than their appeal to the imagination? They were as the King and the Prince, or as the eagle and the flashing swallow. Spooner was one of the cricketers who, when I was very young, made me fall in love with the game; I think of his batting now, in middle age, with gratitude. The delight of it all went into my mind, I hope, to stay there, with all the delight that life has given me in various shapes, aspects, and essences. When the form has gone –for it is material and accidental, and therefore perishable – the spirit remains. And Spooner's cricket in spirit was kin with sweet music, and the wind that makes long grasses wave, and the singing of Elisabeth Schumann in Johann Strauss, and the poetry of Herrick. Why do we deny the art of a cricketer, and rank it lower than a vocalist's or a fiddler's? If anybody tells me that R. H. Spooner did not compel a pleasure as aesthetic as any compelled by the most celebrated Italian tenor that ever lived I will write him down a purist and an ass.

By Three Runs

The most thrilling finish of all the Test matches ever fought at Old Trafford happened on the Saturday afternoon of 26 July 1902. It was the decisive game of the rubber, and Australia won it by three runs, snatching the spoils from the lion's mouth. The match at the end seemed to get right out of the control of the men that were making it; it seemed to take on a being of its own, a volition of its own, and the mightiest cricketers in the land looked as though they were in the grip of a power of which they could feel the presence but whose ends they could not understand. As events rushed them to crisis even Maclaren, Ranjitsinhji, Trumper, Noble, and Darling – most regal of cricketers – could only utter: 'Here we do but as we may; no further dare.' The game, in Kipling's term, was more than the player of the game.

The match was designed, surely, by the gods for their

sport. Even the victors were abominably scourged. On the second day, when the issue was anybody's, Darling played an innings which, as things turned out, must be said to have won Australia's laurels as much as anything else. Australia in their second innings had lost 3 wickets – those of Trumper, Duff, and Hill – for 10 runs and now possessed an advantage worth no more than 47. Under a sky of rags, the fitful and sinister sunlight coming through, Darling let all his superb might go at the English attack. His hitting had not the joyfulness of mastership in it; its note was desperation. He plainly felt the coils of circumstance about him; he plainly was aware of the demon of conflict that had the game in grip. And the defiant action of his bat was like a fist shaken at the unfriendly heavens.

It was in this innings of Darling's that the gods played their first cruel trick. For with Darling's score only 17 he was impelled to sky a ball to the deep field a high but easy catch. And who was the wight that the ironic powers had decreed should shoulder the responsibility of taking that crucial catch? His name was Tate – Tate of Sussex, a kindly fellow who never did harm to a soul. The humour of the gods really began when this cricketer was asked to play for England instead of George Hirst. Tate was a capital bowler, but as soon as he was seen in the company of the great the question went out: 'What is he doing in this galley?' Tate had not the stern fibre of character that can survive in an air of high tragedy; his bent was for pastoral comedy down at Horsham. Tate missed the catch, and never looked like holding it. As he stood under the ball, which hung for a while in the air – an eternity to Tate – and then dropped like a stone, his face turned white. Darling survived to make 37 out of a total of 86.

Had Tate held the catch Australia could hardly have got a score of more than 50, for Lockwood and Rhodes, that Friday afternoon, bowled magnificently. Yet when Tate laid himself down to rest in the evening, can he not be imagined as saying to himself: 'Well, it's nearly all over now, and as far as Tate of Sussex is concerned, the worst must have happened. I never *asked to* play for England – they thrust greatness on me – and I'll be well out of it this time tomorrow, back to Brighton, and who'll remember my missed catch after a week? What's a muff in the field in a cricketer's career – everybody makes them.' If Tate did console his spirit in this way the poor man did not know he was born. The gods had not finished with him; the next day he was to be put on the rack and have coals of fire heaped on his head.

On the Saturday England were left with 124 to get for victory. A tiny score with the cream of batsmanship at hand. But there had been five hours of rain in the night, and Trumble and Saunders were bowling for Australia. Still, England seemed nicely placed at lunch; the total 36 for none and Maclaren and Palairet undefeated. The crowd took its sustenance light-heartedly; everybody lived at ease in a fool's paradise as rosily lighted as Tate's. Here, again, was the humorous touch of the gods: men that are taken suddenly out of contentment are the more likely to writhe in Gehenna. After lunch the sun got to work on the wicket, and straightway Palairet was bowled by an intolerable break from Saunders. Tyldesley came in, and, with Maclaren, the game was forced.

The play of these two batsmen gave the crowd the first hint that all was not yet settled in England's favour, for it was the play of cricketers driven to desperate remedies. The runs, they seemed to say, can only be got if we hurry; there's the sun as well as Trumble and Saunders to frustrate. Tyldesley jumped to the bowling; he hit 16 runs in quick time before he was caught in the slips.

England 68 for 2 – 56 wanted now. And, said the crowd, not yet sniffing the evil in the wind, *only* 56, with Ranji, Abel, Jackson, Braund, and Lilley to come, to say nothing of Rhodes and Lockwood. Why, the game is England's!

Four runs after Tyldesley's downfall Maclaren was caught by Duff in the long field. An indiscreet stroke, yet whose was the right to blame the man for making it? It had come off time after time during his priceless innings of 35, and England could not afford to throw a single possible run away. Maclaren had played like a gambler at a table – not looking as though he were making runs, but rather as one who had ample boundaries at his bat's end to bank on every throw of the dice.

Abel and Ranji were in when at last the multitude unmistakably saw the evil day face to face. For what sort of a Ranji was this? Palsy was on him. You could have sworn that he shook at the knees. It looked like Ranji: his shirt rippled in the wind even as it did on that day at Old Trafford six years earlier than this, the day on which he conjured 154 runs out of the Australians. Yes, it looked like Ranji – the same slight body, the same inscrutable, bland face. Alas! the spirit had gone – here was a deserted shrine. Thousands of eyes turned away from Ranji and looked to Abel for succour. Ah, this is better – the pertness of little Abel lightened the soul. He made gallant runs – a boundary over Hill's head. 'Cheeky' work this – batsmanship with *gaminerie.* 'Bravo, Bobby!' shouted the Old Trafford crowd. At 92 Ranji was ou*t*, leg-before-wicket to Trumble. Well, the sophist crowd told itself, that was bound to happen; he never looked good for any at all. But 5 runs more and Trumble bowled Abel. England 97 for 5 – 27 needed.

'It's quite all right,' said a parson on the half-crown stand; 'there's really no cause for anxiety. To doubt the ability of Jackson, Braund, Lilley, Lockwood, and Rhodes to get a paltry 27 runs would be scandalous. Besides, I do believe that fellow Tate is a batsman – he has an average of 16 for Sussex.' The century went up with cheers to herald it – the crowd made as much of joyful noise as it could, presumably in the hope that cheering would put a better face on the scoring-board. Jackson, who made a century in the first innings, scored 7 in his best 'Parliamentary' manner – neat, politic runs. Then he was caught by Gregory, and now the cat was indeed out of the bag; sophistry passed away from the heaped-up ranks. 'Who'd 'a' thowt it?' said a man on the sixpenny side. Who, indeed? At that very moment of agony at Old Trafford, people far away in the city read in the latest editions, 'England 92 for 3', and agreed that it wasn't worth the journey to Old Trafford, that it had been a good match, that the Australians were fine sportsmen, and jolly good losers.

Sixteen runs – four good boundaries or four bad ones – would bring the game into England's keeping when Lilley reached the wicket.

He was frankly and unashamedly in some slight panic. He hit out impetuously, as who should say: 'For the Lord's sake let it be settled and done with quickly.' Braund was overthrown at 109, and Lockwood made not a run. Lilley lashed his bat about like a man distraught. Rhodes is his companion now, and stands on guard ever so cool. Eight runs will do it, and 'There goes four of them!' affirms the red-hot crowd as Lilley accomplishes a grand drive into the deep.

'Well hit, sir!' shouts our parson. 'Nothing like taking your courage in both hands against these Australian fellows. Well hit, sir!'

Clem Hill is seen running along the boundary's edge as though the fiend were after him. Trying to save the four, is he? – even from as certain a boundary hit as this! Extraordinary men, Australians; never give anything away. Hill, in fact, saved the boundary in the most decisive manner in the world by holding the ball one-handed before it pitched. The impetus of his run carried him 20 yards beyond the place where he made the catch – a catch which put incredulity into the face of every man and woman at Old Trafford that day. 'A sinful catch,' said the parson.

Tate, the last man in, watched Rhodes ward off three balls from Trumble, and then rain stopped play. Yes, rain stopped play for 40 minutes – and England eight runs short of triumph with the last men in. But though it was heavy rain there was always a bright sky not far away – another piece of subtle torture by the gods, for nobody could think that the weather was going to put an end to the afternoon. It would clear up all right in time; the agony had to be gone through.

The crowd sat around the empty field, waiting, but hardly daring to hope. The tension was severe. Yet surely there were calm minds here and there. Why, under a covered stand sat two old gentlemen who were obviously *quite* indifferent to the issue. One was actually reading to the other the leading article from one of the morning papers. Moreover, he was reading it in a controlled and deliberately articulated voice. '"Sir M. Hicks-Beach argued yesterday,"' he read, '"that even if Ireland was overtaxed in 1894, its grievance was less today, because taxation had not increased quite so rapidly in Ireland as in the United Kingdom."' And the other old gentleman, so far was he from troubling his head needlessly over a mere cricket match, promptly took up the points in the argument, and he too spoke in a perfectly controlled and deliberately articulated voice. 'Two wrongs,' he commented, 'do not make a right.' Excited about England and Australia? Not a bit of it, sir! We trust we are old and sensible enough to put a correct valuation on a game of cricket.

In the pavilion Tate was dying a thousand deaths. All depended on him – Rhodes was safe enough. In his head, maybe, notions went round and round like a wheel. 'You've only to keep your bat straight,' he might well have said to himself time after time. 'Don't even move it from the block hole. I've heard tell if you keep your bat quite still it's a thousand to one against any ball hitting the wicket.' . . .

At six minutes to five the Australians went into action again. Saunders bowled at Tate – a fast one. Tate saw something hit the ground and he made a reflex action at it. Click! Tate looked wildly around him. What had happened? A noise came to him over the wet grass, sounding like a distant sea. The crowd was cheering; he had snicked a boundary. Another snick like that and the game is England's and Tate safe for posterity! The ball was returned from the ring, and Darling slightly but impressively rearranged his field, the while Saunders bent down to a sawdust heap. Bloodless, calculating Australians they were.

Tate got himself down on his bat once more, and the wheel in his poor head went round faster and faster. ' . . . Bat straight . . . don't move . . . can't hit wicket . . . block-hole . . . don't move. . . . Bat straight . . . can't hit wicket . . .' And the gods fooled him to the top of his bent – to the last. Saunders's fourth ball was not only good enough for Tate's frail bat; it was good enough for the best bat in England. It was fast through the air and – it was a shooter. It broke Tate's wicket, and, no doubt, broke Tate's heart and the heart of the crowd.

In 20 minutes Old Trafford was deserted save for one or two groundsmen who tended to the battlefield. The figures on the scoreboard had revolved, obliterating all records of the match from the face of it, which now looked vacantly over the grass. The gods had finished their sport – finished even with Tate. Yet not quite. A week later, on the Saturday afternoon following this, Tate met the Australians again in his beloved Sussex, and he was graciously permitted to play an innings of 22 not out against them – and a capital innings at that.

Bill Worsley, Straight from the Pits

Bill Worsley belonged to the hinterland of the county where existence is carried on near to the knuckle, where cobbled streets go up and down hill, where in the pitch-black of cold winter mornings mills' sirens or 'buzzers' awakened the dead, and the rattle of clogs was like the sound of a sort of Last Day or Resurrection. From one of the pits of Lancashire emerged this Bill Worsley, who kept wicket for the county in the great high noon of Maclaren's reign.

He got his chance unexpectedly. The Lancashire Eleven was touring the West of England and the regular wicket-keeper received an injury to the hand which rendered him a casualty for the rest of the summer. A telegram was sent for reinforcements and was received by Bill Worsley on his back in a seam of a coal-mine. He was brought to the surface, where he blinked his eyes to get accustomed to the light of day. After he had slowly read the telegram he said, without emotion: 'It's signed A. C. Maccle-aren' – he always pronounced it that way – 'and it ses Ah've to pack oop and go to Edgbaston, Birmingham, and keep wickets for Lankysheer.' He scratched his head and added: 'Ah'm non so sure as Ah rightly knows where Edgbaston is.'

But his proud and admiring friends saw him to the train and bought the correct railway ticket, and Bill departed, with a farewell message as he leaned out of the carriage window: "Ah reckon Ah'll be back wi' thee all in a day or two. Look after mi whippets.'

He duly arrived at the cricket ground of Edgbaston. Lancashire were about to play Warwickshire. Bill stripped and sat in a corner in the dressing-room. Nobody spoke to him and he, as he afterwards said, kept himself to 'hisself'. He was discerned by Walter Brearley, the fast bowler and an 'amateur', meaning a 'gentleman'. Brearley, the kindest man and the friendliest in the world, hailed the newcomer. 'You are Worsley, aren't you; wicket-keeper for us today?'

'Yes, sir,' replied Bill.

'Come and have a drink,' said Brearley: 'We'll just have *one*, to baptise your first appearance for the county. This is your opportunity, Bill; just you keep a decent wicket and you can say goodbye to the pit, and have a grand life up and down the country. Come on, Bill – this way!' Brearley led Bill to the bar in the members' enclosure. When they reached the counter, Brearley smote Bill on the back and said: 'Now, Bill; what'll you have to celebrate this famous day in your life?'

'Well,' responded Bill politely, 'if you don't mind, Maister Brearley, Ah'll 'ave a Creem de Month.'

Brearley was rather taken aback. 'A what?' he said.

And Bill repeated with equal politeness: 'A Creem de Month, if you please, Maister Brearley.'

Brearley concealed his astonishment and gave the order, including a can of beer for himself, which he picked up and drained at a draught. 'There's luck to you, Bill,' he gulped.

Whereupon Bill drank his green fluid and said: 'The same to you, Maister Brearley, and many of 'em.'

Lancashire lost the toss, and Maclaren led his team into the field. When he reached the middle he as usual spent some time distributing his forces, waving men here and there, while Brearley measured his run and swung his arms and prepared to attack. The two opening Warwickshire batsmen came to the wicket, and Kinneir took his guard. All was ready.

Then Maclaren at first slip withdrew his attention from the bowler and the precise position to an inch of cover-point: he saw Bill Worsley 'standing up', an inch or so from the stumps. 'Worsley,' he said, 'get back a bit – Mr Brearley happens to be pretty quick.'

'Just as you like, Maister Maccle-aren,' said Bill, retreating exactly four inches.

'Farther back still,' shouted Maclaren impatiently: 'he's fast, I'm telling you.'

'Just as you please, Maister Maccle-aren,' reiterated Bill, retreating another four inches.

To himself Maclaren said: 'Well, if he wants his so-and-so head knocked off, very well.'

The match began. Bill 'stood up' to Brearley. Kinneir, a left hander and a most obstinate batsman on a good wicket, was in form. He scored ten in a quarter of an hour – rapid work for him. Then he moved gently over to the off-side and beautifully glanced at a fine angle to leg. Worsley also moved across, made a brilliant catch and, without a change of action or pause, sent the ball high into the air with a one-handed jerk behind his back.

'What the . . . what the . . .' expostulated Maclaren.

But Brearley said, behind his hand, 'Hush, Archie; you'll put him off! Marvellous catch!'

So Maclaren held his peace and the game was resumed. The next batsman was the formidable W. G. Quaife, most notorious of stone-wallers, almost beyond the powers of known science to get out on a hard wicket under six hours. He, too, began well and he, too, presently moved gently across his wickets and glanced exquisitely off his pads, fine to leg. And again did Worsley swoop on the ball, catch it, and with one comprehensive and encircling action jerk it sky-high behind his back.

This was too much for Maclaren. In spite of Brearley's muffled, 'Shush, Archie; you'll only put him off. Marvellous catch!' – in spite of Brearley's kind admonitions, Maclaren approached Bill. 'Well caught, Worsley,' he said, 'but damn it all, what's the idea of this behind-the-back foolery?'

'Well, Maister Maccle-aren,' replied Bill, 'we allus does

it in t' Saturday afternoon league – a little bit o' 'fluence, tha knows, sir.'

'You can't do it here,' said Maclaren, 'in front of all these people. Bless my soul. Now, Bill, get on with your job. You're doing splendidly. But no more bits o' 'fluence, if you don't mind.'

As it happened, one or two Warwickshire batsmen took root, and Lancashire spent a long day in the field. But Bill acquitted himself well, though he did not get any more chances to make a catch. When they all came to the pavilion at close of play, it was discovered that Bill had been wearing primitive gloves. His hands were swollen and black. A pair of scissors was needed to cut his gloves away from his wounded hands.

Brearley's heart went out to Bill. He took him to the bar, the same bar where at the beginning of the day they had drunk to Bill's first appearance for Lancashire.

'Come, Bill,' said Brearley, 'you've won your colours. You'll come with us on the whole tour now. No more pit for you, my lad. You've done "gradely". But for God's sake, get some proper gloves and drop all that behind-the-back business. Can't do it at Lord's – Heaven help us ... Well, here's to you, Bill. Let's celebrate the occasion properly now. What'll you have?'

And Bill replied, polite as ever: 'Well, if you don't mind, Maister Brearley, Ah'll have a Creem de Month.'

Victor Trumper

When Victor Trumper died he was a young man and a cricketer. The death of a cricketer before age has fallen on him is sad; it is even against nature. Well may he look down on our fields from his chill hall of immortality, far removed from the jolly flesh and blood of this life, and cry out, 'Another day in the sun and wind and I not there, I not there!'

It is only a score or so of years since Victor Trumper played a great innings at Old Trafford in a Test match and hit a century before lunch. Can it be true he is now part of the impersonal dust – this Victor Trumper we knew so well? All the little intimate delights belonging to cricket, a man's flannels and his bat, his own boyish enthusiasm for a summer game – surely these are things which ought to hold a cricketer to the friendly earth till he is tired of them? You can never speak to an Australian about Victor Trumper without seeing his eyes glisten with pride and affection;

Trumper will always remain for your true Australian the greatest batsman that ever lived. But it was in England that Trumper achieved his most wonderful play; every lover of the game will pause for a space in the hurly-burly of the present period's Test matches to spare a moment in which to do homage to Trumper.

> The shadow stayed not, but the splendour stays,
> Our brother, till the last of English days.

In 1902, a season of bowler's wickets here, Trumper's batsmanship was by day of a brilliance that beggared description. Lest this language be thought overdrawn (I am not above suspicion in my use of words when it comes to writing of a Trumper), I will draw on the restrained vocabulary used in the MCC's *Cricket Scores and Biographies*:

> For Trumper the season [of 1902] was one long trium-
> phal progress, and those who were fortunate enough
> to witness his amazing brilliance will never be able to
> forget the unrivalled skill and resource he displayed.
> On sticky wickets he hit with freedom and scored well,
> often whilst his companions were puddling about the
> crease, unable to make headway and seemingly content
> if they could keep up their wickets ... He was always
> to be feared on Australian wickets, but followers of
> the game in England were privileged to see him at his
> zenith.

Was it not genius that made Trumper a master batsman in conditions not common to Australian cricket? Only a few of our own batsmen were resourceful and skilful enough to conquer the English pitch as it was in the old days whenever sunshine and rain got to work on it. Trumper learned his game in the land where perfect grounds are the rule; he came to this country, and in a season that saw the wickets of English batsmen of the highest rank falling like corn before the sickle he was masterful. Trumper in 1902 took our finest spin bowlers by the scruff of the neck, usually from the first ball sent to him, drove them, thrust, glanced and 'carted' them, right and left, for all the world as though they had been schoolboys. Amongst these same bowlers happened to be Rhodes, Taigh, Lockwood, J. T. Hearne, Hirst, Barnes, Trott, Wass and Braund.

In the Test match at Manchester, as I say, Trumper scored a century before lunch; even Maclaren, with all his strategy, could not set the field for him. No shibboleth about an 'outer and inner ring' of fieldsmen ever troubled Victor Trumper. He was master of all the strokes, and he could use almost any one of them at his pleasure, no matter the manner of ball bowled at him. He would cut the identical length which a moment later he would drive. It was, indeed, impossible to pitch a length at all to Trumper on one of his great days. 'He would,' says the sober record of the MCC, 'get a yorker to the square-leg boundary, and it was by no means unusual to see him cut a ball off the middle stump for four. Some of his biggest hits, which went over the ring, were made without any apparent effort.'

Let me give a few more prosaic facts about Trumper before I squander words over his art (whoever would not be spendthrift of language about Trumper, let him not write on him at all). In our bowler's year of 1902, Trumper scored eleven centuries, two against Essex in the same match; he hit a century for Australia at Old Trafford before lunch, as we have seen. In the Test match at Sheffield in 1899 he scored 62 out of 80 in 50 minutes. For New South Wales, on a bowler's pitch, he made 101 out of 139 in 57 minutes, at Sydney in 1905. He scored in Test matches 17,150 runs at an average of 45.01, an astonishing figure for a batsman who lived so dangerously at the wicket. In Australia he averaged 84.30 (for 843 runs) in 1912–13; 72.10 (for 721 runs) in 1899–1900; and 69.22 (for 1,246 runs) in 1910–11. Facts, as Mr Bounderby would say. And now let us come to the imperishable spirit of the man.

To change the old saying about the strawberry, God no doubt could create a better batsman than Victor Trumper if He wished, but so far He hasn't. Ranjitsinhji is the only cricketer that might be instanced as Trumper's like in genius. But even Ranji was not so great a match-winner on all wickets. Even Ranji never smashed the best attack of his day with the sudden vehemence of Trumper. Ranji did not rout his bowlers; he lured them onwards to ruin by the dark, stealthy magic of his play; the poor men were enchanted into futility. Trumper put them to the sword . . .

Yet it was a knightly sword. There never lived a more chivalrous cricketer than Trumper. I see his bat now, in my mind's eye, a banner in the air, streaming its brave runs over the field. He was ready always to take up the challenge of a good ball; Trumper never fell into the miserable philosophy of 'Safety first – wait for the bad ball.'

And what of the man's style? He had, as C. B. Fry put it, no style, yet he was all style. 'His whole bent is aggressive,' wrote Fry, 'and he plays a defensive stroke only as a very last resort.' Imagine Spooner's cover drive, Hirst's pull, Maclaren's hook, J. T. Tyldesley's square cut, Macartney's late cut through the slips – imagine a mingling of all these attributes of five great and wholly different batsmen, and perhaps some notion of Trumper will emerge in your mind. The grand manner of Maclaren, the lyrical grace of Spooner, the lion energy of Jessop, the swift opportunist spirit of Tyldesley – all these excellencies were compounded proportionately in Trumper. Do I exaggerate youthful impressions of the man? Then let me give here a tribute to Trumper uttered to me by an English cricketer whose name stands for all that is masterful and majestic in our batsmanship: 'In comparison with an innings by Victor at his best, my best was shoddy – hackwork!'

Trumper's winged batsmanship was seen in the golden age of cricket; he was, at his finest, master of some of the greatest bowlers the game has ever known. When he played for Australia, Clem Hill, Noble, Duff, Darling, S. E. Gregory, and Armstrong were batsmen with him.

Splendid as the cricket of these men might be, day after day, whenever Trumper got out the light seemed to go for a while from an Australian innings. 'The eagle is gone, and now crows and daws.' We make an artist's immortality by thinking upon and loving his work; Trumper was an artist-cricketer; let him live again in the mouths of men whenever Test matches are in action. Since he accomplished some of his greatest innings in this land, English cricket owes much to his ghost.

Ranjitsinhji

Cricketers will never see the like of Ranjitsinhji; he was entirely original, and there is nothing in all the history and development of batsmanship with which we can compare him. His style was a remarkable instance of the way a man can express personal genius in a game — nay, not only a personal genius but the genius of a whole race. For Ranjitsinhji's cricket was of his own country; when he batted a strange light was seen for the first time on English fields, a light out of the East. It was lovely magic and not prepared for by anything that had happened in cricket before Ranji came to us.

In the 'nineties the game was absolutely English; it was even Victorian. W. G. Grace for years had stamped on cricket the English mark and the mark of the period. It was the age of simple first principles, of the stout respectability of straight bat and good-length ball; the flavours everywhere were John Bull's. And then suddenly this visitation of dusky, supple legerdemain happened; a man was seen playing cricket as nobody born in England could possibly have played it. The honest length ball was not met by the honest straight bat, but there was a flick of the wrist, and lo! the straight ball was charmed away to the leg boundary. And nobody quite saw or understood how it all happened. Bowler stood transfixed, and possibly they crossed themselves. I once asked Ted Wainwright, the Yorkshire cricketer, what he thought of Ranji, and Wainwright said, 'Ranji, he never made a Christian stroke in his life.' Why should he have done? The style is the man, and Ranji belonged to the land of Hazlitt's Indian jugglers, where beauty is subtle and not plain and unambiguous.

Marvellous game of cricket that can give us a W. G. Grace, English as a Gloucestershire tree, and George Hirst, Yorkshire as a broad moor, and Ranji as true to his racial psychology as any of them!

The game has known no greater spectacle than that of C. B. Fry and Ranji as they made a great stand for Sussex. I notice that Mr. J. A. Spender has described the Ranji-Fry combination as 'the perfect display of the first-wicket stand'. But Ranji never went in first with Fry; he always batted second wicket down, and thereby hangs a tale – and again the teller of it is Ted Wainwright. 'Ranji and Fry', he would murmur as memory moved in him, 'every year it were the same owd story. We used to go down to Brighton with the sun shining and the ground hard as iron. And Sussex allus won the toss. And we all went on the field and

47

started bowlin', and, sure enough, we'd get Vine out and the score board would say Sussex 20 for 1. And then George Hirst would get Killick out quick, and we all on us said, "Come on, Yorkshire, we're going grand; Sussex 31 for 2!!"' Wainwright paused here in his narrative, and after a while he added, 'But, bless you, we knowed there were nowt in it. Close of play, Sussex three 'undred and ninety for two, and the same owd tale every year.'

Bowlers have never known a problem so heartbreaking as the problem of Fry and Ranji on a perfect Brighton wicket. Happy the man who today can close his eyes and see again the vision of Ranji, his rippling shirt of silk, his bat like a yielding cane making swift movements which circled round those incomparable wrists. He saw the ball quicker than any other batsman; he made his strokes later, so late, indeed, that Lockwood almost saw his great breakback crashing on the leg stump while Ranji remained there at his crease, apparently immobile. Then, at the last fraction of the last second, Ranji's body leaned gently over his front leg, the bat glinted in the sun, and we saw Lockwood throw up his hands to heaven as the ball went to the boundary, exquisitely fine to leg, with the speed of thought. This leg glance was Ranji's own stroke, but it is a mistake to say he could not drive. Usually he was too indolent for forcible methods, but none the less his front-of-the-wicket play could reach unparalleled range and precision; and his cut was a dazzling lance of batsmanship.

He caused a revolution in the game: he demonstrated

the folly of the old lunge forward to a ball seductive in length. Ranji's principle was to play back or to drive, and his many imitators contrived in the course of years to evolve the hateful two-eyed stance from Ranji's art, which, of course, was not for ordinary mortals to imitate. He is today a legend. Modern lovers of the game, jealous of their own heroes, will no doubt tell us that Ranji, like all the old masters, was a creation of our fancy in a world old-fashioned and young. We who saw him will keep silence as the sceptics commit their blasphemy. We have seen what we have seen. We can feel the spell yet, we can go back in our minds to hot days in an England of forgotten peace and plenty, days when Ranji did not so much bat for us as enchant us, bowlers and all, in a way all his own, so that when at last he got out we were as though suddenly wakened from a dream. It was more than a cricketer and more than a game that did it for us.

The Greatest Test Match

On a bright day in the spring of 1921 I went to Lord's, hoping to see the first practice of the Australians. But the place was deserted, save for the man at the gates. He told me Armstrong's men were being entertained that afternoon somewhere in the City, and that they wouldn't be in the nets till after tea. Still, he added, with a touch of human nature not too common at Lord's, if I liked I could enter the ground and sit and enjoy myself in the sun till they came.

I sat on a bench with my feet spread out so that they touched the soft grass. A great calm was over the field. The trees beyond the Nursery were delicate with fresh green, and the fine old pavilion seemed to nod in the sunshine. It was an occasion for a reverie, and I fell to affectionate thoughts upon the great days of cricket, of the history that had been made on the field which stretched before me. I thought of Grace, of Spofforth, of Hornby, of A. G. Steel ... Maybe I dozed for a while.

Then I was conscious of a voice. 'Would you mind moving up a little? This seat is rather congested.'

I looked around and saw sitting by my side a man in a tight black coat which buttoned high on his chest. He had sidewhiskers and wore a low turned-down collar and a high bowler hat. A handkerchief was showing from a breast pocket in his jacket. Not quite awake yet, I moved up.

'Thank you,' he said. 'I'm sorry I disturbed you. A nap carries one comfortably through a long wait at these matches. What a crowd there is!'

I looked round. I was in the middle of a big crowd indeed. In front of me sat a parson. He was reading *The Times*. I glanced over his shoulder and saw the headline: 'Egyptian Campaign: Sir G. Wolseley's Dispatch.'

The man at my side said, 'Were you here yesterday, sir?' and before I could reply he added, 'It was a considerable day's cricket, and the *Post* has an excellent account. Perhaps you've seen it?' He handed me a copy of the *Morning Post*, and, thanking him, I took it. The paper was dated 29 August 1882. In a column headed 'England v Australia' I read that on the day before, Australia had been dismissed for 63 by Barlow and Peate, and that England, captained by A. N. Hornby, had made in reply 101. Then I understood my situation. And what is more I now understood it without the slightest astonishment. Even the aspect of the ground, which told me it was Kennington Oval and not Lord's, did not embarrass me. It was enough that I was one of the crowd that was to witness the second day's cricket in the ninth Test match – the most famous Test match of all.

I gave the *Post* back to my companion in silence. 'A considerable day's cricket indeed, sir,' said the parson. 'But England ought to have made more runs. Our batting was distinctly mediocre – almost as bad as the Australians'.' A loud cheer disturbed his argument. Down the pavilion steps walked the England Eleven in single file, led by Hornby. With him was WG, and he passed along the field with an ambling motion, and the wind got into his great black beard. He spoke to Hornby in a high-pitched voice and laughed. Then he threw the ball to a tall, graceful player just behind him and cried, 'Catch her, Bunny.' Following Grace and Hornby were Lucas, C. T. Studd, J. M. Read, the Hon. A. Lyttelton, Ulyett, Barlow, W. Barnes, A. G. Steel and Peate. The crowd quietened, awaiting the advent of Australia's first two batsmen, and I again heard the parson's voice. ' ... The English total was distressingly poor. Rarely have I seen poorer batting from an All England Eleven. The fact is, sir, that for some little time now English cricket has been deteriorating. Our batsmen don't hit the ball as hard as they used to do, and even our bowling ...' Another cheer drowned his discourse. 'Bannerman and Massie,' said my companion. 'I should imagine Bannerman's the youngest man in the match.'

The parson was prompt with his correction. 'I believe S. P. Jones, who was twenty-one on the first of the month, is the junior member of the two teams. Studd is,

I fancy, eleven months older than Jones. Bannerman is twenty-three at least, and Giffen is six days younger than Bannerman.'

My companion was silenced, but I ventured a question. 'How old is Spofforth?'

Pat came the answer, 'Twenty-seven on the ninth of next month.'

The crowd, including even the parson, went as quiet as a mouse as Barlow began the English bowling to Bannerman. Lyttelton, behind the wicket, crouched low. It was exactly a quarter past twelve. The text half-hour was a tumultuous prelude to the day. Bannerman was all vigilance, while Massie played one of the great innings of Test cricket. He hurled his bat at every ball the slightest loose, and his hits crashed ponderously to the boundary. He was the living image of defiance as he faced the Englishmen, glaring round the field his challenge. At one huge drive from Barlow's bowling my companion murmured, 'I've never seen a bigger hit than that at the Oval.'

But the parson overheard him. 'When the Australians were here in '78,' he said, 'W. H. Game, playing for Surrey, hit a ball from Spofforth to square-leg right out of the ground.' Still, he admitted that this Massie fellow hit them quite hard enough. In half an hour England's advantage of 38 was gone. Hornby called up bowler after bowler, Studd for Barlow, Barnes for Studd. Steel tried his hand at 56 – the sixth bowler in less than three-quarters of an hour. When Australia's score was 47 Massie lifted a ball to long-on.

'Lucas is there,' said the parson; 'he'll get it all r—— Good Lord!' For Lucas dropped the ball and blushed red as the crowd groaned out of its soul.

'Sixty-six for none,' murmured the man at my side; 'they're 28 on with all their wickets intact. If Massie prevails – ah, bravo, sir, well bowled, well bowled!' A ball from Steel had tempted Massie, and just as he jumped out it broke back and wrecked the wicket. Massie walked to the pavilion, roared home by an admiring but much relieved crowd. His innings was worth 55 to Australia, made out of 66 in less than an hour.

Bonner came next, and the English out-fields dropped deep and had apprehensive thoughts. Would not Massie's example make this bearded giant a very Jehu? But Hornby has an inspiration. He asks Ulyett to bowl instead of Steel. And Ulyett moves to the wicket like a man ploughing against a breaker, puts the last ounce of his Yorkshire strength into a thunderbolt of a ball that sends Bonner's middle stump flying. The crowd is only just getting back the breath lost in approval of this feat when Bannerman is caught by Studd at extra mid-off. Bannerman has batted 70 minutes for 13. 'Quick work for him!' says the parson. And with the broad bar of Bannerman out of the way the English bowlers begin to see daylight. Peate's slow left-hand deliveries spin beautifully, as though controlled by a string. The Australians now, save Murdoch, are just guessing. The fourth wicket falls at 75, the fifth at 79. Australia are all out 122. 'Only 85 to win,' says the parson. 'It's our game after all, though Lucas did his best to lose it.'

It was a true autumn afternoon going to its fall in grey light when WG and Hornby went to the wicket to face Spofforth and Garratt. The crowd filled the ground, but so silent was it as Grace took his guard that one could hear the *tink-tink* of a hansom cab coming closer and closer along the Vauxhall Road. Spofforth's first over was fast – he let the ball go with a quick leap, dropping his arm at the moment of release. Blackham 'stood back' when Grace was batting, but crept up for Hornby. 'Beautiful wicket-keeping', murmured my companion.

'Pinder was not less gifted,' said the parson. And he added, 'I have not seen Spofforth bowl as fast as this for some time. He has latterly cultivated medium-pace variations.' Both Hornby and Grace began confidently, and at once the tension lifted. Hornby made a lovely cut from Spofforth and a dainty leg stroke for a couple.

Spofforth uprooted Hornby's off stump with England's score 15, and with his next ball clean bowled Barlow. The crowd gave out a suspicion of a shiver, but the advent of bluff George Ulyett was reassuring, especially as Grace welcomed him with a fine leg hit from Garratt for three and a beautiful on drive to the boundary from Spofforth. 'Thirty up,' said my companion; 'only 55 to get.' England was still 30 for two when Spofforth crossed over to the pavilion end. Now I was behind his arm; I could see his superb break-back. And he bowled mainly medium pace this time. With each off-break I could see his right hand, at the end of the swing over, finish near the left side, 'cutting' under the ball. Sometimes his arm went straight over and continued straight down in the follow-through – and then the batsman had to tackle fierce top spin. There was the sense of the inimical in his aspect now. He seemed taller than he was a half-hour ago, the right arm of him more sinuous. There was no excitement in him; he was, the parson said, cold-blooded. Still Ulyett faced him bravely while Grace, at the other end, time after time moved from his crease with a solid left leg and pushed the ball away usefully.

'Fifty up,' said my companion, 'for two wickets. It's all over – we want only thirty-four now,' And at 51 Spofforth bowled a very fast one to Ulyett, who barely snicked it. It served, though; Blackman snapped the catch, and his 'H'zat!' was hoarse and aggressive. Lucas came in, and with two runs more WG was caught at mid-off.

'What a stroke!' said the parson. 'I'm afraid he's not the Grace he was.'

Four for 53, and Lyttelton and Lucas in. Lyttleton hits out big-heartedly, but the field is like a net tightly drawn. It is suddenly understood by every man of us that the game is in the balance.

'The wicket must be bad,' says somebody.

Lucas stonewalls, with a bat as straight as a die. Spofforth bowls a maiden; Boyle bowls a maiden; Spofforth bowls another maiden. The air is growing thick.

'Get runs or get out, for the Lord's sake,' says somebody.

The field creeps closer and closer to the wicket. Spofforth and Boyle are like uncanny automatons, bowling, bowling, bowling . . . Six successive maidens.

'This,' says the parson, 'this is intolerable.'

One's heart is aching for an honest boundary hit . . . And the human bowling machines send down six more successive maidens. Think of it: twelve successive maidens, and the game in that state, the crowd in that purgatory.

'When Grace was a boy of eighteen I saw him make 50 on this very ground and he played every ball he got.' It was the parson again, but he sounded a little strained, a little unhappy.

At the end of the twelfth successive maiden, a hit was purposely misfielded that Spofforth might have a 'go' at Lyttelton. The batsmen fell into the snare. Four more maidens, and spinning is Lyttelton's wicket.

'Anyhow, that's over and done with!' thankfully breathes the crowd. Better all be dead than dying! England five for 66 – 19 needed. Steel comes next and Lucas hits a boundary. Roars the crowd 'Bravo!' then catches breath. Steel caught and bowled Spofforth none – Maurice Read clean bowled second ball. England 7 for 70.

'Incredible!' say 20,000 people in dismal unison.

Barnes, the next man, hits a two. Thirteen to win. Heaven bless us, Blackman has blundered! He allows three byes. Run Barnes, run Lucas! Spofforth is inscrutable as the crowd makes its noises. His next ball is too fast for eyes at the boundary's edge to see. Lucas comes down on it, though – hard, determined. And the ball rolls ever so gently on to the wicket and disturbs the bail. Poor Lucas bows his head and departs, and blasphemy is riot throughout the crowd and is communicated by stages to the outer darkness of Kennington Road.

The stars are set against England – our cricketers are for the first time on English soil face to face with a victorious Australian XI. With ten to struggle for, Blackman catches Barnes off his glove, and the last man is here – poor Peate, who is the best slow bowler in England and not a bit more of a cricketer than that, and what good are his mysteries of spin now! Studd is there yet, though; only ten runs and it is our game. Perhaps *he* – Peate has hit a two. It was audacious, but maybe the ball was a safe one to tackle. A bad ball's a bad ball at any time. Peate has nerve (so we are telling ourselves, desperately): he's the right man: he'll play the steady game to good stuff and leave the job to Studd . . . The stark truth is that Peate hit out wildly yet again at a slow from Boyle, missed it, and was bowled. There was a hollow laugh somewhere as the wicket went back, but whether it came from this world or the next I couldn't say. Studd did not get a ball. 'Why, man, did you try to hit: why couldn't you just stop them?' they asked Peate.

'Well,' he replied, 'I couldn't trust Maister Studd!'

As Peate's wicket was broken, ten thousand people rushed the rails and hid the green field. Spofforth was carried shoulder-high to the pavilion, and there the mob praised a famous man. I, too, wanted get up and shout, but somehow I was rooted to my seat. I was probably the only man in that multitude on the pavilion not standing up, and as I sat there I had a strange sense of making a lonely hole in a solid black mass.

The parson was standing on the seat beside me. His boots were not more than two feet from my eyes and I could see the fine ribbed work on the upper edge of the soles. The cheering came downwards to me, sounding remote. I lost grip on events. It seemed that I sat there till the ground was almost deserted, till over the field came a faint mist, and with it the vague melancholy of twilight in a great city. Time to go home, I thought . . . a great match . . . great days . . . great men . . . all gone . . . far away . . . departed glory . . .

A hand of someone touched my shoulder and I heard him say: 'The Orsetralians are on the way, and they'll be in the nets at four o-clock. Nice in the sun, isn't it?'

On a Fresh Cricket Season

The beginning of cricket was fixed by Lord's for round about the first of May, and ostensibly it began then, and was duly reported in the newspapers. But here and there a cricketer of spirit was made to understand that the season was upon him before this; it came, for him, a day sooner at least than the rest of us were aware; the very instant, in fact, that a spring light woke him one morning and stirred in his mind a solitary thought: 'Today we leave for the South; today we set out on the summer's first tour.'

Nothing can go wrong with him on this blessed morning. He packs his bag blissfully, beholds the faded labels on it, eloquent of many a golden Odyssey. Lovely sequence of names – Canterbury, Taunton, Worcester, Horsham, Tonbridge! It was at Horsham, our happy cricketer tells himself, he saw the season die last August. How far away did May seem on that afternoon when the sun burned out and he packed the bag for the last time and said 'Goodbye' to his companions! Did he not wish then with all his heart for Maytime back again? Did he not then ask himself why, when the season's beginning was with him, he had not shouted for joy the day long? Well, a spring morning is here for his delight again. Let him hang on to every minute of it, revel in a delighted sense of the time of the year, tell himself over and over: 'I am getting the best out of the day as it passes; I am missing nothing!'

Observe, happy man, from your bedroom window, at this moment as you prepare yourself for a journey to the South – observe the passers-by along the road opposite. They are going to work, going to the city, there to live stuffily in one dingy spot, while you – while you are going away for the beginning of cricket. Tonight these poor souls will pass by your house again, back from the city, but you will not be there to see them return. By then you will be at the other end of England; perhaps you will have just been taken by the hotel porter to your room, just have unpacked, washed, and gone out into the delicious streets, to ravish yourself in them with the feeling of the miles you have covered that day, and also with the feeling of romantically settling down now in a new place.

Does it matter that as the tour begins our cricketer finds a train crowded as it leaves London Road Station behind, with its mile's view of slate roofs on every hand? Not a bit of it. The other people in the compartment are plainly the veriest birds of passage; prosaic shortness of distance is to be their portion. They must depart at Stockport, or at the most at Crewe. When Market Street and Deansgate are at their crisis of unloveliness and congestion, our happy cricketer is moving through green fields; he is getting intimate glimpses into country life, as from the spacious rolling view outside the carriage window his eye detaches a thatched cottage with a postman knocking at the door, or a village street lazy in noon warmth – it is underneath him now, for the train rattles thunderously over a bridge. And now it is gone!

At Wellington, or in some such place deep in the garden of our land, the journey is broken; there is a change here. The Manchester train goes out, leaving you exquisitely aware that you are now quite out of touch with Manchester. Your connection arrives – a train that obviously has never been in Manchester. The people on it have just as obviously never been in Manchester. Here, unmistakably, you are in a fresh hemisphere, entering on the journey's last lap through a drowsy landscape. And how peaceful the closing hour of a day's railway travel is! The mild agitations of the morning – felt even by a happy cricketer have spent themselves. The senses are tired at last of responding to new scenes, new sounds, new odours. Through too much unfolding of strange life about him our pilgrim feels an agreeable tedium; he drops into a reverie ... After Oxford, Cambridge, and then Leicester – always lots of fun at Leicester. Must look out for Astill's swinger, though. Yorkshire after that; suppose they'll give us the usual hot stuff. Where do we play Kent this year? Good Lord, at

Gravesend! Why not on the Angel Ground at Tonbridge – glorious place! Wonder if my off-drive will be better this year. Must get my foot to it more. That's a nice piece of wood Smith picked for me; must get it going tomorrow at Oxford. Might easily pick up runs for nothing at Oxford; always a few green bowlers there this time of the year. A good start's everything . . .

On the carriage seat he notices a newspaper, and there is a paragraph in it giving the County XI for its first match. He sees his name and is thrilled. After the winter's obscurity he is to become an item in the public news once more. In a day or two from now men in Newcastle and Woking, men he has never seen or heard of, telegraphists, sub editors, and compositors by livelihood, will be bandying his name about. 'Blank drove Benskin and completed his fifty in sixty-five minutes.' This will be read on the Manchester Exchange, in the Reform Club even, in Back George Street among the grey cloths, in Gorton, and in Westhoughton.

Will he run into form quickly? But he has no use for misgivings in this hour of May content. He is master of his fate, captain of his break-back. He sees, in his splendid vision, a hundred moments that the summer holds for him – the yellow stumps standing upright as he reaches the crease at the fall of the first wicket, with the white line of the popping crease just broken in the middle where Smith took his guard; the fieldsmen moving back to position as he gets his bat ready; the trees away in the distance behind the bowler. He sees the bowler coming towards him, face set; he feels his bat circling in the air, feels the ecstasy that comes with a hit clean in the blade's middle; he sees a fieldsman on the off-side boundary picking up the ball after it has been thrown back into the field from the crowd. He sees Lord's again, basks in the sense of walking to it on a June morning down the St John's Wood Road; he sees himself 'going on at the Nursery End', the while the score-board announces 'Bowler 7' and the pavilion bloods look at their cards and pronounce his name. He sees all the lovely cricket fields in England beckoning to him; he sees the sun mellowing on an afternoon somewhere in brown Sussex as cool drink is brought and bowlers slake their thirsts, while away on the field's edge a man in white lies prone on the grass even as he, our happy cricketer, stands erect at the wicket, 86 not out. And, best vision of all, he sees himself 'not out' even to the close of play, privileged to remove his pads, to change from his warm flannels, to leave the ground, to go here, there, and everywhere that evening, to go to bed, to get up in the morning; privileged to pass through all these spaces between one day's play and another and to remain not out all the time! Moments of vision indeed. Tomorrow and tomorrow – days in the sun, luscious grass to walk on, wind running over the body. Happy man, this is the time of the year for you; August will never seem so far away again.

The train's whistle blows; pace slackens. Here you are, and the others, cricketers all, with the season well and beautifully launched. No runs yet, maybe, and no wickets down; but a paradisal day already lived through.

The Cricketer as an Artist

We are supposed to be well on the way towards decadence
in an art as soon as we allow the parts to fascinate us rather
more than the whole – when, for instance, a Debussy so
falls in love with the attractiveness of his whole-tone scale
harmonies that he neglects the main job of music, which
is the expression of some sort of emotion. But decadent
or no, it is only human to find great joy in a new technical
dodge for its own sake. A man may decide to buy a cycle,
meaning really to save money in railway fares from and
to the city; none the less, the day the machine arrives he
will take the thing out and ride it to nowhere in particular,
simply exulting in a new toy. Probably he will also take it
to pieces and lose a few important screws and things – out
of what is at the bottom the artist's preoccupation with the
way of doing things simply for the fascination of that way.

This love of technique for technique's sake is a charac-
teristic in English cricket today – perhaps more than it has

ever been before. The parts of cricket – bowling, batting, and fielding – are now reaching an almost over-developed stage. In the beginning, we can imagine, 22 men met on a field, took sides, and had no other interest in cricket than to win the match. No matter how 'old Lumpy' bowled 'Nutty' out – grub or full toss – the great point was that he was out. And the lucky snick past slip looked just as well on the score sheet as the neatest of cuts. In its earliest period, the parts of cricket were too crudely organised to invite specialism and all those distractions which specialism can easily engender to take a cricketer's attention from the job in hand – that of beating the other men. Played on a village green, rudely if lovingly, one could say of cricket, borrowing from Kipling, that 'the game was more than the player of the game.' Nothing but the lust for conquest and contest here – no wiredrawn appreciation of the fine shades; simply the wigs on the green and our team against the world.

There is a different viewpoint from this among cricketers now, and, indeed, among watchers of cricket. Who cares about the tussle for championship points if a Ranji be glancing to leg? Even the man who wants Surrey to get beaten cannot find it in his heart to complain if Hobbs scores a hundred. And what modern bowler that has felt the joy which comes of breaking a ball from the off with a leg-break action can resist the temptation of bowling his googly in season and out – aye, even if he suspects that a good straight length ball would get his man out quicker?

A summer or two ago the writer was coaching little boys at a public school. They chafed at having to pass through a course of conventional bowling. 'We'd rather get wickets with breaks and swerves than the straight stuff that the old 'uns used to bowl' – that was their view of the matter at the bottom. And only the other day, a great batsman in one of our counties, when he was bowled trying to hook an off ball, explained his failure in these words: 'Well, you simply can't go on hitting off-balls past mid-off. Any fool is able to do that. One gets tired of doing things in the easiest way.' The divine discontent of the artist, this, surely. Who that has a soul at all, be he bricklayer or maker of sonnets, is happy just moving along the lines of least resistance? Had Ranjitsinhji been content with fat scores made in the fashionable way, he could easily have gone on hitting balls from the middle stump straight to long-on. But he was ever an artist, 'tired of doing things in the easiest way', ever seeking to widen the scope of his craft, experimenting, creating obstacles for the sheer fun of overcoming them.

Was ever cricket so well off in the so-called classical days for artists, especially artist-bowlers, as the game has been these last few years, since the advent of B. J. T. Bosanquet and his disciples? Surely a man had to have an axe of partisanship to grind before he could rave for aesthetic reasons about the bowling of the Attewell school. A good length outside the off stump all day – why, one of those new-fangled bowling machines would have been as interesting to watch. It was all right, of course, if you were watching the game for no other reason than to shout Nottinghamshire home, for undoubtedly Attewell did get his bags of wickets. But the man who goes to cricket solely to witness a contest is mistaking his game. Football can work off more combative energy in ten minutes than cricket in a summer.

The summer game has, of course, its tight finishes – moments in which it is the team and not the individual that matters, moments in which one will cheer a full toss that gets a wicket and groan at the bowler whose fine off-break gets clouted for six. But these seasons of crisis come rarely in cricket. Normally the game is a spectacle as much as a contest. And because of that we must have our artist cricketers – men who can get us interested in themselves, who can get interested in themselves, even though no finish of the game is in sight, and all is moving to the drawn match which bores the uninitiated onlooker. With Attewell bowling like an automaton and Scotton always taking the line of least resistance, the game needed to be won and lost. There was little, surely, in these cricketers but match-winning qualities. And, significantly enough, with the coming in recent summers of the great individualists like Fry, Ranji, Trumper, Bosanquet, the ancient lament about incompleted games has been heard less and less.* Nobody worries about the draw – the uncompleted match which satisfies no lust for conquest – if an artist-batsman happens to be on view. Not long ago the most attractive

---

* Written in 1920.

side in the country was Sussex, with, of course, Ranji in the eleven. Yet they drew all, or nearly all, their matches.

Our grandfathers had, of course, their artist-batsmen in no small numbers, and perhaps it is in bowling that modern cricket is infinitely more interesting* than cricket of yesterday to the onlooker who does not happen to be a partisan, but watches simply out of a love of the fine shades. Certain, anyhow, that our grandfathers never knew the googly. When county groundsmen a few years ago started to make their pitches as perfect for batsmen as they knew how – mainly with an eye to a three days' gate – they probably broke the hearts of scores of average bowlers, who found that length and spin were not much use on those 'shirt-front wickets'. But the artist-bowler found only another occasion for joy in this new obstacle, and set himself to get over it. Then the googly came, the whole point of which is to deceive the batsman before the ball has pitched. What matter the state of the ground if you can beat your man in the air? And the perfect modern wicket saw also the development of the swerve – another device calculated to enable a bowler to snap his finger at the groundsman and his marl.

Thus did bowling take on finer and finer points. Today people actually go to a match to watch Parkin bowl – it is not only the batsman that is in the picture now! Mind you,

---

* 'Interesting,' I say – from the spectators' point of view; I do not mean that bowling now is better technically.

they go not merely to watch Parkin bowl somebody out. Folk doubtless went to look at Alfred Shaw get wickets. It was the wickets going down that they liked; not bowling for its own sake. A few summers ago scores of cricketers flocked to Lord's keen on Parkin's bowling and found it interesting whether or no he was getting wickets.

Specialism always makes the parts more and more interesting, and we have arrived at the time when cricket is in the hands of specialists. There is even a danger that the whole will suffer. You can get so much in love with the art of spinning the ball 'the wrong way' that you begin to forget that without a good length a bowler is no match-winner. And as a long-hop is not even pretty to watch, you might even cease to be worth looking at. It is well, then, that in cricket, too, nature in the long run distributes equally her Platonists and her Aristoteleans – the men who walk by faith and the men who walk by reason. We have yet such sturdy upholders of first principles as William Quaife and J. W. Hearne. But even Hearne bowls googlies. There is no getting away from it – it is the heyday of the cricketer artist, the man who simply will not do the job in the old fashioned and easiest way.

Cricket Fields and Cricketers

There is surely some interaction between a cricket team and the ground it mainly lives on – does not the play of the side assume tone and colour from the scene? Yorkshire cricket has the aspect of Bramall Lane and Leeds – dour, and telling of stern competitive life with smoke and real industry about. Can you imagine the shrewd Lancashire game quite at home under a June sky at the Saffrons? Does not there come through the cricket of Sussex the brown and sunny flavour of Eastbourne and Hove when the time of day is noon and the earth seems humming with heat? The plain homeliness of the Midlands is expressed by Leicestershire cricket: it has no airs and graces, no excessive refinements. See an innings by Cole, of Leicestershire, and you ought not to be long guessing from the smack of rotund nature about it that he has passed the main portion of his days in the sun on a field with rustic benches running intimately round. No, it is not mere fancy to say: 'Show me a cricket team in action and I'll tell you where is its native heath.'

Take Lord's, for example. The country spirit, the circumscribed life denoted by country, is not for Lord's. For your good cricketer the ends of the earth have come to a resting-point at Lord's, and wherever he may be at the fall of a summer's day his face should turn religiously towards Lord's. Lord's is the Cosmopolis of cricket. And which county do you find playing the bulk of its games at Lord's? Why, naturally enough, the team that, less than them all, gives us the definite county flavour. Middlesex has ever been as cosmopolitan as Lord's itself – a side gathered from the earth's corners, West Indians, Australians, even Yorkshiremen! A man from Huddersfield sat in the crowd at Lord's a season or two ago, and as he watched Middlesex beating his own county he was stirred to a protective derision – a derision which he cultivated as balm for the wound that defeat at cricket must always bring to Yorkshiremen. 'Middlesex? he asked of the throng around him. 'Wheer's Middlesex? Is it in Lundon?'

His barb was well directed; London obliterates the county boundaries, and neither at Lord's nor at the Oval do you feel the clannishness that stings you in the atmosphere of Old Trafford or Bramall Lane. To be eloquent of authentic county demands a certain narrowness, a contentment with those things of the earth, and that part of the earth, which providence has placed immediately at one's doorstep. County means nature and at Lord's cultivation borne on the winds of the world has rather expelled nature. Watch Hearne move fastidiously towards a century; watch Bruce or Crutchley batting, and you are looking on cricket played in the drawing-room of civilised men and woman. And at those times when Bosanquet bowled at Lord's there came into the game the touch of exquisite decadence that marks a true Cosmopolis. Frankly, I have never yet been able to fix Hendren into my notion of Lord's; he is quite indecently provincial in his relish of a thumping boundary.

There is, of course, in the life of a cultivated cricketer little that is sweeter than a summer morning at Lord's, a morning when the sky is a blue awning blown out with soft wind, and the trees at the Nursery End make a delicate motion. 'The Nursery End at Lord's!' The phrase sets memory astir, for have we not read in days of old in those evening papers our boyish eyes scanned that 'Richardson went on at the Nursery End,' that 'Ranjitsinhji glanced Noble to the rails at the Nursery End'? Because Max Beerbohm has never written an essay called 'Going to Lord's on a July Morning' we have proof he has never in his life walked down the St John's Wood Road with a day of cricket in sunny weather before him.

But perhaps it is not given to the man who lives only round the corner from Lord's and can visit it every day to feel its appeal as keenly as the man from the North, who not more than three or four times a year walks down the St John's Wood Road. Let the morning be quiet and mellow and there seems in the air about the St John's Wood Road, at least to one not too familiar with the place, a sense of the dead old days, causing a melancholy which no doubt one ought to be ashamed of. The mind is made by this something in the St John's Wood air to play with fancies of Victorian greatness hanging about the spot; of a gleaming hansom cab at the entrance and a black-bearded man, looking mountainous in everyday clothes, getting out while folk standing round murmur 'WG!'; of simple-faced men in wide, uncreased trousers proceeding along the pavement – the names of them, likely enough, Lockwood, Lohmann, Richardson – all keen to 'get at the old 'un.'

No lover of cricket as he wanders about Lord's can very well keep the thought of Grace from his mind, for though Grace was a Gloucestershire man surely he larded the green earth at Lord's till the very spirit of him may be said to have gone into the grass. You see, just as Lord's is too large in spirit to stand for any one county or for any one space of time in cricket's history, so did the amplitude of Grace transcend Gloucestershire and his little day. At Lord's, with a June morning spending its warmth, one feels a kind of resentment that there should ever have been a bourne put by nature on WG's capacity to endure and play the game till he was utterly tired of it. Is not Lord's here for him now just as ever it was, and a summer day here also, one so fresh that it casts clean out of the understanding the thought of years that pass away? Why could it ever happen to a cricketer that a June morning comes on which the sun begins in the old comfortable way to climb the sky, and

Lord's stands in the light, full of summer-time animation, and he no longer there to know of it?

II

Leave Lord's one day and tomorrow discover Bramall Lane and you enter another world. Frankly, the cricket field at Sheffield is a blasted heath, but, as Shakespeare knew, it is on blasted heaths that matters of grim moment come to pass. A Lancashire and Yorkshire match is not to be thought of at Lord's; here at Sheffield the scene tells a plain tale of the stiff energy of North Country life, and it provides the right setting for a battle between ancient hosts where the informing spirit is of a dour and combative blood feud. Squat chimneys outside the ground loom black, and even on a Bank Holiday the air contains a hint of furnaces and steel smelters. And to the man who likes his cricket moving dramatically on the right stage the Bramall Lane crowd is a work of art. It is a multitude which seemingly throws out a white heat and causes the game to boil over prodigiously.

Who at Sheffield on Whit Monday in 1922 will ever forget the great crowd that watched Yorkshire struggling for a first innings' advantage over Lancashire the day long? It was a crowd unashamedly partisan. No room had the red-hot ranks for the equanimity that can look on an issue and say: 'May the best side win.' This vast gathering lived the violent afternoon through to one thought, to one thought alone: 'Down with Lancashire. Trample the Red Rose in the dust.' Here we had a partisan temper which sought to persuade events in Yorkshire's way. There was surely not a man on Bramall Lane's desolate plain that afternoon who would not have held up his hands to the sky till pain scourged him had he believed that such a martyrdom would keep the hurly-burly favourable to his county. Not magnanimous, you might well say; still, there is an aspect to partisanship as brittle as this which is not entirely to be despised. If the Sheffield crowd cannot attend to the amenities at the sight of an advance by the ancient foe, if it is driven in the hour of Yorkshire's adversity to a fury and apprehension that have no use for a magnanimous admiration of the skill of the conquerors, we may wish ourselves far away from such a crowd, and thank our stars cricket does not breed many like it, but we certainly cannot deny that here is 'character', here is rich red blood and abundant spirit.

I have heard folk from the South say of cricket at Sheffield that it simply is *not* cricket. Their preference has been for the game as it is played with trees and country graciousness around. But why put a limit to cricket's appeal; why deny her infinite variety? Lancashire and Yorkshire at Bramall Lane is not less cricket than any match in an old meadow at Little Slocombe on the laziest day in June. Cricket, indeed, has many facets; it can satisfy most of the human animal's interests and emotions, and, as we have seen, it is sensitive to most of our moods and our habitations. It can stir one, at Sheffield, into a very man of war;

it can soothe one, at Tonbridge, to the sweetest peace. In turn, it can sound a clarion note that sets the combative spirits in the blood running agog like hey-go-mad, as Tristram Shandy would say; and in turn it can capture the summer's own music.

Lord's in Wet Weather

JUNE 1920

For want of something better to do during these last two incredibly wet days at Lord's, I have been trying to understand why that place so forcibly recalls Charles Dickens' *Bleak House*. It is not merely that the rain has turned the place into another Chesney Wold; that the view from the pavilion window as I write is alternately a lead-coloured view and a view in Indian ink; that the heavy drops fall, drip, drip, drip, upon the pavilion terrace, which might be named the Ghosts' Walk, since the shades of so great cricketers of other days make it murmurous. No, not simply these external and quite accidental effects are responsible for the mind's jumping back to Dickens' novel. Lord's is capable of reminding you of Sir Leicester Dedlock and Chesney Wold in fine weather as well as in wet, so inflexibly aristocratic is the place, so proud of the ceremonies, so insistent on blue blood.

Unless one happens to be definitely of Lord's, and a member of the mighty MCC, one is outside the pale here. You are inexorably kept at a distance. The place is a mass of signboards, teaching you your manners and position in life. Like Sir Leicester Dedlock all over, Lord's is as old as the hills, and, so it would appear, infinitely more respectable. The place, indeed, carries a general air of believing that the world might get on without hills, but would be done up without the MCC. Since Nature made the grass which grows there, Lord's would, no doubt, admit with Sir Leicester that, on the whole, Nature is a good idea, but an idea just a little low when not enclosed with a fence. There is even to this day at Lord's a kind of fence which separates amateurs from professionals. A man from the unfashionable North, carrying with him a suggestion of real industry, feels that Lord's is all the time eyeing him curiously from a safe point of vantage, and mentally putting him down as a possible Wat Tyler, or, at the most generous estimate, an Ironfounder.

It is hard to imagine there is any place in the world where class distinctions are so firmly stressed as at Lord's. During a University match this is more apparent than ever. That is why possibly no painter in the school of Frith has given us a canvas depicting Lord's on a fine summer's day during the occasion of a 'Varsity match. The picture would certainly give scope for something of the multitudinous panorama in Frith's too much abused *Derby Day*, but it would be bound to miss the broad universal appeal of the racing picture. Human nature on a large scale could hardly be got into a view of Lord's – only one aspect of it, well bred and exclusive. A race meeting, on the other hand, annihilates class distinctions.

What would happen to a man in corduroys (supposing for the sake of argument such a phenomenon possible) – what would happen to him if he smote a Viscount on the back in the throes of some enthusiasm for a leg hit?

Yet at a race meeting such events have been known to happen, to nobody's consternation. One touch of Epsom with the favourite in fourth at 6 to 4 on makes the whole world kin. Still, these fine aristocratic ways at Lord's do not really annoy. Possibly an American writer would find them objectionable. That is because he would not regard them, as they are regarded by the average outsider, who pays his couple of shillings at Lord's, as just a pretty decoration on the main structure of affairs.

Lord's will not allow the man in the street to come right into the swim, but they can't keep him right out. I saw a few working men this morning at the ground gates waiting for the rain to stop. They variously wore light and dark blue colours. How each man decided whether Oxford or Cambridge should be the vent for the expression of his inveterate partisanship I could not say. His interest in both elevens might have been merely academic. But it was not so – these same working men were rather hot with argument about the respective qualities of Bettington, Marriott, Hedges and Partridge.

Obviously the game is more than the player of the game, in Kipling's words, even at Lord's, and common human nature will creep in. The terrible rain today could not quite keep it out.

Spooner at Old Trafford

AUGUST 1920

The innings of Spooner in the Lancashire and Yorkshire
match on August Bank Holiday will not quickly be forgotten. It was his return to the crowd that loves him after
a long absence, and the magic of his art made everybody
on the packed ground that day into a jubilant, shouting
schoolboy. Such batsmanship had not been seen at Old
Trafford since the Augustan days before the war. He went
in first with Heap. Waddington gave him some trouble
before he found the pace of the drying turf. We hung on
to his every movement. If he should fail! Ah, be careful,
Reggie, with that swinging off ball! For a while we sit in
purgatory. And then the master drives Waddington glo-
riously to the on boundary, and we are in paradise. The
master is now in tune with himself. Two off drives to
the rails from successive balls off Rhodes – and then the
sheerest poetry of cricket. 'Wrist-work! Wrist work!' is the

usual comment on Spooner's cricket. And it really does seem that he makes his forcing strokes even as an artistic housemaid uses a feather duster. But no man could urge a ball in front of the wicket, with Spooner's strength, by wrist-work alone. There must be some latent body energy in the hit; the muscular mechanism works so smoothly that it deceives us. A fountain is a thing of fairy spray to the eye, but underground some violent pressure goes on. It may be in such wise with Spooner batsmanship.

The great man in cricket, as in all other arts, is an individualist, whose game is as much a part of him as his physiognomy (to echo Fenélon), his figure, his throbbing pulse – in short, as any part of his being which is subjected to the action of the will. In and through the art of batsmanship we have come know Spooner as intimately as if he had written 'Sonnets to a Dark Lady'. Walk at random on a cricket field and see Spooner make his off-drive. You have no need to be informed that Spooner is batting. The stroke can be 'attributed' with as much certainty as any canvas by Paul Véronèse. That graceful forward poise, the supple play of the wrists! Ranji himself was not more graceful than Spooner. There was, in fact, a disturbing melodramatic element in Ranji now and then. When he glanced to leg that straight ball dead on the middle stump, you gasped amazedly. And emotion is never pricked as sharply as that by sheer grace. In Spooner's batting, at his best, we see the unities observed (as the gentleman in Dickens would say): the harmony, the eternal fitness of the game, suffers no shock. For Spooner just puts bloom on the orthodox. His cricket has a classical purity in these days. But if his decorative formality makes him a Pre-Raphaelite, so to say, he is a Pre-Raphaelite of the Millais order – the Millais who painted *Autumn Leaves*. There is warm colour in his play as well as the clear natural outlines.

The Defeat at Eastbourne

August 1921

From the pains which entered the body of English cricket at
Trent Bridge in May the good Lord has at long last delivered
us. This afternoon, on the sunny Saffrons cricket field, the
Australians' colours have been hauled down; the mighty
men that authentic England elevens have found uncon-
querable in ten successive Test matches have been beaten,
beaten by a fictitious England eleven under the leadership
of our greatest cricket captain, and, moreover, beaten by a
side that was routed in a first innings for 43 paltry runs.
Who on Saturday could have got the faintest glimpse of
such an end to the match, even in the wildest flight of
fancy? All cricketers know well the infinite changefulness
of the great game, but to overthrow the might of Australia
from no better base than a first innings total of 43 – why,
the miraculous is here, black magic, the very imps of mischief. There were the most thrilling fluctuations in the

day's play; now the game was safe in Armstrong's keeping, now it slipped from his grasp, now, by a desperate motion of the will, Armstrong clutched it again, and then, as, indeed, it looked his for good, out it slipped and MacLaren and his men stuck greedily to it.

At the morning's outset Bardsley and Carter played the bowling comfortably. Gibson was seemingly harmless, and from his first three overs 16 runs came. Would other English captains have taken Gibson off after so bad a beginning? MacLaren did not – and, true, he had no great amount of bowling at hand to embarrass him. But MacLaren has had faith in Gibson throughout the summer, and today the young University cricketer was to justify, as Barnes and Dean once justified, the insight of the master. With Australia's score 52 Gibson clean bowled Bardsley by a glorious ball that pitched on the off stump and hit the leg. Falcon then bowled a fast short one to Carter, who cut it powerfully. In the Test matches such a stroke from an Australian invariably went to the boundary. Today young Claude Ashton was in the slips; he saw the ball as a swallow sees a fly, darted forward, and caught it magnificently. The outlook for Australia was darkening, but soon the confidence of Macartney's and Andrew's cricket made slight sunshine for Armstrong. And with the total 73, Falcon bowled Macartney, who produced a weird stroke with a cross bat. Pellew and Andrews added just 30 for the fifth Australian wicket, which fell when Hubert Ashton brilliantly caught Pellew at slip. So to lunch with no man's appetite keen for food. Australia needed now 87, with five wickets in hand.

Half-an-hour's play after the interval, and surely the victory was Armstrong's entirely. Andrews and Ryder scored 34 runs in this short space, and, worst of all for MacLaren's prospects, they hit Falcon's bowling all over the field. The score was 140 for five when MacLaren asked Faulkner to bowl in place of Falcon. The move was made at the last moment, still at the right moment. Gibson broke the Ryder-Andrews partnership at last, but it was Faulkner, in his third over, that placed the Australians completely against the wall by upsetting Andrews' off stump with an excellent ball which whipped across the wicket from leg. Andrews was eighth out at 158, with but 43 wanted now for his side's victory. He was in such fine form that had he endured another fifteen minutes, especially against Falcon, he would most certainly have won the match.

Armstrong was the last hope of his team. Was it just MacLaren's good luck, or was it MacLaren's superb knowledge of cricketers that ordained that Faulkner should be bowling when Armstrong came to the wicket? For Armstrong never has been able to cope with Faulkner. Today he was sorely troubled by the South African's 'googly'. He used all his cunning to avoid Faulkner, but he had to face the music at last. And Faulkner pitched him a ball whizzing with spin on the leg stump. Armstrong lost it hopelessly, and the ball would have hit the off wicket but for Armstrong's obstructing pad. Faulkner shook the skies with a triumphant "How's that?' and Armstrong had to go. Macdonald and Mailey added nine more or less nondescript runs for the last wicket, which fell to Gibson, and rightly so. He bowled beautifully without a rest throughout the Australian innings. He has a ball which is a good imitation of Barnes's famous ball, the one that pitches on the leg stump and swings away to the off. He stuck to his task gallantly, and never allowed the crisis to upset him. In the very throes of the crisis Faulkner exploited his finger spin audaciously.

At the finish, Armstrong, in a speech to the jubilant crowd, said his men had been beaten by the better side. It is certain that England in the Test matches could not show the superb fielding, the skilful and intelligent bowling of this side of MacLaren's. The fielding indeed was up to Australian standards. The crowd roared for MacLaren at the close, but MacLaren was rather overcome with emotion, and through a deputy announced this was his farewell to cricket. A beautiful farewell it has been, putting the crown on his greatness. Not in his hey-day did he give us finer captaincy than he has given us in this match. It was plain this afternoon that his very presence in the field gave his men hope and courage.

Let nobody get the impression that the Australians flung this game away through a casual attitude towards it. Possibly there was just half-an-hour of negligent batsmanship when the Australians went in against a total of 43. But from the fall of Collins' wicket on Saturday, Armstrong had his men strung taut enough. And this afternoon Armstrong's face as he witnessed the breaking of Andrews' wicket – which was a certain omen of the end – had a profoundly sombre expression. Gone the old affability! Where were his quips and oddities now?

The main causes of the Australian defeat, as it seemed to the writer, were fielding just as brilliant as the Australians' own, captaincy that put every fieldsman in the proper place, and clever spin bowling. As one watched the Ashtons, fleet of foot, sure of grasp, one thought of the heavy, plodding wanderings of England's Test match outfielders. And as one saw MacLaren move his men here and there by the most deliberate yet the gentlest waves of the hand – gestures telling of a perfectly composed mind – one thought of Douglas's volubility as he sought to obtain a tactful disposition of his men. There was, indeed, a tincture of bitterness in the sweet as one watched the afternoon proceed to its superb consummation.

The bowling of Gibson and Faulkner in the Australian second innings was just of that kind Australian batsmen have never really mastered. Barnes could put even Trumper at his mercy by the ball that broke away from the bat after pitching somewhere near the leg and middle stumps. Both Gibson and Faulkner exploited this dangerous ball this afternoon and by excellent fortune they both managed also a capital length. The Australians did not again find Falcon troublesome, though he bowled not a bit below his Saturday's form. Fast and fast-medium bowling, right arm, that comes more or less straight through, is the stuff Australian batsmen thrive on. They waxed fat on Howell, Douglas, Jupp and Parkin (when he bowled fast). To these bowlers they could play forward confidently. Even the slow-medium off-break rarely troubles an Australian batsman. He commonly is good at leg-side play and can get back to the wicket and force the ball away in the spin's direction. The ball that pitches on the wicket and breaks away he has never mastered. One might add, what batsmen have? This delivery demands the most discreet use of the 'two-eyed stance', of back play supported judiciously by the pads. And though the Australians can play back cleverly enough on slow wickets, back play is not so much in the blood of them that they can play back easily on a fast wicket.

The finger spin used by Faulkner and Gibson today is to be tackled safely only by the perfect back-play technique employed, say, by Taylor, the South African, against Barnes, a year or two ago. Armstrong's struggles with Faulkner were pathetic; he merely lunged at the ball when it was in the air, lost it as it spun, then desperately changed his stance at the last minute. Bardsley played forward beautifully to the ball that bowled him, and had it come through straight he would have hit it. The ball spun several inches on pitching, and Bardsley had no pads there as a second line of defence. A lot of abuse has been hurled at the 'two-eyed stance', and rightly, since it has too often been exploited against fast bowling. But, as this afternoon's Australian batsmanship has shown, there is not much hope against a ball spinning away at a good length if one uses the old-time lunge forward.

But the impressions of this glorious match likely to last longest are of Maclaren. One will see him, white-haired and beautifully calm, standing in the slips beckoning a man to a more judicious place in the field. One will see him plucking at his trousers' knees in the old way, hitching them up before he slightly bends into the classic slip position. One will see him moving across the pitch at the over's end, taking now and then one of his bowlers by the arm and giving him a word of encouragement and advice. And if these impressions should fade in a while, surely one will never forget his walk to the pavilion at the game's end, the crowd pressing round him and cheering – MacLaren with his sweater over his shoulders, his face almost lost in the folds of it, looking down on the grass as he moves for good from the cricket field, seemingly but half aware of the praisegiving about him, seemingly thinking of other times.

Woolley: An Appreciation

You must see Woolley batting on one of Kent's cricket fields to enjoy thoroughly the charm of his delightful art. Of course Woolley can spread beauty about him wherever he goes, but at Bramall Lane – even at Old Trafford – one thinks of him as one thinks of a butterfly in a city street on a summer's day. The writer once saw Woolley the batsman set ideally, and never will he forget it. It was while an August afternoon turned to evening in Kent. The tumult and the shouting of the day were over, and now we all sat in quiet, just waiting for stumps to be drawn while Kent played out time in the calm light. Woolley made gentle movements with his bat. His body would fall a little forward as he flicked a ball to the off-side; there seemed no weight in him when he negligently trotted down the pitch.

And as the sun shone more and more aslant, the light seemed to put this batsmanship of Woolley's under a glass; we had cool and polished contours given to it, the hard outlines of reality were lost in soft shades. Woolley's batting is frequently called 'brilliant'; it is the wrong word for his art at any time. Brilliance hints at a self-conscious gesture, of some flaunting of ability. And nobody ever has seen the touch of the braggart, or even of the coxcomb, in Woolley. The condition whereby grace has its being is a perfect unawareness of the fact that it is graceful. In grace there is always a sense of modesty; the arrogance that masterfulness breeds does not go with grace, which is one of the gentler virtues.

This is not to hint that in Woolley's batsmanship there lurks a timid spirit. We all know that Woolley is one of the world's greatest match-winning batsmen. One wishes to establish nothing more than that a batsman so winsome as Woolley is not properly to be called 'brilliant'. The word's very mention fills the mind with lurid colour. In Woolley's batsmanship there is radiance, but never a light that is garish. Even when he drives in front of the wicket the softest splendour falls over the field. None of us of these times has seen a left-handed cricketer play a handsomer game than Woolley's. To describe his forward hits one is tempted to borrow Nyren's words about Silver Billy Beldham: 'One of the most beautiful sights that can be imagined, and which would have delighted an artist, was to see him make himself up to hit a ball.' Yet the phrase will not quite fit Woolley. 'Make himself up' is too strong a term: it denotes a sudden accumulation of energy to be seen by the eye – an act of violence. Woolley has not been known to look violent or to seem stung suddenly into effort. He does not, like, say, a K. L. Hutchings or a Hirst, use a bat as a rod of punishment and flog boundaries by force out of bowlers. Rather a bat is a wand in Woolley's hand: he makes enchanting passes with it.

Woolley causes batting to appear the easiest pastime in the world. A fast bowler, pounding heavily to the crease, bowling at Woolley with the loud grunts of unloosened energy, working himself to death in the hot sun in quest of Woolley's wicket – and Woolley, all restful curves, making his easy opposition! What a contrast, and what a nice irony in it! Woolley hardly ever seems to hit a ball: of him you can really say that his strokes are *strokes*. Surely he just caresses the ball with a bat of velvet surface. One day an assertion of some primitive nature left somewhere in Woolley will impel him to smite once with all his might, and then the ball will pass far beyond the fields of Kent. For the force even of his caresses is strong enough; the secret of his motive power is timing.

He gives us the lyrical in batsmanship, just as Trumper gave us the dramatic. When Trumper batted, he met the onslaught of the bowler with an onslaught of his own as vehement. There was a conflict of will and skill when Trumper and a fast bowler were face to face, and so we had the dramatic, which thrives on conflict. As we have seen, Woolley does not look to be in stern opposition against a furious attack; he meets it effortlessly. And because drama cannot be felt unless we are made to understand that conflict hot and bitter is present, we get no drama from Woolley. He just goes his own sweet ways. While other batsmen turn the wicket into a battleground, the bowlers into an enemy to be plundered for runs, Woolley makes a soothing music that lures everybody after him, bowlers and all, as he moves along his happy track. He does not bat for his runs; he bats a serene course to them. So easeful and natural does a long innings strike you, when Woolley passes through one, that you well might think of some act blessedly predestinate.

And it is likewise when Woolley fails; you are not outraged, you are not made to think that here ambition and skill have been frustrated. In Woolley's failures there is no jar that hurts you – they are as becoming as his conquests. Grace, one has already said, is modest, and has the air of fragility always. Rude human nature, such as Hirst showed us in his pulls to the on boundary, never peeps out of Woolley. His batsmanship has been through a purifying fire; refinement one day came to Woolley

'And whipped the offending Adam out of him . . .'

The point for technical men about Woolley's batting is important; he achieves his style mainly by back play – and have we not been told time after time by the dons of the game that if a batsman would own a beautiful style he must cultivate the forward method? In Woolley you find working to perfection the modern principle: 'Play back if you cannot drive.' How many times in a long innings does Woolley exploit the forward lunge, made from a rigid back foot? The writer does not recollect having seen Woolley use this stroke. Woolley has a great height and consequently a wide swing for all his hits – so wide that in the curve of one full swing are included the three points at which a half-volley, a good-length ball, and a rather short one may be struck. Woolley, then, does not need to move his feet extensively; he has only to 'time' accurately his swing down as the three different lengths come to him – which three lengths, of course, are the common lengths of bowling. Granted the slightest readjustment of the feet, Woolley's swing will serve in itself for a strong hit from any of these lengths.

His height, then, makes grace hard to miss by one so naturally willowy (let us overlook the faint suggestion of gawkiness in him); the small batsman – a Bobby Abel – is compelled to nip backwards and forwards on his feet, as the varying lengths come along, and though his animation is often thrilling, it must of necessity let the graceful go hang. Woolley has all the strokes; his leg glances, with his tall body half turning and drooping ever so slightly over to the on-side, are not magical like Ranji's were, but they are, in a quieter way, as precious. But discussion of Woolley in terms of technique is abominable. Who would talk of the *Mona Lisa* in the painter's jargon? And speaking of the *Mona Lisa*, is there not always about Woolley's dark face an inscrutable hint of a smile held back, like that we get from the lady sitting among the rocks?

Woolley's bowling was fashioned by the Tonbridge nursery, and Blythe served as the model. But the way of Nature after she has turned out a masterpiece is to break the mould. She does not let her best things get common: a solitary Blythe was enough for her; she made him once and for all. Woolley as a bowler is excellent on doubtful wickets, but he is plainly a bowler who is happier with a bat in his hands. He first trod a county cricket field at Old Trafford in Whit Week, 1906. And some of us that were in the crowd thought we had seen the beginning and the end of this tall, pale boy's experience in big cricket. It was the match in which J. T. Tyldesley cut and drove the Kent bowling for 295 not out. On the first day Woolley missed two catches; his bowling analysis when 'JTT' had finished with it was 1 wicket for 103; and in Kent's first innings Cuttell bowled him first ball. On the last day, though, he hit 64, and discerning men on the ground said the innings heralded a new glory coming into Kent cricket.

Woolley is the most stylish professional batsman in the country; his style carries the Tonbridge stamp. Kent have rarely, in fact, had an uncultivated professional batsman. They consider in Kent that a boy needs to be taught to use his blade in the way that a boy with music in him is taught in other places to use a violin; batsmanship at Tonbridge, in short, is regarded as an art and a science and therefore a matter for culture.

Cricket at Dover

KENT V LANCASHIRE, 1, 2 AND 3 JULY 1926

Wednesday

The distance from Lord's to the Dover cricket field is farther than the crow flies or even than the train travels. Here
we find a different habitation than cosmopolitan Lord's:
here is Kent and real England. The Dover field is tucked
away in hills along which Lear must have wandered on
his way to the cliffs. There are green lawns and terraces
rising high behind the little pavilion, and you can sit here
and look down on the play and see the cricketers all tiny
and compact. In such a green and pleasant place as this,
with June sunlight everywhere, slow cricket by Lancashire
has not seemed quite so wearisome as usually it does. The
absence of animated play has gone well in tune with the
day's midsummer ease and generous warmth. We have
been free to watch the game idly and give ourselves up with

lazy delight to the June charm and flavours of a field all gay with tents and waving colours; and we have been free to observe the delicious changes in the passing hour – the full light of noon, the soft, silent fall to mellow.

The gentle tap-tap-tapping of the Lancashire bats has made the quiet music proper to this gracious Kentish place and occasion. On a perfect wicket Lancashire made a poor prelude to the innings. Hallows was twenty-five minutes getting his first run, and with the total 24 he sent a puny stroke to short leg and was caught at leisure. Ernest Tyldesley and Makepeace then played the steady Kent attack with a like steadiness. At lunch, after ninety minutes' action, Lancashire's score was 60 for one, and on the whole Makepeace had revealed himself our quickest maker of runs.

Between lunch and tea, two hours and a quarter, Lancashire added 135 for the loss of the wickets of Makepeace and Tyldesley. These batsmen built a partnership worth 100 in 105 minutes. They showed us good cricket enough, but it was always kind to the bowling. Tyldesley was missed in the slips at 15, and got himself out by a half-hit to mid-on. I wish his batting were a little more masculine this year. Tyldesley and Makepeace persisted for the same period – two hours and 35 minutes. After Watson had let us see half a dozen strokes I chanced with myself a half-crown wager that he would make 50 at least. Watson's cricket, though slow, had always a more certain touch than anything he has done of late. One or two of his cover drives possessed a decisive strength I have not seen him use since last year he played an innings of a century at Lord's and delighted the heart of poor Sydney Pardon, who, alas! did not live to see his dreadful Australians considerably humbled yesterday on the cricket field he loved so dearly. Watson reached 50 in one hour and three-quarters, which apparently is the standard rate of movement nowadays in the making of a cricketer's innings. Watson seemed to give a chance to the slips at 28. Halliday struck too late at a fast medium length, after giving some hint of an ability to get his bat well over the ball. Lancashire's score arrived at 200 in ten minutes short of four hours – Poppy and Mandragora of cricket.

The Kent attack rarely fell for accuracy. Collins, Ashdown and Wright each exploit the fast to medium length which drops cannily just on the short side. Only batsmen with late, wristy strokes are able to get rapid runs against this style of attack, and, truth to say, Lancashire is not rich in wristy cricketers. Freeman's spin came from the ground with little venom, but his pitch and direction were reliable throughout all his labours. His flight has scarcely the clever variations of Mailey's bowling. To the lovely afternoon's close the Lancashire batting remained true to type.

Lancashire 307 for 8 (F. Watson 78, H. Makepeace 71, E. Tyldesley 69).

Thursday

We have had another lovely day and plenty of fascinating cricket. The Kent innings began at noon under a sky that was like a dome of glass all stained blue. On such a morning as this, a batsman is certain to see visions and dream dreams as he comes to the ground eager for the game. And Hardinge and Ashdown started to make runs with easy, confident strokes. In half an hour the Kent score reached 39, and the Lancashire men must quickly have resigned themselves to hours of sweaty toil in the warmth of a sun whose rays of light hit the hard earth like blows from a golden rod. But the chances of cricket hang on a hair's breadth. McDonald's first 41 balls were hit for 29 runs, and he did not seem to be in a conquering mood. Another six balls without a wicket would, I think, have ended with McDonald going out of action and taking a longish rest. It was at this period of incipient crisis for Lancashire and McDonald that Ashdown was guilty of a foolish mistake. McDonald had been trying to bump them — a certain proof that he was not feeling at his best. Ashdown tried to hit one of these bumpers to leg, and instead of standing up straight and to the side of the ball and exploiting the authentic hook stroke, he scooped with a blind bat, ducked his head, and sent a skier to the leg side, where Duckworth held a clever running catch.

This unlooked-for success obviously caused McDonald to lift up his heart. His pace became faster immediately, and yet again was he encouraged by thoughtless batsmanship.

Hardinge once or twice held out an indiscreet bat to quick lengths on the off side and was lucky not to touch them. The warnings taught him no lesson: again he put forth a highly experimental bat to one of McDonald's fast rising balls, and Duckworth caught him behind the wicket, crowing in glee like a cock as he did so. McDonald realised, in the style of a good opportunist, that he was in fortune's good books: he worked up a lot of his true speed, pitched a length on or near the off wicket. Seymour made a sheer reflex action and sent a slip-catch to Richard Tyldesley. Chapman also flicked a speculative bat, though this time the ball was much too close to the wicket to be left alone. Chapman was Duckworth's third victim in ten minutes.

The match in this brief space of time wheeled round dizzily in Lancashire's way. McDonald got the wickets of Ashdown, Seymour, Hardinge, and Chapman in nine balls for three runs. This merciless exposure of Kent's want of acquaintance with authentic fast bowling reduced the crowd to a silence which was broken – at least where I was sitting – only by the emphatic statement of an old gentleman to the effect that modem cricketers cannot cut, and, moreover, that Jack Mason and Burnup would have cracked this bowling of McDonald far and wide – a strong opinion indeed, announced with much ferocity of tone and addressed to nobody in particular.

The Kent batsmen, no doubt, played McDonald feebly. Several of them merely thrust out their bats to the line of the ball, using arm strength only, and not getting the body over and into a resolute stroke. Woolley threatened for twenty minutes to stem the onrush of McDonald. He drove him to the off boundary with rare power and beauty, and then sent a cut past point like the flash of valiant steel. I settled myself down to enjoy a dramatic sight – Woolley and McDonald as antagonists: Woolley standing erect at the wicket waiting with his curving bat as McDonald ran his sinuous run along the grass: Woolley flashing his lightning and McDonald hurling his thunderbolts. This spectacle of grandeur did not, as they say, materialise outside of the mind's eye: Watson suddenly and comprehensively bowled Woolley even before some of us were aware he had begun to take part in the Lancashire attack. The ball scattered Woolley's leg wicket out of the earth: it pitched between the off and middle stumps and went with the bowler's arm. The Australians would gladly pay Watson £100 for the sole rights to that excellent delivery.

The downfall of Woolley, fifth out at 74, knocked the decisive nail in the coffin of Kent's first innings. It is true that Hubble batted brightly for a while and also Freeman, but the lustre of their cricket was only like that of a sort of brass plate on the aforementioned coffin. The innings closed at three o'clock for a total which was an insult to the splendid turf. Duckworth was in reliable form: he made five catches and also accomplished a very easy case of stumping. His high-pitched shout of 'How's that' was constantly in the summer air: shall we call him chanticleer of wicket-keepers?

The other day Mr Warner wrote that English batting has improved vastly since Armstrong beat us in this country. As I watched McDonald get his wickets today I was convinced that Collins would win the Test matches almost as comfortably as Armstrong did if he commanded the McDonald and Gregory of 1921. English batting has not improved since then against really fast bowling – a melancholy truth which McDonald will demonstrate for us on any day that finds him in his strongest form.

Green rightly did not compel Kent to follow on: McDonald was tired and the wicket perfect. Makepeace and Tyldesley forced the runs excellently after Hallows had got out: 50 was reached in little more than half an hour. Makepeace scored 37 in 50 minutes – furious driving for him. Ernest Tyldesley was brilliant: not for many a long day has his cricket been so powerful, so handsome, so masterful as in this innings. He played Lancashire's proper game from the outset, drove in front of the wicket with a superb poise of body, and reached 50 in 70 minutes. No English innings in the Test at Lord's the other day, save perhaps Woolley's on Tuesday, could compare with this by Tyldesley in point of beautiful and versatile strokes. Moreover, the Kent attack was on the whole as good as the Australians', at any rate until Tyldesley hammered it off its length. This is the kind of batsmanship we need for the winning of Test matches within three days.

Tyldesley arrived at his century in two hours and five minutes without a shadow of a mistake. Iddon played strong cricket, too, and this time his forcing drives were proportionately blended with strokes of sound defence. He has still much to learn of the art of picking out the right ball for a safe hit, but he is going along nicely. In Lancashire's second innings Cornwallis did not field because of an injury to his leg. Cornwallis, by the way, is a true Kent captain – keen, chivalrous, and always in love with the game, Iddon and Tyldesley scored 122 for the fourth wicket in 90 minutes. We have seen a Lancashire eleven today in which we could take a pride indeed.

Lancashire 336 and 243 for 5 (E. Tyldesley 144 not out); Kent 154 (E. A. McDonald 7 for 81).

Friday

Green closed the Lancashire innings last night, and Kent had the whole of this cool and pleasant day for the making of 424 needed to bring them a famous victory. Five hours and ten minutes of play were to be gone through. A bad beginning happened to the innings; with only a dozen scored Ashdown tried a leg hit from Sibbles, and the ball seemed to swing in from outside his legs astonishingly, and it clean bowled his leg wicket. Seymour, who is not at all a defensive batsman but needs must play the old Kentish game of chivalry, hit ten runs off three balls from Sibbles, and attempted a stroke to the on from a short bumper sent by McDonald. He skied the ball high to leg, and Halliday, running from somewhere near mid-wicket on the on-side, made an admirable running catch, taking his prize as it dipped away from him in the wind. Even with this unfortunate prelude Kent's score reached 80 in an hour – cricket is always a game for Kent, rarely a penitential labour.

Woolley and Hardinge joined partnership at five minutes to twelve, and in ninety-five minutes they lifted the total from 41 to 181 – which brought us to lunch. The cricket was never in the least rash or demonstrative; indeed, Woolley batted half an hour for eleven. The runs came by play in which defence and offence were mingled with the most accurate judgement conceivable. The good ball was treated soundly and cautiously; the indifferent ball was seen quickly by both batsmen, and hit hard by means of a splendid range of scoring strokes. On present form Hardinge is one of the best batsmen in the land. Today his cricket was beyond criticism – solid yet antagonistic. He plays as straight a bat as any English cricketer; he can cut, drive, and glance to leg with the best of them. His batsmanship always shows to us the pre-war stamp.

Hardinge made his fifty in ninety minutes; Woolley was twenty minutes quicker over the same score. Just before lunch Woolley in getting his fifty sent a hit to third man that Hallows might possibly have caught had he made ground with some alacrity. Hardinge came to his century after two hours and three-quarter's handsome activity. At twenty minutes to three Kent wanted 224 with two and a half hours still to go. A slight drizzle hereabout damped the grass, and probably added to the hardships of a failing Lancashire attack. Woolley was badly missed by Richard Tyldesley when his score was 82, and Kent's 220 – a blunder which must have caused the whole Lancashire side to shudder from head to foot. Woolley got his beautiful hundred out of a total of 239 in two hours and ten minutes; his next stroke, a great on-drive, made the Woolley-Hardinge stand worth 200 – hit in 140 minutes. At three o'clock Kent were 170 runs from victory's goal, and two hours and ten minutes remained.

Green rung the changes on his bowlers, but all of them seemed merely so much fuel to the brilliant bonfire of batsmanship which was burning for the glory of Kent cricket before our eyes. Three fieldsmen stood on the edge of the offside field for Woolley – a rare sight in these days. The Lancashire cricketers looked rather broken in wind now: there was little hurry in their feet and apparently not much hope within their breasts. Every other ball bowled, it seemed, was hit to the distant parts of the ground: it was the fieldsmen near the wicket who had least work to do.

At 294 Woolley was leg before wicket: in two hours fifty minutes he had shown us his own delectable art and helped Hardinge to make 253 for the third wicket. With no increase in Kent's position R. Tyldesley broke through Hardinge's defence and missed the wicket by an inch: his face, red as a moon of blood, wore the aspect of anguish as he saw Hardinge escape.

It was a bolt out of Kent's blue sky that finished Hardinge's great innings – a lion-hearted quick throw-in by Green from long-on hit his wicket with Hardinge out of his ground. But for this mishap I imagine Kent would have won easily. Hardinge batted ten minutes short of four hours and a half, and deserved a more fortunate end. The cricket of Hardinge and Woolley taught a lesson which at the moment is needed in our game – the ancient lesson that offence skilfully exploited is the best form of defence. Collins was bowled, fifth out, at 327.

Tea was taken at four o'clock with Kent 341 for five – 20 minutes to be wasted, 85 runs wanted by Kent, and five wickets by Lancashire. Anybody's game and a moment of palpitating crisis in which a tea interval was an absurd irrelevance. Why should there be tea intervals at all on the closing day, on which, of course, stumps are drawn at half-past five? The heady situation challenged the audacity of Chapman, who flashed his bat like a sword at McDonald's off ball: he cut and carved 49 in fifty minutes, and then, as the game was coming again well into Kent's grip, he was neatly caught at cover by Makepeace, sixth out at 361. The next ball bowled Deed: thus a sudden heave of the game's great wheel landed the laurels at Lancashire's grasp. And McDonald's next ball shattered Wright's stumps – a hat-trick for McDonald at the very moment every Lancashire cricketer must have been praying for the miracle which alone could pull our county out of the fire lit by Hardinge and Woolley.

As Hubble and Freeman took up the defence of the Kent ninth wicket the band on the edge of the grass made the mellow music of the madrigal out of *The Mikado*. The moment was too tense, perhaps, for these golden strains, yet their sweetness was in tune with the afternoon's lovely English flavour. To my dying day I shall remember gratefully these afternoons in Kent, afternoons full of the air and peaceful sunshine of imperishable England. McDonald bowled at a noble pace during this last act of a memorable game, and as he ran his silent run of sinister grace the scene was one of those that do cricket honour – the crouching slips, the dogged batsmen, and the crowd watching, hoping, and fearing, now dumb and now making exuberant noises as some lightning stroke beat the field. McDonald bowled Freeman at 390: the little man had shown himself a fighter. Two runs afterwards Hubble was stumped exactly on the stroke of five o'clock.

And so a noble match was nobly won and, what is as true, nobly lost by 33 runs. Both sides did the grand old game service on this July day. Every cricketer played hard and passed through his difficult hours. The running out of Hardinge was the afternoon's turning-point: the splendid feat of McDonald settled the issue. He bowled finely at the finish, and Richard Tyldesley bowled finely too. A match well worth remembering – the brilliance of Hardinge, Woolley, and Ernest Tyldesley, the changeful hurly-burly of Kent's Titanic second innings – and everything done in a beautiful cricket field.

Lancashire 336 and 243 for 5 dec.; Kent 154 and 392 (F. E. Woolley 137, H. T. W. Hardinge 132, McDonald 5 for 106). Lancashire won by 33 runs.

Hobbs in the Nets

Not long ago I had the good fortune to see Hobbs at practice. He used a beautiful white bat, and as he made stroke after stroke he would glance solicitously at the face of his blade as though he were reluctant to do it hurt. The noise made by his hits was music to every cricketer present – a clean, solid noise, with no overtones. One could imagine, and envy, the thrill of delight that passed through Hobbs as he made these strokes – delight running its current from the bat's end up the arms, down the spine, and all over the body. Batsmen in other nets ceased their ineffectualities as Hobbs practised; they ceased them for very shame and also because the art of Hobbs held them in thrall.

Hobbs himself was not in serious vein. He was merely improvising like the pianist who lets his fingers move irresponsibly and experimentally over the keyboard; like the artist who in a 'rough study' will indulge in bold 'chancy' sweeps of the crayon. But it is during these improvisatory moments that we sometimes get a peep that takes us deeper into the mind and character of an artist than his finished work permits. The finished work often gives you the artist 'dressed up for the occasion', so to speak. He is, of course, himself in a finished work, but plus something conditioned by his medium and his public. It is by means of his improvisations that the artist can break free from the tyranny of his medium.

A quarter of an hour of Hobbs in the nets revealed to us a Hobbs above that ruthless law which, by the grim paradox of all art, is the source of perfection and the death of it. Here was a Hobbs free to use his bat as waywardly as he chose, and every stroke he made was made to serve no ends other than the artist's. The strokes were worth nothing in runs – no Surrey axe had to be ground in the nets. They were strokes thrown away on the air, squandered by our greatest batsman in a moment that found him free to the uttermost. In a quarter of an hour only three balls passed Hobbs's bat. The practice almost guaranteed that this summer will find him as masterful as ever.

From behind the net the technique of Hobbs is, so to speak, seen under a magnifying lens. Or it is as though one were looking at a painting with one's eyes almost glued to the canvas. You can see that now more of energy, even of roughness, goes into Hobbs's cricket than is apparent when watching him from a distance. He grips his bat in the middle of the handle as he waits for the ball, but frequently when he plays back the right hand drops almost to the bottom of the handle. This denotes strong right forearm leverage in Hobbs's defensive strokes. Immediately the bowler begins his run Hobbs seems to have some instinct of what manner of ball is on the way; rarely does he move his feet to an incorrect position. His footwork is so quick that even from behind the nets it is not always possible to follow its movement in detail.

And he covers a lot of ground – forward and backward. No wonder it is almost impossible to pitch a length to Hobbs when he is at his best. His style, like the style of the master of every art, and of every fine art, seems to sum up all that has gone before in the development of his technique. Hobbs's batsmanship has enough in it of the straight bat and the forward left foot to link it up with the batsmanship of Grace and the other old masters. Yet his on-side strokes, which he makes from a full-fronted stance, are sufficiently modern. The glorious truth is that many an honourable sowing by cricketers of the past comes to a fine flower in the batsmanship of Hobbs.

Bradman, 1930

The power of genius in cricket is not to be measured by the scoreboard, and not even by the clock. A Trumper, a Spooner, will reveal art and energy in one or two personal strokes or by some all-pervading yet indefinable poise and flavour. At Leeds Bradman announced his right to mastership in a few swift moments. He made 72 runs during his first hour at the wicket, giving to us every hit of cricket except the leg glance.

But long before he had got near the end of his innings he was repeating himself; it was as though the sheer finish of technique was a prison for his spirit. He could not make a hazardous flight; he reminded me of the trapeze performer who one night decided to commit suicide by flinging himself headlong to the stage, but could not achieve the error because his skill had become infallible, a routined and mechanical habit not at the beck and call of anything so volatile as human will or impulse. When Bradman passed

200 at Leeds I felt that my interest in his play might break out anew at the sight of one miscalculated stroke. But none was to be seen. His cricket went along its manifold ways with a security which denied its own brilliance. Every fine point of batsmanship was to be admired; strokes powerful and swift and accurate and handsome; variety of craft controlled by singleness of mind and purpose. Bradman was as determined to take no risks as he was to hit boundaries from every ball the least loose – his technique is so extensive and practised that he can get runs at the rate of 50 an hour without once needing to venture romantically into the realms of the speculative or the empirical. The bowler who had to tackle Victor Trumper was able to keep his spirit more or less hopeful by some philosophy such as this: 'Victor is moving at top speed. Well, I'm bound sooner or later to send along a really good ball. Victor will flash at it in his ecstasy-and I'll have him.' The bowler toiling at Bradman cannot support himself by a like optimism. For hours he will see his ordinary balls hit for fours along the grass; then his good one will wheel from his arm, by the law of averages which causes every bowler to achieve one moment of excellence in every hour.

But is Bradman ever likely to be so blinded by the radiance of his own visions that he will throw back his head at the good ball, confuse it with the others, and lose his wicket through a royal expense of spirit? Not he; he sees the dangerous ball with eyes as suspicious as those of a Makepeace. Down over his bat goes his head; the blade becomes a broad protective shield – and probably two pads will lend a strong second line of defence. It is not a paradox to imagine some bowler saying to Bradman, with strict justice, after Bradman has punished five fours in one over and cannily stopped the sixth ball: 'For the Lord's sake, Don, do give a fellow a chance and have a hit at her!'

The genius of this remarkable boy consists in the complete summary he gives us of the technique of batsmanship. In every art or vocation there appears from time to time an incredible exponent who in himself sums up all the skill and experience that have gone before him. It is not true that Bradman has inaugurated a new era in batsmanship: he is substantially orthodox in technique. Nearly all his strokes at Leeds could very well have been used as illustrations to C. B. Fry's thoroughly scientific and pragmatic book on batsmanship. But Bradman shows us excellences which in the past we have had to seek in different players; nobody else has achieved Bradman's synthesis. It is, of course, a synthesis which owes much to the fact that Bradman stays at the wicket longer than most of the brilliant stroke players of old ever dreamed of staying.

Perhaps he is marked off from the greatest of his predecessors not so much by technique as by temperament. It is hard to believe in the possibility of a more masterful stroke player than Trumper was, or Hobbs in his heyday. But when Trumper and Hobbs were great batsmen it was customary for cricketers to try to get out when their scores went beyond, say, 150. How many times has Hobbs thrown his wicket away after reaching his century? Bradman brings to an extensive technique the modern outlook on cricket: a hundred runs is nothing to him; he conceives his innings in terms which go far beyond Trumper's or Macartney's most avaricious dreams. He has demonstrated that a batsman can hit forty-two boundaries in a day without once giving the outfielders hope of a catch; he has kindled grand bonfires of batsmanship for us. But never once has he burned his own fingers while lighting them.

When I think of an innings by Macartney I do not think entirely of cricket. My impressions of Macartney's batting are mixed up with impressions of Figaro, Rossini's Figaro, a gay trafficker with fortune, but a man of the world; hard as iron though nimble of wit; an opportunist wearing a romantic feather in his cap. And when I think of an innings by Trumper I see in imagination the unfurling of a banner. Not by Bradman is the fancy made to roam: he is, for me, a batsman living, moving, and having his being wholly in cricket. His batsmanship delights one's knowledge of the game; his every stroke is a dazzling and precious stone in the game's crown. But I do not find his cricket making me think of other and less tangible things: the stuff of his batsmanship is skill, not sensibility. In all the affairs of the human imagination there must be an enigma somewhere, some magical touch that nobody can understand and explain. You could never account for Macartney, Ranjitsinhji, Spooner, Trumper, in terms of even a marvellous technique. Bradman, as I see and react to him, is technique *in excelsis*. I could write a textbook on him with comprehensive and thoroughly enlightening diagrams. Could anybody have written a textbook saying anything that mattered about the batting of Johnny Tyldesley?

The really astonishing fact about Bradman is that a boy should play as he does – with the sophistication of an old hand and brain. Who has ever before heard of a young man, gifted with quick feet and eyes, with mercurial spirits and all the rapid and powerful strokes of cricket – who has ever heard of a young man so gifted and yet one who never indulged in an extravagant hit high into the air? Until a year or two ago Bradman had seen little or no first-class cricket.

Yet here is he today, bringing to youth's natural relish for lusty play with a cricket bat a technical polish and discretion worthy of a Tom Hayward. A mis-hit by Bradman – when he is dashing along at fifty runs an hour – surprises us even as a mis-hit by Hayward did when he was in his most academic vein. How came this Bradman to expel from him all the greenness and impetuosity of youth while retaining the strength and alacrity of youth? How did he come to acquire, without experience, all the ripeness of the orthodox – the range and adaptability of other men's accumulated years of practice in the best schools of batsmanship? The cricket of Trumper at the age of 21 could not be accounted for, but we were content to accept it in terms of spontaneous genius. Besides, there was always the rapture and insecurity of the young man in Trumper. But while we can account for Bradman's batting by reason of its science and orthodoxy, we are unable quite to accept it – it is too old for Bradman's years and slight experience. The genius who thrills us is always unique but seldom abnormal. If Bradman develops his skill still further – and at his age he ought to have whole worlds to conquer yet – he will in the end find himself considered not so much a master batsman as a phenomenon of cricket.

As I say, the remarkable fact about Bradman's batsmanship is its steady observance of the unities. At Leeds he was credited with the invention of a new kind of hook. But there was no scope at Leeds for any sort of hook, ancient or modern. The ball never rose stump high on the first day; how can any batsman hook a ball that does not rise at a sharp angle from the ground? I have never yet seen Bradman perform the hook stroke, but I have seen him pull often enough. The pull, indeed, is one of his most efficient hits; it is timed to perfection, and the sound of it is as sweet as a nut.

At Leeds more than half of his 46 fours were drives in front of the wicket. His drive and cut, indeed, were much more frequently to be seen than his pull and leg hit. The secret of his stroke-power lies in his ability to move quickly backwards or forwards, making the length short or overpitched. The area of the wicket wherein a ball can be pitched that is a good length to Bradman is considerably narrower than that which is defended by all our county batsmen, Woolley excepted. He judges the direction of the attack rapidly; never is he to be seen lunging forward, stretched speculatively out; never does he fall into that 'two-minded' state which compels a batsman to make 'A-shaped bridges down the wicket feeling awry in the air for the ball,' to quote C. B. Fry. Bradman clinches Fry's celebrated Fallacy of Reach:

> The Fallacy of Reach is fatal to true cricket. None but a giant by advancing the left foot and pushing out down the wicket can reach within feet of the pitch of a good length slow ball or within yards of the pitch of a good length fast ball. Why, the very thing the bowler wants one to do, what he works to make one do, is to feel forward at the pitch of his bowling.

Bradman plays back or else goes the whole way of the forcing stroke on punitive decisive feet, When he is as a last resort compelled to play forward, he actually goes back on his wicket to do so, and his legs are behind the bat, and his eyes are on the ball. So strong is his back play, and so quick his eyes and feet, that it is fatal to bowl a short length to him. Yet, so far, that is the mistake the English bowlers have made against Bradman. Frankly they have not stood up to his punishment. Flattered by everyday batsmanship (right foot rooted behind the crease), English bowling has wilted at the sight of a bat that is busy and resolute; hence an attempt to take refuge in short bowling, a safe enough dodge in front of a cricketer who cannot cut. Bradman has thriven on bowling which he has been at liberty to see all the way, to see pitch yards in front of him.

If he has a weak point, Robins, by accident or design, found it out occasionally at Trent Bridge. Every time (which was not often) that Robins sent a well-flighted ball to Bradman, pitched on the middle stump and spinning away, Bradman was observed to be thinking hard, entirely on the defensive. It is not, of course, for the pavilion critic to presume to know the way that Bradman can be got out cheaply. But it is surely not presumptuous for anybody to suggest that the short-pitched ball is about the last of all to send to a batsman with Bradman's voracious appetite for fours and his range of hits.

He has all the qualities of batsmanship: footwork, wrists, economy of power, the great strokes of the game, each thoroughly under control. What, then, is the matter with him that we hesitate to call him a master of style, an artist who delights us, and not only a craftsman we are bound to admire without reserve? Is it that he is too mechanically faultless for sport's sake? A number of Bradmans would quickly put an end to the glorious uncertainty of cricket. A number of Macartneys would inspire the game to hazardous heights more exhilarating than ever. . . . But this is a strain of criticism that is comically churlish. Here have we been for years praying for a return of batsmanship to its old versatility and aggression; we have been desperate for the quick scorer who could hit fours without causing the game to lapse into the indiscriminate clouting of the village green. In short, we have been crying out for batsmanship that would combine technique and energy in proportion.

And now that a Bradman has come to us, capable of 300 runs in a single day of a Test match, some of us are calling him a Lindrum of cricket. It is a hard world to please. Perhaps by making a 'duck' some day, Bradman will oblige those of his critics who believe with Lord Bacon that there should always be some strangeness, something unexpected, mingled with art and beauty.

Grimmett

He is an unobtrusive little man, with a face that says nothing to you at all; seldom is he heard by the crowd when he
appeals for leg-before-wicket. He walks about the field on
dainty feet which step as though with the soft fastidiousness of a cat treading a wet pavement. He is a master of
surreptitious arts; he hides his skill, and sometimes, when
he is on guard at cover, he seems to hide himself. He knows
a trick of getting himself unobserved, and he darts forward
to run a man out like somebody emerging from an ambush.

'Gamp is my name and Gamp my nature.' That is a dark
metaphysical saying; the meaning cannot be put into
words, but none the less we can grasp it by the instinct
for eternal substances. It is like that with Grimmett;
the name penetrates to the quiddity, like 'curl', 'twist',
'slithery'; his name is onomatopoeic. I love to see him
bowl a man out behind his back, so to say – round the legs;
the ball gently touches the stumps and removes perhaps

only one bail. The humorous cunning of it reminds me that the Artful Dodger used to walk stealthily behind his master and extract the handkerchief from the coat-tails without Fagin's ever noticing it. Compare Grimmett with the wonderful leg-spin bowler he succeeded in the Australian eleven, Arthur Mailey. An Australian once said to me: 'Mailey bowled the googly stuff like a millionaire; "Clarrie" bowls it like a miser.' Mailey tossed up his spin with all the blandness in the world; his full-tosses were like a generous sort of fattening diet – before the killing and the roasting. Mailey did his mischief by daylight. Grimmett goes to work with a dark lantern; his boots are rubbered. Mailey's wickets were like a practised and jolly angler's 'catch'; Grimmett's wickets are definitely 'swag'. When he goes off the field after he has had 7 for 57, I can see the bag he is carrying over his shoulder.

He is the greatest right-handed spin-bowler of our period. The comparison with Mailey was employed to stress not resemblance but difference; Grimmett is less a 'googly' than a leg-break bowler. He uses the 'wrong' one sparsely; he is content to thrive on the ball which breaks away and leaves the bat; that is the best of all balls. A straight ball, wickedly masked, is Grimmett's foil to the leg-break. He makes a virtue of a low arm; his flight keeps so close to the earth that only a batsman quick of foot can jump to the pitch of it. And then must he beware of Oldfield, the wicket keeper who stumps you with courtesy; he does not make a noise to the umpire, but almost bows you from the wicket. Or he is like a perfect dentist who says when your heart is in your mouth: 'It's all over; I've already got it out; here it is.' To play forward to Grimmett, to miss the spin, and then to find yourself stumped by Oldfield – why, it is like an amputation done under an anaesthetic.

Moments come to all of us when we are uplifted beyond the ordinary; we become touched with grace for a while; we become vessels of inspiration. Felicity descended on Grimmett at Trent Bridge in June 1930, on the first day of the Test match. I have never seen cleverer bowling on a good wicket against great players. Hammond was batting; he made two of his own great forcing off-side hits, off the back foot. These strokes told us that Hammond was in form. Grimmett bowled him a straight ball which sped sinfully from the beautiful turf. Hammond lbw to Grimmett. Next came Woolley. Left-handed batsmen love leg-spin bowlers: the break turns the ball inwards to the middle of the bat. But Grimmett did not send a leg-break to Woolley: he sent the 'googly', whipping away. Woolley's forward stroke was seduced by the fulsome length. Woolley was stumped by Oldfield. A few minutes afterwards Grimmett drew Hendren a yard out of his crease like a mesmerist; then, having got Hendren where he wanted him, not far enough down the pitch, but yet too far, he bowled him. Grimmett will remember in his old age how he spun and 'floated' the ball that day; by the chimney corner he will babble of the way he turned a batsman's smooth lawn into a 'sticky dog'. By sheer craftsmanship he overthrew three great batsmen; nothing to intimidate, no brute force (as George Lohmann called fast bowling of sorts); nothing but a slow spinning ball bowled by a little man with an arm as low as my grandfather's.

The first sight of Grimmett bowling arouses mild laughter. His action recalls the ancient round-arm worthies, or it recalls cricket on the sands with a walking stick for the wicket and a father of six playing for the first time for years. A few steps, a shuffle, and Grimmett's arm seems to creak. But watch his wrist and his fingers: they are sinuous and beautiful. The wrist twirls and swivels; the fingers seem to adore and caress the ball, with the touch of a parent. Grimmett's fingers are always light and wonderfully tactile; when he passes the salt at dinner he imparts the 'fluence'.

He is, I believe, a sign-writer by profession. Can't you see his right wrist at work, sweeping the brush along the ornamentation? Can't you see the fingers intimately putting the finishing flick to a full-stop? Or can't you see the skeleton key at work, finding the way through the locked door of Sutcliffe's bat? He is, as I say, a master of surreptitious arts. His countenance expresses no joy when he confounds his opponents. But I imagine that long after close of play, as he lies in bed and thinks about it, he laughs far into the night. That apparent half-volley which Walters tried to drive; that obvious long-hop that Hendren tried to hook. Confidence tricks! O my lungs and liver, the wickedness of the world!

He seldom gets a man caught in the deep field. That is an

open and a brazen way to rifle the English house. Better by far a swift catch at first slip, or at the wicket best of all lbw; nobody knows anything about it away from the scene of the burglary. He is a great character, not only a great bowler. Sometimes he fancies himself as a batsman. He thrusts his left foot across and drives. Or he waits for it and cuts elegantly. Occasionally he plays late and sees his stumps all awry. Then, and only then, does he wear his heart on his sleeve.

Everybody cherishes private ambitions; we all wish to be what we are not. Dan Leno sighed to play Hamlet; Henry Irving enjoyed himself best when he sat on his top hat and pretended to be Jingle in a farce derived from *Pickwick*. Grimmett made fifty in a Test match at Nottingham in June; perhaps in his old age he will remember Trent Bridge not for his great bowling of 1930, but for his preposterously stylish and first-class half-century of 1934. The rest of the world will dwell for ever on his spin, learned in Australia, where a slow bowler must do his own work and not depend on nature and friendly wickets.

For my part I shall think of him always as I saw him at Worcester in May, taking the county's last wicket and winning the game. A catch was missed from him, and in the same over another lofty chance was skied near cover. Grimmett would trust nobody but Grimmett this time; he ran after the ball himself, and when he caught it he put it in his pocket and glided from the field, concealed entirely amongst ten other victorious Australians.

The Ashes 1936–37:
On the *Orion* to Australia

Life on the ship during the voyage out was not according to my expectations; I began it with some romantic ideas lingering in my mind since my boyhood about the talks and intimacy which would occur amongst a company of cricketers setting forth to play Australia. The team merged with the rest of the passengers until you scarcely knew where they were or which was which; Allen rightly encouraged his men temporarily to avoid cricket. The fun of the voyage was at times not easily to be marked off from the fun of a fashionable hotel on any evening at Folkestone after a day at the September festival. It became boring, and I gladly escaped from it. I even left the captain's table – not disrespectfully, I hope. The captain was charming and a marvel of tact. But the time arrived when I was ready either to laugh outright or become sarcastic at the efforts of the social climbers who each evening vied with one another to obtain the captain's recognition. The snobbishness on an ocean-going liner is appalling. I imagine that most captains in the service would like at times to leave the captain's table. But this is another digression.

When we reached the Red Sea, I decided to begin a diary; I did not keep it up, of course, for the simple reason that on a ship nothing often happens, Mark Twain achieved the perfect summary:

> Oct. 13, Got up, washed, went to bed.
> " 14, "   "   "   "   " "
> " 15, "   "   "   "   " "

and so on and so forth.

My own entries are a little fuller; here they are:

September 25

'Passengers may sleep on deck in the vicinity of the forward lounge between midnight and 6.30 a.m.' – so runs, with much confidence, the notice that has today been given prominence in the various premises of the *Orion*. We are in the Red Sea as I write, and there is scarcely a soul on board, not including the ship's cat, who is capable of any form of sleep, either on deck or below the deck, in cabin or under the starry heavens; the Red Sea is at its hottest, its stickiest, its cruellest. There is no air in the world, except fetid breath from the desert; the *Orion* makes not a wisp of a breeze as she goes her patient course. The sun is merciless, and when we escape the chastisement of its fiery rods by going under awnings or inside the lounge or drawing-room or tavern or café, then we are suffocated, or, rather, put under some evil drug of the Orient. There is one place only where we can find momentary release from the torment – in the dining-room (only we don't want to dine), where the atmosphere is marvellously chilled. Here the temperature is 75 degrees, and as we enter it we feel as though we have gone into a refrigerator; we expect, even hope, to see frost and snow appearing over our bodies. When at last we reluctantly leave the dining room and pass out through its swing doors, we go straight, without a second's break, into an oven.

I have never before dreamed that the world could become so hot, that people could endure such miseries, that nature could go its ways so indifferent to mortal needs. For three days the sun has hurled down on us the light and heat that destroys; for three days the sky has contained not a cloud, nothing but the pitiless blue of endless and indifferent space. And hour by hour the sea has grown hotter, so that at night, after the sun has gone down and a lovely silver horn of a moon has enchanted the sky, even then we have had no peace, for the waters hold the day's scorchings and throw them back. 'Passengers may sleep on deck' – may, indeed! I did not try; I kept to my cabin and hopefully manipulated the device that blows air upon you, risking sore throat, stiff neck, double pneumonia. Anything would be better and more merciful than to 'pass out' from Red Sea humidity, either by oozing away or by going mad and diving overboard with such despair that one hit the floor of the ocean and perished as much from concussion of the brain as from drowning.

The other evening, a quarter of an hour before dinner, I met Captain Howard on the staircase; the manager of the MCC team had only ten minutes ago changed into his dinner jacket. His collar was already a rag; Mr. Gladstone, after four hours or so of eloquence, never more drastically reduced stiff linen to this state of shapeless wetness. From the foreheads of all of us waterfalls have descended, splashing and dashing like the cascades of Southey's poem. (Was it Southey? – it is still too hot to think here, though at last we are emerging from the Red Sea and a breeze is stirring, giving us a sense of resurrection of all the world from the dead.) At the first hint of this heaven-sent zephyr R. W. V. Robins stripped off his evening jacket and, regardless of dignity and braces, went to the promenade deck and, feeling the faintest suggestion of a wind, said to me: 'We seem to be cooling as we direct our course towards the Antarctic'. Robins has suffered much and has borne it all with humour and an Alfred Lester sort of fortitude.

Everything that science can do towards the defeat of the Red Sea is done on the *Orion*, but nature, as Mr Squeers said, is a 'rum 'un'. 'She's a lovely ship,' said Hammond, 'but I wish she – well, had wings!' I tell of these hardships not out of a desire to present ourselves as martyrs and heroes but to console those we have left at home on the brink of an English winter. 'Lucky you!' they said as we departed from Southampton a fortnight ago; 'oh, lucky, to be going into the sunshine, while we shiver in the east winds and hug our hot-water bottles!' At the moment of writing, there is scarcely an English man or woman on the boat who would not cheerfully give pounds and pounds sterling for one hour of Manchester's wettest rain and coldest cold. Happy days are probably waiting for us in Australia – we shall deserve them, for we have suffered in the Red Sea's cauldron.

But such is human nature that while we were writhing and dissolving in the Red Sea, we persuaded ourselves that the Red Sea was really behaving with unusual moderation; then the moment we sniffed a wind of the Indian Ocean we agreed unanimously that the Red Sea had broken records in heat and life-destroying humidity, and we went about amongst ourselves distributing medals for patience, endurance, and philosophy, so to say. The probability is that we revealed ourselves as so many comfortable creatures of the temperate zone of the earth; it is said by the knowing ones of these parts that the more intelligent inhabitants of the Nubian Desert sometimes visit the Red Sea to enjoy its bracing climate – to them the Red Sea is the Skegness of the Tropics.

Pleasures there have been for us, of course; lazy days in the Mediterranean, when the sunshine has been friendly and the swimmers in the bathing-pool have splashed about, before stretching themselves luxuriously in the lovely slanting light of the late afternoon. Then the evenings. First the sunsets, and the peacefulness that comes over the ship before dinner; people have retired to dress, and the solitary watcher, leaning on the ship's side, has the sense for a moment that he is being divested of personal identity and absorbed into the deepening beauty of the hour of twilight over the ocean as the evening star appears. At night the dancing begins, and here again it is good to escape from the glitter and animation, to withdraw and watch from a point apart. Then it is possible to feel the pathos of contrast – the light and happy intimacy of life brought together for a moment by chance; and the surrounding and lasting immensity of the Indian Ocean.

And while all the laughter of young people goes on, and the elders sit domestically in lounge and drawing-room enjoying familiar comforts, the ship moves on, a beautiful sensitive creature, with the flexibility of a canoe and the power and grandeur of an ocean-going liner; through the night it moves, throbbing with a poised life of its own, making a wake in the water delicate as a chain.

At the moment we are well beyond Aden, a sun-cursed pile of brown rock, oleaginous, with the refuse kites flapping in the air – a place where the White Man's Burden, and the Black Man's Burden too, can be felt as a weariness to flesh and spirit. We are following the track of a monsoon, and the ship is rolling. In the middle of the night it is thrilling for the landsman to listen from his cabin to the surge outside, and to feel the whole of the boat's nervous system working; you can hear the heart of it. I have grown to love the ship and the quiet certainty of the men who control its strength, grace, and nobility.

October 17

... Life on a ship is concentrated in so small a space that in a month a man exceeds the common length of days. The distractions and responsibilities of the world come for a while to an end; as the hours go by we can almost count each pulsation of existence; consciousness and sense of personal identity become pure and absolute. And a strange sort of pathos falls on the little world we make for ourselves during the voyage; we know it cannot last long, that friendships almost certainly will come to an end soon, that all our efforts to reproduce the world we have left on land must end in irony – yet we do indeed reproduce it, I am afraid, with as many as possible of its foibles and pretensions. We live as though in a bubble which we have ourselves blown up, and as the voyage goes on the more does the bubble swell to bursting-point.

I have loved the evenings sitting in the 'Tavern' before dinner, watching the swimmers in the bathing-pool while the sun sank over the Indian Ocean and the sky turned to a sudden purple and stars appeared as though kindled one by one. I loved the careless fun of the games deck, the fun with the children in their own playground. I loved to go at half-past ten every morning into what I called the 'Market Place', because it was there that C. B. Fry held court amongst the deck-chairs and the passing life of the ship; where we discussed all things under the sun. Perhaps our arguments were rather too contrapuntal to be easily followed by the listening throng; we each went our way, talking for art's sake, keeping count of our own bull's eyes. But one day, just to tease him, I said: 'Well, Charles, good morning. No hemlock yet? Give us your views on the origin of the Iambic.' It was a pure piece of banter; the word 'Iambic' came to my mind by the merest chance. I might as well have asked him to explain the origin of King Cole or green cabbages.

But Fry, without a moment's hesitation, launched into a remarkable piece of virtuoso exposition; in half an hour he sketched, with a swift touch and comprehensive illustrative detail, the history of prosody. And he had not finished when I left him and went for my morning walk seven times round the deck, making the mile. Each time I passed the ship's centre (the 'Market Place') he was still at it – 'You see what I mean? However . . .' He wore a confusing variety of clothes day by day, clothes of strange dyes, patterns, and purposes. Only once did he appear (save at dinner) in tolerably reasonable guise, and that was at a fancy-dress ball, when he simulated an ascetic yet genial scoutmaster. The next day he wore what I called his deep-sea fishing attire, and I said: 'Glad to see you back in fancy dress, Charles'.

The team went quietly about their pleasures. Verity read *Seven Pillars of Wisdom* from beginning to end. Hammond won at all games, from chess to deck quoits. Maurice Leyland smoked his pipe, and Duckworth danced each evening with a nice understanding of what, socially, he was doing. Wyatt took many photographs and developed them himself. Fry, armed with a most complicated camera, also took many photographs, and none of them could be developed.

After we left Colombo the heat mercifully cooled down and a fresh wind blew. We came upon the Cocos Islands suddenly on a windy morning. Never shall I forget the romantic beauty of this experience. All the adventure stories of my youth sprang to life; here was Stevenson, Ballantyne, Defoe. On the little beach, silent and empty, there was surely Man Friday's footprint; the colours on the water evoked visions of enchanted lagoons, treasure, and coral. In a towering sea two little boats came bravely to take a barrel from the *Orion* containing the quarterly supply of rations for the handful of men who work on the islands, supporting the Empire and the White Man's Burden. The barrel was taken on board, and mighty waves swept past the two boats, sometimes hiding them from our view. On the *Orion* we all leaned over the side and waved farewell. And the last we saw of the little boats was their plungings and swayings as they returned to the island, with the men waving farewell in return; there was not a person on board the *Orion* who did not feel the emotion of the scene. 'It makes a lump come into your throat,' said William Voce of Nottinghamshire.

When we reached Fremantle it was seven in the morning. We had to be up and about early. Many times on the voyage I had wakened in the dawn and looked through my porthole. There is magic in things seen from a ship's porthole; it becomes a magic mirror. I saw the sunrise on the Indian Ocean through my porthole, and felt ashamed to be prying into an act of beauty so secret and removed from human interference. Through my porthole I saw Australia for the first time.

When Cricket Changed

For twenty years I went to cricket matches north, south, east and west, and I saw the blossom come upon orchards in Gloucestershire, as we journeyed from Manchester to Bristol; and I saw midsummer in full blaze at Canterbury; and I saw midsummer dropping torrents of rain on the same lovely place, the white tents dropsical: 'Play abandoned for the day.' I saw the autumn leaves falling at Eastbourne. I have shivered to the bone in the springtime blasts at the Parks at Oxford. In a *Manchester Guardian* article I congratulated the keenness and devotion of two spectators who at Leicester sat all day, near the sightscreen, from eleven until half-past six, in spite of an east wind like a knife. Then, as I was finishing my notice, a thought struck me. 'But', I added in a final sentence, 'perhaps they were only dead.'

I have seen English summer days pass like a dream as the cricketers changed places in the field over by over.

Sometimes I have seen in vision all the games going on throughout the land at the same minute of high noon; Hobbs, easy and unhurriedly on the way to another hundred under the gasometer at the Oval; Tate and Gilligan at Hove skittling wickets while the tide comes in; Hendren and Hearne batting for ever at Lord's while the Tavern gets busier and busier; at Southampton, Kennedy bowling for hours for Hampshire – Kennedy never ceased bowling in those days; he could always have produced a clinching alibi if ever circumstantial evidence had convicted him of anything:

'What were you doing on July 17th at four forty-five in the afternoon?'

'Why, bowling of course.'

From Old Trafford to Dover, from Hull to Bristol, the fields were active as fast bowlers heaved and thudded and sweated over the earth, and batsmen drove and cut or got their legs in front; and the men in the slips bent down, all four of them together, as though moved by one string. On every afternoon at half-past six I saw them, in my mind's eye, all walking home to the pavilion, with a deeper tan on their faces. And the newspapers came out with the cricket scores and the visitor from Budapest, in London for the first time, experienced a certain bewilderment when he saw an *Evening News* poster: 'Collapse of Surrey'.

In these twenty seasons I saw also a change in cricket. It is not fanciful, I think, to say that a national game is influenced by the spirit and atmosphere of the period. In

1920 cricket retained much of the gusto and free personal gesture of the years before the war of 1914-1918. Then, as disillusion increased and the nation's life contracted and the catchword 'safety first' became familiar and a sense of insecurity gathered, cricket itself lost confidence and character.

My own county of Lancashire provided a striking example of how a mere game can express a transition in the social and industrial scene. When Manchester was wealthy and the mills of Lancashire were busy most days and nights, cricket at Old Trafford was luxuriant with Maclaren, Spooner and Tyldesley squandering runs opulently right and left. It was as soon as the county's shoe began to pinch and mill after mill closed, that Lancashire cricket obtained its reputation for suspicious thriftiness; care and want batted visibly at both ends of the wicket. Not that the players consciously expressed anything; of course they didn't. But a cricketer, like anybody else, is what his period and environment make of him, and he acts or plays accordingly.

The romantic flourish vanished as much from cricket as from the theatre and the arts. I even reacted against the romanticism in my own cricket writing. The lyric gush, the 'old flashing bat' and 'rippling green grass' metaphors gave way to, or became tinctured with, satire if not with open irony. Hammond no longer inspired me into comparisons between him and the Elgin marbles; I saw something middle-class and respectable about his play, and was vastly amused and relieved when occasionally he fell off his pedestal and struck a ball with the oil-hole of his bat, or received a blow from a fast ball on his toe.

Bradman was the summing-up of the Efficient Age which succeeded the Golden Age. Here was brilliance safe and sure, streamlined and without impulse. Victor Trumper was the flying bird; Bradman the aeroplane. It was the same in music, by the way: the objective Toscanini was preferred to the subjective Furtwängler. In an England XI of 1938, A. C. Maclaren would have looked as much an anachronism as Irving in a Noel Coward play.

Interlude: 'That Means War'

I have looked into an account I wrote of a journey from Manchester I went upon to write about cricket:

> Observe, happy man, from your bedroom window, at this moment as you prepare yourself for a journey to the South, observe the passers-by along the street opposite. They are going to work, going to the city, there to live stuffily in one dingy spot, while you-while you are going away for the beginning of a new cricket season. Tonight these same poor souls will pass by your house again, back from the city, but you will not be there to see them return. By then you will be at the other end of England; perhaps you will have just been taken by the hotel porter to your room, just have unpacked, washed and gone out into the delicious streets, to delight yourself in them with the feeling of the miles you have covered that day . . .

At Wellington [continues this diary of a pilgrimage], or in some such place deep in the garden of our land, the journey is broken; there is a change here. The Manchester train goes out, leaving you exquisitely aware that you are now quite out of touch with Manchester. Your connection arrives – a train that obviously has never been in Manchester. The people on it have just as obviously never been in Manchester. Here, unmistakably, you are in a fresh hemisphere, entering on the last lap of your journey, through a drowsy landscape. And how peaceful is the closing hour of a day's railway travel; the mild agitations of the morning have spent themselves. The senses are tired at last of responding to new scenes, new sounds, new odours . . .

Anybody reading that passage in cold blood might imagine that I had travelled on a magic carpet, to realms of gold, over minaret and hanging gardens. If I am not mistaken I had gone to Kidderminster to watch Worcester v Lancashire. I confess that when I journeyed from England to Australia by air, on the most marvellous of magic carpets, one you could dine on, and have an excellent hock for lunch, I was not once inspired to such an Odyssey as the one described above, written in 1921. 'Delicious streets', you will observe. Perhaps they were delicious, a quarter of a century ago. I saw them in time, whether streets of Kidderminster, Worcester, Canterbury, Leicester, Taunton, Tonbridge, Gloucester or Ashby de la

Zouch — I saw them looking far from delicious, as the last rays from the summer evening sunshine fell like naphtha on pavements full of pimply youths in thirty-shilling suits and suede shoes, with their girlfriends, nearly all bad of tooth, either going into or coming out of a Palais de Danse or Plaza.

And the inns and hotels where I unpacked and washed in subsequent years: the same can for hot water, the same night commode with a tin clasp, the same wardrobe that came open suddenly after resistance, the same dressing-table with signs on the top of it that some former guest had been careless with his cigarettes, the same glass and water-bottle, and the same sickly pink counterpane. And in the breakfast-room next morning, the same cloistered dyspeptic gloom, and fried eggs like baleful yellow eyes, and the same resigned waiters. It was an England day by day losing character and all joy in life generated by the individual. It was an England becoming more and more unfriendly and shut up in itself and resigned.

Even at cricket matches in these country towns, I often felt a sense of dejection. The local caterer supplied the lunches for the crowds at a good profit, poor feeble stuff washed down by bottled beer brought miles. The people sometimes hardly seemed to possess strength to cheer boundary hits, when at intervals they happened. The last time I sat on the rustic benches of Taunton cricket field in summer, I watched two Somersetshire professionals, both entirely of the town clerkly, pushing and poking their bats at spiritless long-hops and half volleys. And I imagined the ghost of Sammy Woods looking on helpless to get at the bowling.

I came before long to dislike these miasmas of urban monotony. There was at least character at Old Trafford and Sheffield. But at last I made Lord's my headquarters, though never a member of the MCC and never free to go into the pavilion during a Test match except by special dispensation. Lord's conceded to the march of progress only on her own terms, holding the balance between tradition and change. The tulips were brought up to wear the MCC colours. I always felt that the MCC did not in its heart of hearts approve of a big crowd present at Lord's. When rain fell at Lord's, putting an end to play for hours, the crowd was in God's good time informed whether further cricket would take place that day; a man was sent round the field propelling a contraption on wheels, like a velocipede, carrying a board on which were chalked some tidings from the captains or the umpires as to their intentions and the state of the wicket.

I have known Australians to visit Lord's for the first time and loathe the feeling they received there of custom and prerogative. But after a while I have known the same Australians thoroughly assimilated, in love with the old order it stood for; they became more royal than the King. They enjoyed seeing the patricians in the Long Room at lunch, eating meat pies and drinking cans of beer-like patricians. Lord's was not, of course, all school-tie and

patrician; it was a microcosm of London itself. There was
the East End-near the Tavern – as well as the West End of
the Long Room. When the promenade on the grass took
place during lunch, Seven Dials was free to move with
Belgrave Square; a Hendren is as symbolical of Lord's as
ever the Hon. C. N. Bruce. Still, there is a limit to things;
you can have J. W. Hearne at Lord's a sort of butler; you can
have Patsy a head-groom or coachman; you can have big
genial Jim Smith, out of the garden, so to say, or something to do with the buttery. But at Lord's you could not in
decency have an Emmott Robinson permanently on the
premises or any other embodiment of industry or trade.
Cricket, I say, honours the *habitat*; the social historian will
find in a study of it and its environment much that the blue
books omit.

A hundred times I have walked down the St John's Wood
Road on a quiet morning – that's the proper way to enjoy
Lord's: choose a match of no importance, for preference
one for which the fixture card promises a 'band if possible'. I have gone a hundred times into the Long Room
out of the hot sun and never have I not felt that this is a
good place to be in, and if the English simpl*y had* to make
cricket a national institution and a passion and a pride,
this was the way to do it, in a handsome hall and pavilion,
a resting-place for the game's history, with its constitution
to be found as much in *Debrett* as in *Wisden*. I have looked
through the great windows on the field of play and seen the
cricketers in the heat, moving like creatures in another

element, the scene as though suspended in time; the crowd a painted canvas; the blue sky and the green of the trees at the nursery end; the lordly ones slumbering on the white seats of the pavilion, or quietly talking.

On the Friday morning when Hitler invaded Poland, I chanced to be in this same Long Room at Lord's watching through windows for the last time for years. Though no spectators were present, a match was being continued; there was no legal way of stopping it. Balloon barrages hung over Lord's. As I watched the ghostly movements of the players outside, a beautifully preserved member of Lord's, spats and rolled umbrella, stood near me inspecting the game. We did not speak of course; we had not been introduced. Suddenly two workmen entered the Long Room in green aprons and carrying a bag. They took down the bust of W. G. Grace, put it into the bag, and departed with it. The noble lord at my side watched their every movement; then he turned to me. 'Did you see, sir?' he asked.

I told him I had seen.

'That means war,' he said.

The Roses Match

On Saturday next I shall go to Leeds to watch the forty-second match since the war between Lancashire and Yorkshire; the occasion will complete my twenty-first year as a commentator in this paper on the greatest of all tussles between county rivals.

In most matches the critic endeavours to be impartial; he sits aloft in the press-box, like an impersonal god, seeing all things moving, towards their predestined end. The Lancashire and Yorkshire match is an exception; I step down from the pedestal of impartiality. I become for a few days as prone as anybody else in the crowd to the passions of the partisan. If two Yorkshire batsmen make a long stand (and if one of them happens to be Arthur Mitchell by name and by nature) I do my best to exert an influence of will over the field of play – some current of hate and malice calculated to cause mishap, if not death and destruction, to take place at the wicket for the benefit of my native county.

I have found that a partnership can often be broken by leaving the press box and retiring for a moment (usefully) behind the scene. I have this way taken a hundred wickets for Lancashire in twenty-one successive seasons.

The mind holds events in these games vividly; they remain coloured by imagination in a frieze of memory, set against a grim and humorous background of North of England life. No other match expresses so much character. The crowd is part of the whole; it exults and it suffers – especially does it suffer. A year or two ago Lancashire defeated Yorkshire somehow at Sheffield. When the winning hit was about to be made, when the fact became clear that no power on earth could save Yorkshire, a man wearing a cloth cap was sitting miserably amongst the litter on the great and forbidding mound which stands one side of the ground. And his wife said to him: 'Well, tha would come, wouldn't thi?'

Many years ago another Lancashire victory happened at Leeds in surprising circumstances. On August Bank Holiday Lancashire, according to long custom, collapsed. I wrote severely about the weak play exhibited by our batsmen. Next morning Yorkshire needed only a few runs to win, and everybody thought they would get them without the loss of a wicket. We turned up at Headingley merely as a matter of form. I believe that Emmott Robinson resented having to go through the ritual of changing into flannels. 'Waste o' time and money,' he probably said. Yorkshire collapsed incredibly, and Lancashire won by some twenty runs. That evening I received an anonymous postcard from a patriot who had read my diatribe on Lancashire's batting; it was brief and to the point, but not entirely fit for publication: 'You ——— fool,' it said; simply that and nothing more.

I shall remember all my life the finish of this match. After Yorkshire's last wicket fell I rushed from the Headingley ground and got on a tram, eager to carry the good news, hot from the burning, to Manchester. The tram guard came jauntily to me for my fare; he was whistling. 'What ha' they won by?' he asked.

I said, 'They haven't won; they've lost.'

He replied, 'Ah mean t' cricket match – did they lose any wickets?'

When I assured him I had referred to t'cricket match, and that Yorkshire really had been defeated he suspended business on the spot; he did not give me a ticket, but turned his back on me and walked to the front of the tram, where he opened the door and told the driver. Then the tram proceeded a mile or so into Leeds by its own volition.

In Leeds the dreadful news had travelled before me; you could see the effect on most faces. I went to the railway station, and as my train would not come for half an hour I entered the refreshment room. Shortly a few of the crowd dribbled in, sadly returning home. A Yorkshireman sat down at my table. He looked at me and said, 'Hey, this is a reight do. Fancy Yorkshire put out for fifty. Ah thowt better of them.' There was no anger in his voice, only sorrow.

Then he looked at me again, harder. 'Tha doesn't seem to be takin' it to 'eart very much,' he said.

I told him that, as I was from Lancashire, I naturally could not see the disaster from his point of view.

He inspected me now from a different angle. 'Oh,' he said, 'so tha comes from Lancashire?'

Once more I admitted that I did.

'And tha come specially to see t' finish this mornin'?'

I answered in the affirmative.

'Ah suppose tha's feelin' pleased with thisen?'

I did not deny it.

'And tha's goin' back to Manchester by this two-twenty train?'

Yes, I said, I was.

'Goin' back reight now?'

Yes, I reiterated.

'Well,' he said, slowly and in measured terms, 'Ah 'opes tha drops down dead before thi gets theer.'

There is no crowd in the world to equal the Lancashire and Yorkshire cricket crowd. Sutcliffe once stonewalled at Old Trafford for half an hour, almost without scoring. The afternoon was warm, and a huge multitude sat in silence. The game seemed to become suspended out of time and space. Nothing disturbed the illusion of eternity. Suddenly a voice addressed Sutcliffe, not critically, but with simple, honest inquiry: ''Erbert,' the voice solicited, ''Erbert, coom on; what dost tha think thi are, a ——— war memorial?'

In August, 1919, the first season after the war, two-day county matches were played, and at Sheffield on the Tuesday after Bank Holiday Hallows batted from noon till evening and saved the match for Lancashire. The crowd worked hard to get him out. Twenty thousand of them emitted a staccato noise as soon as each ball bowled at Hallows left the bowler's hand. 'Hoo!' they said (I cannot find an onomatopoeic sign eloquent enough). At six o'clock the crowd gave up the bad job and began to leave the trying scene. Rhodes vainly sought to tempt Hallows, but Hallows continued to push the ball away with his own stately ease and insolence.

A solitary man remained on the mound. He was black in the face. All the afternoon he had done his utmost with his 'Hoo!' Rhodes bowled the last over of the day. The lonely man on the mound let out six desperate 'Hoo's!' The final one exploded in the darkening air. Hallows patted the last ball of the last over, and the players began to leave the field. The man on the mound surveyed Hallows, gathered together all his remaining energy and passion, and howled forth, 'Oh, ——— you!' and went home.

Walter Hammond

Walter Hammond was one of the truly great cricketers in the game's history; it would be hard to leave him out of any recorded England XI, though blasphemy might be committed if we altered a single name of the magnificent membership of the England XI which played at Birmingham in 1902; who of these could with justice and decency stand down even for Hammond – A. C. MacLaren, C. B. Fry, K. S. Ranjitsinhji, F. S. Jackson, Tyldesley, Lilley, Hirst, G. L. Jessop, Braund, Lockwood, Rhodes? Do I hear a whispered suggestion that Tyldesley was not greater than Hammond as a batsman and no bowler at all? But I cannot argue reasonably on behalf of J. T. Tyldesley. In his heyday he was the only English professional player who by batting alone could retain his position in the England team. I flatter Hammond by bringing his name into contact with Tyldesley's, even as I honour Tyldesley by the same verbal conjunction. Hammond indeed was the complete cricketer in his superb physique, which combined power and lissome movement; his batsmanship attained in time classic poise and the habit of long domination. He was a dangerous medium-paced bowler who, given the ambition, might have vied with George Lohmann in all-round and elegant skill; for I doubt if even Lohmann was Hammond's superior as a slip fieldsman.

He looked the part too, even as Lohmann looked it. His shoulders were broad; the physical frame as a whole maybe at first hinted of top-heaviness somewhere, and there seemed a tendency of his legs, as he stood in the slips, to go together at the knees. At the first sight of a snick from the edge of the bat his energy apparently electrified the shape and substance of him, he became light and boneless, and down to the earth he would dive, all curves and balance, and he would catch a ghost of a 'chance' as if by instinct; quick though it moved, the body no doubt lagged behind the born gameplayer's intuitions. He could take a slip catch as the ball flashed rapidly away, wheeling on the ballet Lancer's toes and not so much gripping or seizing the ball as bringing it back, so to say, with time to spare. Only A. P. F. Chapman of Hammond's contemporaries equalled Hammond at catching close to the wicket.

I first saw Hammond in 1923 playing against Lancashire Gloucester; he was an unknown youth, and he batted low in the innings, amongst the tail-enders. He drove one four to the off, then got out; but I had seen enough. I wrote half a column in the *Manchester Guardian* about the boy and ventured a prophecy of greatness to come. It was easy to look into his future; there is no mistaking the thorough-bred. We needn't look for hours at quality. The scoreboard and the statisticians must wait for results; and medioc-rity needs the proof of print and percentages before it is recognised even as mediocrity. Hammond was born to distinction on the cricket field; before he had been playing Gloucestershire long most of us knew that here was one of the elect, the chosen few. But not everybody knew; in 1924 I argued with John Sharp of Lancashire, then on the England selection committee, that already Hammond was worth his colours. But Sharp thought he lacked discretion; 'He's a bit of a dasher,' he said. In Hammond's career as a batsman can be divided into periods, much as the career of Hobbs can be divided.

First he was all swift aggression, even to the verge of reck-lessness. Then followed the illness which in 1926 nearly put an end to his cricket. And now he merged into maturity just as Test matches were changing in temper and atti-tude according to what I shall herewith call the Jardinian theory, the theory taught by the strongest-willed of all the captains of England Elevens, the theory of the survival not so much of the fittest but of the most durable. The great batsman for the purposes of Test matches, according to this theory, was he who stayed in for hours and compiled large quantities of runs, not necessarily by commanding and beautiful strokes but by the processes of attrition.

Hammond remained to the end a batsman handsome to look at, a pedigree batsman, monumental and classic.

But I shall continue to try to remember well the young Hammond who in 1927, when the Gloucestershire cause seemed lost beyond repair, hooked the pace of MacDonald with a savage power I had seldom seem before and have never seen since. At this point I imagine the eyebrows of most of my more experienced readers are going up questionably – 'Hammond hooking? But Hammond didn't use the hook. If he had a weakness at all it was lack of resourceful strokes to leg. O'Reilly could keep him quiet by bowling on his leg stump.'

On the morning of Friday, 20th May, Gloucestershire, with two wickets down in their second innings, were only 44 ahead. The Lancashire professionals planned to get the match over quickly, so that they could go to the Manchester races. From the first over of the day, bowled by MacDonald with the velocity and concentration of a man determined to get to Castle Irwell in time to back a certain winner at 5 to 1 against, Hammond drove five fours from five consecutive balls. The sixth ball would also have counted for four, but it was fielded on the boundary's edge at the sight-screen behind MacDonald's arm. A straight drive from the first over of the most dangerous fast bowler of many decades! Hammond punished MacDonald so contumaciously that short 'bumpers' soon began whizzing about Hammond's head. He hooked them time after time as ferociously as they were discharged at him. I watched this death-or-glory innings standing in the dusty earth near the Manchester end of the ground, near long leg. Several of Hammond's hooks crashed into the earth, sending gravel flying about us like shrapnel. In some three hours Hammond scored 187, with no chance, four sixes and twenty-four fours.

In August 1924 at the age of 21 he wrecked the Middlesex attack on a dreadful wicket at Bristol. Gloucestershire, in first, scored 31, then dismissed Middlesex for 74. In Gloucestershire's second innings Hammond scored an unbeaten 174 out of 294 for 9 (declared), in four hours, winning the match. It was cricket of this dauntless kind, with strokes blinding to the eyesight, strokes of controlled power and strokes of controlled imagination, all kaleidoscopic and thrilling to the romantic vision, which impelled me to a column article I sent to the *Observer*, then edited by J. L. Garvin, who also became convinced of young Hammond's genius. But we couldn't convince yet the England selection committee that here was the greatest England batsman since the high noon of Hobbs. The philosophy of 'safety first' was at this time in full swing and sway. By the by, when Hammond first got married, Garvin wrote to me: 'For the next few months he'll probably not do very much – but afterwards, better than ever.'

Because of illness Hammond did not play for England until 1927. Then as one of Chapman's team – in Australia in 1928-29 – Jardine, the vice-captain, he scored 905 runs in the rubber, with an average of 113.12. He began modestly in the first Test Match of the series, played at Brisbane:

44 and 28. Next at Sydney he scored 251, followed by 200 and 32 (run out) at Melbourne, followed by 119 not out and 177 at Adelaide (two hundreds in the same game), followed by 38 and 16. The world of cricket was staggered, not realising of the wrath to come from Bradman. So far in cricket's history no one human batsman had amassed runs in Test matches with this insatiable appetite and with Hammond's austerity of purpose and disciplined technique. For he had now put childish things behind him, at least while playing in Test matches. The glorious uncertainty of cricket was a term no longer to be sensibly applied to Test matches between England and Australia; the wickets all this time were anaesthetic, somnolent couches stuffed with runs. We must bear these wickets in mind as we make an estimate of the bowling of W. J. O'Reilly, who was doomed to go to work on them and to toil on them for hours, if he could not spin. In the circumstance his record of performances well bears comparison with that of the unparalleled Sydney Barnes.

Hammond fitted himself into the new economy and the new ethic of sport; and he lost nothing of the grand manner while making the adjustment and the ordered concession to the mathematical and the mechanical. He cut out all but his safest strokes; he became patience on a pedestal of modern concrete; Phoebus Apollo had turned fasting friar. He reserved for matches of lesser importance flashes or flickers of his proper brilliance. His stately and pillared centuries and double-centuries were as classic as the Elgin marbles and about as mobile and substantial. With the ease of absolute mastery he batted maiden over after maiden over, his body bending to the ball almost solicitously, making strokes of cradled gentleness. For the Cause he clipped his own wings; but there is something majestical in wings in repose. He played henceforward mainly off the back foot. His terrific punches to the offside received their strength from a propulsion or a swift thrust of the body beginning at a bent right knee, then steely wrists directed the energy, so that none was wasted; it all ran like a current of power into the bat and through it into the ball.

At Lord's in 1938 his greatest Test match innings may be said to have added to the ground's lustre and history. When he went to the wicket England had lost Hutton, Barnett and Edrich to the alarming pace of McCormick, and not many more than twenty runs had been scored. Hammond at once took charge of the game and after due scrutiny and circum-spection he hammered McCormick and Fleetwood Smith and O'Reilly to shapeless helplessness, never seeming to hurry himself or use his strength combatively; no; he went a red-carpeted way to 240, his cover-drives thundering against the rails under the sign of Father Time.

This innings announced that for Hammond ripeness was all that mattered now; the early and dazzling shooting-star had by some astronomical decree changed into the benign satisfying and fulfilled harvest moon. His batting at Lord's this day was marmoreal; an appeal against him for leg-before wicket, a raucous appeal at that, sounded so incongruous that I was there and then strangely inspired to a satire, in the form of Meredithian parody:

Hammond leg-before-wicket – has anybody noticed that he *has* a leg? Usually the leg of the modern batsman is ever before us, obscure it as you will, dressed degenerately in pads of breadth and length, inordinate unvaried length, sheer longinquity ageing the very heart of bowler on a view. Most cricketers have their legs, we have to admit. But what are they? Not the modulated instrument we mean simply legs for leg-work, legs of an Emmott Robinson. Our cavalier's leg – our Hammond's – is the poetic leg, a valiance, a leg with brains in it, not to be traduced by the trick they ken of at Sheffield . . .

After Hammond put an end to his innings this day in June 1938, everybody stood up as he returned to the pavilion, stood up to render tribute to a cricketer who had ennobled Lord's. After the second war, Hammond again visited Australia, this time as captain. He suffered physical ailment and mental worry, so could not make a good end. But during the 'Victory' Test matches in England, not regarded as official, the original Hammond was seen, riding on the crest of his youth; or, to drop the metaphor, he attacked as of yore, the bat swinging free of care again, sure of aim, and, best of all, a source of enjoyment to himself as well as to all others.

One of his more remarkable innings was played on an absurdly difficult wicket at Melbourne, during the 1936– 37 rubber; the ball broke most known laws of geometry, trigonometry and suchlike. Now it shot along the earth like a stone thrown over ice; now from the same length would it rise upward at an acute angle threatening batsman's skull or thorax. On this turbulent pitch Hammond maintained his customary poise and calm; his innings of 32 came like oil in raging waters. He stayed in easefully for an hour and a half, never once obliged to hasten a stroke. The irony of it all was that all this mastery was really a service to Australia; much more good would have come England's way had Hammond driven and hooked, defying every tabulated principle of science, and scored his runs in a quarter of the time – so that Australia might have had to go to the wicket and face the music. J. T. Tyldesley in 1903, also on a foul pitch at Melbourne, made 63 out of England's total of 103, and by brilliance and versatile if sometimes indiscreet strokes, won the match, or at least brought victory within England's reach.

Hammond in his pomp occasionally suggested that he was batting lazily, with not all his mind alert. When he at times scored slowly on a perfect wicket he conveyed to us the impression that he was missing opportunities to get runs because of some absence of mind or indolence of disposition. He once said to me after he had made a large score on a comfortable wicket, 'It's too easy.' He preferred a worn dust-heap at Cheltenham, where he would put the most dangerous attack to the sword, and where fielding in the slips he was Nijinsky and a myriad-armed Indian god at one and the same animate time.

His career had its pungent ironies, apart from the disillusionment of the curtain's fall. When he first met Fleetwood-Smith, a googly bowler of rare and enchanting art, Hammond nearly knocked him out of cricket for good and all. Then in 1937 at Adelaide, when the rubber was at stake, Hammond and Fleetwood-Smith came face to face; and we knew that the decision rested with one or the other. On the closing morning, England needed 244 to win, with 7 wickets in hand, Hammond not out. It was the fourth match of the series, England had won two, Australia one. All our eyes were riveted on Hammond as he took the bowling of Fleetwood-Smith in a gleaming sunshine. To the third ball of the day Hammond played forward and was clean bowled. Australia won, drawing equal in the rubber; they also won the fifth. As Hammond's bails fell to the ground, Fleetwood-Smith danced, walked on his knees, went nearly off his head. And I heard Duckworth's voice behind me: 'We wouldn't have got Don out first thing in the morning with rubber at stake.'

'Too easy.' He was an artist of variable moods. But he was greater than the statisticians suspect. Perhaps all of a beautiful batsman's innings should be of brief duration as Edgar Allen Poe said all poetry should be short. At least no innings by a master and artist should seem longer than any ever played by Trumper, Woolley or John Tyldesley. There were more things in Hammond's cricket than are dreamed of in the scorebook's economy.

The Melbourne Test, 1950, Third Day

This was one of the most astonishing and thrilling days in the annals of cricket, and it ended with the balance so precarious that the merest wisp of a straw from luck would sway it decisively, England's or Australia's way. Yet again Australian batsmanship was rendered poverty-stricken; the second innings was all over at five minutes to five for 181. England counter-attacked grandly from the position to which they were thrown back on Saturday; the wicket, though not altogether after a contemporary batsman's heart, was on the whole true – in spite of a ball that kept low now and again and easy for run-making. Keener bowling than Bedser's, Bailey's and Brown's, and keener fielding, couldn't be imagined; and the raging battle was infused by a spirit of sportsmanship that honoured the finest and oldest traditions of cricket, the Melbourne crowd contributing a generous if ear-shattering part.

After a two days' pause the match began again in hot

weather, the sun streaming from a sky of blue satin stretched without a crease in it. From the heights of the members' pavilion, looking straight down and behind the line of the ball's flight, the wicket resembled a light-brown oblong coffin in which, you might have said, reposed the hopes of all bowlers. But it was a deceptive wicket really good enough for a good batsman, but, as I say, a ball occasionally kept low; and there was always enough hardness in the rolled baked earth to create that illusion in cricket of increase of speed after the ball has pitched. A Test match wicket in Australia, let alone Christmas Day and Boxing Day, could scarcely be expected to remain sober all the time. So once again we were privileged to enjoy a fair fight between bat and ball, fortune never distributing her favours unequally among the opponents.

At first I resigned myself to hours of slow attrition while Morris and Archer set themselves to reduce Bedser, Bailey and Wright to limp, moist, ineffectual bodies. Only one wicket fell before lunch, and in ninety minutes not more than 57 runs were scored; and now Australia were 79 ahead, nine batsmen to come. Morris played back to a well-flighted length from Wright, got into position for a glance to leg, changed his mind, and allowed his pads to stop a 'googly', and to his unconcealed surprise was given out lbw. Still, nobody foresaw the wrath to come. Archer suggested obduracy if not a technical control that has been taught by experience to work at leisure and by instinct.

The fun began at half-past two when the great ground

was packed and inflammable. Archer was caught a few yards from the bat by Bailey, off Bedser in the 'gully', and five minutes afterwards Harvey backed-up impulsively as Miller stabbed defensively for ward at a surprisingly quick one from Wright. Washbrook, at mid-off, fielded swiftly, threw at one wicket and struck it with Harvey yards out. I was obliged to ask the brilliant fielder's name; he was so thoroughly disguised in a white hat that he might have been wearing the Tarnhelm. Miller also protected himself from the sun by use of a cap; and Miller with his hair invisible is as though W. G. Grace had appeared without his whiskers.

Indeed, Miller was not happy; his aggression hinted of some mental unease. Clearly the occasion was not going to be a sort of extra Christmas dinner for Australian batsmen. He made two great strokes off Wright, a voracious sweep to leg, the whole man coming full circle, and a leap of a drive to the off. Then Bailey clean-bowled him with dramatic abruptness. Miller tried to change from offence to defence, but the ball's speed was even quicker than Miller's eyesight; the middle stump was hit before the bat could intervene.

Now Brown came into action again, rolling to the crease like a man-of-war. A rasping ball removed Loxton, caught at the wicket: Australia 5 for 131, and what with the boiling temperature of the afternoon and the roars and the zoological screams of the women in the crowd, the wonder is that typewriters in the Press Box were not dislocated and infinitives split asunder. The frenzy of it all was intensified by the impersonal tranquillity of the stainless blue sky. Brown next got rid of Lindwall, also caught at the wicket; and in the same over Brown, insatiable and very warm, defeated Tallon, who played back to succumb lbw.

After tea Bailey held a catch worth going miles to see, even by transport in Melbourne. Hassett, who was batting belligerently, edged a ball from Brown low to the grass and Bailey grasped it one-handed, flinging the heart and soul of him at the chance. Brown's antagonistic bowling, which had disposed in rapid sequence Loxton, Lindwall and Hassett and changed the day's course, was all done with an old ball and less by the arts of length and variation of pace (which were excellent) than by vehemence of will and power of a good right arm. With every run invaluable and every ball a nail in somebody's coffin for certain – England or Australia's – a stand by Johnson and Johnston (only Iverson to come) came as more and more fuel to the flames of a game which burned and singed us as though all of us, crowd, cricketers, bats and balls and surrounding nature, were being caught up in the conflagration of an Australian midsummer. The ninth wicket added 25; Ian Johnson's portion was 23; and England tomorrow, so it was written, but mercifully we couldn't know it, would lose by 28. A day of irony, a day of cricket long to be remembered.

Brown again sent Simpson in first with Washbrook to begin England's task (if it couldn't be called a duty); a mere 179 to win a victory. It was a risky move surely, for if ever an

England innings needed a masterful lead it was now. But Washbrook was the first to fall, well beaten by Iverson with a ball that kept low. Hassett lost no time before he brought his spin-bowlers into action, but I fancy he was as hopeful of collaboration from the batsmen's fears or imaginings as from the wicket itself, which if it didn't reject spin, scarcely imparted the pace or 'snap' that kills. Bailey, sent in twenty minutes before close of play, was bowled by Ian Johnson for nothing, stretching forward to an off-break. Why was Bailey asked to bat in a position so responsible at the end of an afternoon on which he had not spared himself in the field? Hutton, who was possibly becoming accustomed to arriving at the crease not with a clean, confident sheet behind him but in the midst of falling wickets, dallied calmly with the last long agonising minutes, as the sun cast the shadows of the great stand over the grass in stark black blocks.

Denis Compton

From time to time, in most walks of life, a man appears who rises above his particular job and attracts the attention of people who are not intensely interested in his vocation. He has the appeal of what we conveniently call 'personality', though few of us are able to define the term. 'Handsome is as handsome does' is an old and very sensible saying, so true indeed that even a Denis Compton is obliged to prove his skill day after day, as he and the rest of us have found cause ruefully to realise only yesterday. It is, apparently, not enough that he should 'look well' and embody charm and appeal in all his actions in the field. Some cricketers, on the other hand, may show abnormal technique perpetually, breaking records by rote; yet they fail to achieve 'glamour' in an age that insists on it. Also, there's something in a name.

Would our Denis seem to smell as sweet if it were Septimus Tomkinson? He has had all the help from the fairies in the cradle (though, of course, the fairies can take away capriciously, as well as give). He was baptised Denis Charles Scott Compton, a Barrie title, and he was born only a mile or two from Lord's in the month of May, the month when the cricket season blooms and blossoms; and his father not only loved the game but was good at it himself. He was endowed with sturdy loose limbs, square shoulders and strong wrists enlivened with suppleness. He was born with an inexhaustible flow of spirits and an eye that sees swiftly and can usually seek out the bright lining of a cloud; and not only that, it is an eye that wins friends at a glance. He is not tall but not short; just the right build, mingling the physical attributes of cricketer *and* footballer. Nature came to him with her cornucopia pretty full, and she let him help himself to it – for a while. Best of all, she brought to him a modest mind, without which the straight bat is only a symbol of vanity – not that Compton's bat is always straight. As we shall see, he has his own way of rendering first principles up to date.

Only the other year, it seems – time flies quickly in the cricketer's life, with wars ripping out whole chunks of summers – people going to Lord's and entering the ground at the W. G. Grace gates were buying scorecards from a bright-eyed boy, and he was Compton. Yes, his career has contained all the romantic ingredients: upward flight from the bottom rung. But no writer of a boy's story would risk a sudden eclipse of his hero at the height of his fame, in Australia too! Let us keep to the main pattern – 'Card of the match, sir'; then, at the age of eighteen, our hero is playing for Middlesex at Lord's, the historic place shaded by great ghosts; and all London around him on a June day, all granted him without a hard fight, gift added unto gift, the plant in the proper soil from the start. For in his first season he scores 1,004 runs, average 34.62. He gets a century in his sixth match. At the age of 20 he is chosen to play for England, and, facing Australian bowling in a Test match for the first time, he gets a century. War merely gives him the schoolboy's second wind; there seems no summit beyond his reach. He lowers the record of the one and only Jack Hobbs, 18 hundreds in one memorable summer. After beating at home the record aggregate in a season of Tom Hayward, 3,816 runs to the Old Master's 3,518, he goes on to score two centuries in a Test match against Australia, when he first plays there.

Today he is 33 years old and should have been rather in need of crutches. He throws off vicissitude without a shrug; he even throws off a sudden dreadful blow from his deceitful fairies, and throws it off without spite. He sometimes seems to trust his stars dangerously, grateful if they are ascendant but apparently scarcely aware if they are not.

But genius – even genius – needs to choose the right moment. Compton came to the high summer of his renown in a period when we all badly wanted the like of him on our fields for the purpose of rejuvenation. His cricket, in 1947, gave a nationwide pleasure which was somehow symbolical. In a world tired, disillusioned and bare, heavy with age and deprivation, this happy cricketer spread his favours everywhere, and thousands of us, young and old, ran his runs with him. Here at any rate was something unrationed. There were no coupons in an innings by Compton. He was contagious; he liberated impulses checked for long amongst all sorts and conditions of English folk – women as well as men, girls as well as boys. He embraced a new public in search of entertainment and release, a public which knows nothing of the old divisions that restricted sport to 'men's games'. Denis hath his fans not less dewy-eyed than those of Hollywood.

Is he a great batsman? I would prefer to describe him as a richly gifted one who is a stroke-player of distinction and some originality. He certainly isn't Hutton's equal in technique, and nature didn't intend that he should be. Hutton is obviously the more organised batsman of the two; he possessed what I call (and I hope I won't scare away my schoolboy) power of conception, ability to see a long way ahead in an innings. A big score by Hutton is thought out, or is the consequence of deliberation, either before or during the execution of it. Compton seems frequently to play according to mood, or what once on a time was called the inspiration of the moment. Hutton's cricket is old in the head, rational and responsible. Compton's cricket is never old in the head; for all its schooling and skill it simply will not grow up. If Hutton had run into half of Compton's appalling misfortunes in Australia during the Test matches of 1950-1951 he would have extricated himself by a severe bracing of the will. Compton was soon at a loss – an Aladdin who had forgotten how to rub the lamp and pronounce the necessary Abracadabra.

It is the failing of all sorts of criticism to consider an artist's or performer's technique apart from the individual who is using it, and to regard skill as a thing in itself which moves of its own volition and always in the same way. The truth is that if the technical equipment of Hutton could somehow be given to Compton, inoculated into his bones and being one night while he slept, and his own taken away from him, we should see little essential difference in his cricket next day. With Hutton we have the order and fulfilment of science; with Compton we have the short-cuts and spontaneous illuminations of temperament. Compton one day is so quick on his feet, in and out of the crease, that the bowler seems now and then to have to change his mind while running ball in hand to the wicket. Sometimes Compton prances down the pitch, only to find a length altogether too short for forward stroke; he will run back to cut it, and sometimes it is a scurry to save himself.

He is a superb driver between the left hand of mid-off and point. He is not always too particular about placing his left foot near the line of the ball: he is trustful of the enormous power and steering-wheel suppleness of his wrists. But on his ill-starred days he may very soon be caught because his bat has gone out to seek the ball on the off-side with no guidance apparently from Compton himself; it is as an artificial limb. On these inexplicable days he falls under that evil spell which reduces others not fit to tie his laces to immobility of the right foot, so that, he, Compton, yesterday as impertinent and ubiquitous of movement as a young terrier tackling a mastiff, is bird-limed. Or his bat has become leaden. Not often, though, is he so reduced and chap-fallen. Yet, you see, the margin of error is there. He needs always to be 'seeing' the ball with the clearest and most rapid and comprehensive eye. A Hobbs or a Hutton, because of sound grasp on the fundamentals, is able to go on and on until the age of spectacles and ear trumpets. Compton's cricket at his best belongs to youth.

He has, in fact, been called the Peter Pan of the game. But the point about Peter Pan is not that he would not, but could not grow up.

The operation on Compton's knee has been a serious hindrance; still, I fancy that even if he hadn't incurred this physical damage he would today just the same be under the compulsion to face a transition period in his development as a batsman. As youth leaves us – and no man lives for ever – we must overhaul our catechism, as that great thinker, Captain Cuttle, advises. He has already proved his harder metal. In Australia five years ago, on his first visit there, he was put under the obligation of adopting a method and outlook foreign to his nature as then supposedly known and revealed. He found himself bowed down somewhat in heavy armour, his job grimly to 'hold the fort'. Nobly, if not grimly, he obeyed the orders of the day, and at Adelaide on a perfect wicket he was professionally clever enough to score 43 in two hours and a quarter, and compile two centuries in one Test match. At Trent Bridge in 1948 he defended a broken bridge for England for six and a half hours against Australians 'on the kill', while darkness fell on the earth from the sky. This innings was one of the greatest ever played in all the annals of Test cricket, both for extensive skill judiciously applied and for disciplined mind and temperament.

Maybe we shall not again look on the gay Lothario Compton of 1947; but let us console ourselves that 'ripeness is all'. He has the humour to adapt himself. When he first played Iverson at Melbourne in 1950 he was for a while completely at a loss; he tried all ways and means to deal with Iverson's peculiarly spun off-break, hopping about the pitch forward and backward, quite bereft, hitting and missing. At the other end of the wicket was young Sheppard playing Iverson in the middle of the bat. But as runs were not coming England's way and nothing being done to push the game forward, Sheppard between overs asked Denis for some advice or 'lead' in procedure.

'It's all right, David,' said Compton. 'Don't worry. You go on as you are, and I'll attend to the antics.'

When gloomy view was taken of his future, and on an afternoon that really did see him hobbling around Lord's on crutches, he told me he'd be playing again in a fortnight. 'You can't keep a good man down, can you?' he said without the slight affectation.

His wonderful year, as we all know, was 1947, in a season of glorious summer. When he came down the pavilion steps at Lord's on his way out to bat, the schoolboys crowed like cocks. An innings by Compton played this year of 1947 against Kent takes its place on the sunlit frieze of all that memory holds of gallant, accomplished and beautiful batsmanship. Kent declared on this enchanted afternoon and Wright bowled at his very best. Compton consumed him, leg-spinners, 'googlies' and all. His strokes were as shooting stars, gliding and skimming according to an astronomy of their own. The same sort of ball was treated in different ways and sent to different parts of Lord's. No effort, all grace; no flamboyance, but brilliance in the dress of courtesy. E. W. Swanton has written of this innings for the posterity of cricket.

He scored his last 71 . . . in 40 minutes. The Kent captain and his bowlers did not make the mistake of splitting the field. If they attacked the leg-stump they had six or seven men on the leg-side, or vice versa. But Denis countered every manoeuvre. Perhaps he would move sufficiently quickly to get outside the ball and chop it past slip, or, if the field were on the off-side, he drew the ball across his body to fine-leg. He was always on the move, either up the wicket or laterally and, as often as not, changed his direction as the ball left the bowler's hand.

When he got out, Kent quickly won the match, and so this great innings assumed the lustre which shines on bravely lost causes.

For my part I don't wish to think of Compton as one of the persistently masterful players. In spite of what recent trials and ordeals may have taught him, and in spite of the technical adjustments demanded by increase of years and some inevitable check on physical elasticity, he will never, I am sure, surrender to middle age. He will continue, at least this is the hope in the hearts of thousands of us, to convey the impression that he is capable, while batting, of

(1) making a superb stroke with his feet in the 'wrong' place;

(2) making a mighty pull while falling flat on his stomach;

(3) suddenly achieving a flawless execution so that the textbook black-and-white examples of Hutton seem to be given the illumination of colours;

(4) getting out to the easiest ball because after having gone halfway down the pitch he has forgotten exactly what he has ventured so far to do;

(5) running himself out or somebody else by yards, or

(6th and last) performing all these remarkable actions at one and the same time.

Denis Compton contributes to England life and holiday at the crown of the year; he is part of an English summer. In spite of his conquests, his record and scores, his cricket has always contained that hint of brevity which is the loveliest thing in the summer's lease.

Letter to the *Telegraph*, 1958

13 December 1958

Reflections on the Brisbane Display

SIR – Congratulations to my friend Mr E. W. Swanton on his brilliant and sensible comments from Brisbane.

'A bowler,' he reminds us, 'will only bowl as well as he is allowed to.' As one who once was himself a professional off (better than Burke!), may I heartily say, 'How right you are, Swanton!'

Various apologetic experts on the spot have assured us that it is unreasonable to expect our modern scientific batsmen to make strokes if:

a) the bowling is accurate;
b) the bowling is inaccurate;
c) there is too much grass on the wicket;

d) there is not too much grass on the wicket;

e) the field is set 'tight';

f) the field is spread out.

How do our contemporary heroes of the willow expect to receive the ball – on a plate with parsley?

Neville Cardus
London W1

Richie Benaud

At the beginning of June 1961, before the first Test match between England and Australia, Norman O'Neill, playing under Richie Benaud against Sussex, injured a knee while fielding, and was obliged to retire. At first the damage threatened to remove for some lengthy period this brilliant young cricketer from the Australian team. The news of O'Neill's and Australia's misfortune upset me so much that I wrote at once to Benaud hoping that O'Neill would quickly be fit again. I was as much concerned about the loss, even for a while, to the game of an artist as I was about this threat to Australia's chances of victory in the rubber.

The reply of Benaud to my letter was true to his character and to the character of most Australians. He thanked me for my sympathy but finished by saying: 'I'm not worrying unduly. I think that you'll find we'll be there when the chips are down.' And so, at the decisive moment in the rubber, they indeed were there. At Old Trafford, where the rubber's issue was settled, England were winning easily on the fifth afternoon, 150 for 1 wicket, Dexter riding the storm and only 106 needed now in as many minutes. Moreover, the Australian attack seemed pretty bankrupt: Davidson weary, Mackay physically handicapped. Benaud actually called for a breathing space, and drinks were brought into action, under a hot Manchester sun. (In 1934, two Australians were afflicted by sunstroke at Manchester during a Test Match.)

With the afternoon apparently lost for Australia, Benaud became a vessel of plenary inspiration. He bowled round the wicket and pitched his spin on the places on the pitch worn by Trueman's footmarks at the other end. As every cricketer and history knows, the trick came off. But it is not generally realised, even yet, how cleverly, how artfully, Benaud played it. He clean bowled the obstructive Subba Row the last ball, or thereabouts, before tea with a full-toss. He knew well enough that, an interval due, Subba Row would take no risk, offer no stroke, to a good ball. When Dexter was racing ahead, and defeat stared Australia in the face, Benaud said to himself, 'We can't possibly save this match but we *could* win it!'

He has been called a 'lucky' captain of cricket. The truth is that he, at his career's beginning, had to suffer hard blows to his confidence. At the age of 21 he played in his first Test match v West Indies at Sydney in January, 1952. He bowled only four overs, three balls and took Valentine's wicket for 14, of which number Valentine's share was exactly none. And he scored 3 and 19. His baptism to Test cricket in this country, in 1953, was scarcely memorable – three matches, five innings, 15 runs, average 3; 68 overs and two wickets for 174. He, supposedly a leg-spin bowler, failed to use the dusty wicket at Lord's when Willie Watson and Bailey retrieved a lost cause for England by hours of superbly dour defence. A famous player that afternoon was emphatic that Benaud never would reach top-class as a leg-spinner. 'He's a roller. Give him time,' I said. For I had seen young Benaud, months before this forlorn afternoon for him at Lord's – I had seen him in the nets at Sydney. Moreover, Arthur Mailey was putting faith in his potentiality as a back-of-the-hand spinner. But Benaud again disappointed his prophets during Hutton's and Tyson's triumphant invasion of Australia in 1954-55. He bowled 116 overs and 7 balls in the Tests for 202 runs and 10 wickets. And in nine completed innings he scored merely 148. For Australia in the West Indies, in 1955, he opened out his promise as a bowler, with 18 Test wickets, average 27.

Nonetheless, he was still on the doorstep of international achievement as recently as 1956, when he came to England for the second time. Another failure now could easily have seen the last of him amongst the Top People. He was nearing his 26th birthday. An Australian Test cricketer is usually established by this time of his life; in fact, many of them have looked towards retirement from the International scene by then – whatever Clarrie Grimmett may say to the contrary. Even in 1956, despite a resonant prelude to the season to the tune of an innings of 160 v Worcestershire, Richie for a while still could not raise himself above the level of the team's subsidiary resources. He was useful week by week, but in the first of the summer's Tests, at Nottingham, which had no result, he was not particularly useful. He scored 17, and bowled (in England's second innings only) 18 overs, and took none for 41. Between this and the second and Lord's Test he played in one match, scored 7 and 15 v Northamptonshire; and his one wicket cost 91. Conceivably he might not have been chosen for the Lord's Test if the Australian reserves had been stronger.

On the fourth morning of this match Australia, in a second innings, had lost six wickets for 115 and were only 229 ahead. On the evening before a morning on which Richie was destined to deal England a more or less death blow (with bat not ball), I met him for the first time at a dinner given by the most generous of hosts – John Arlott. We scarcely spoke. Benaud was not yet the confident Benaud of today. But there was a 'something' about him which impressed me, a suggestion of latent and alluring personality. The impression was strong enough to urge me to write an article, to appear before the game was resumed next morning, in which I risked a forecast ... 'Before we are much older Benaud will do something forcibly to demonstrate his natural and unmistakable gifts.'

Well, on this fourth morning, in a ticklish moment for Australia, with the day fresh and Trueman after blood with 4 wickets already rendering him even more than usually voracious — (4 for 38) — Benaud arrived at the ground almost late and had to rush into action at once, pads buckled breathlessly. Immediately he attacked, risking a long-armed drive. Also he hooked Trueman for six — and Trueman was the first of thousands to applaud the stroke. Benaud trusted to his eye daringly. In two hours twenty minutes he scored 97, swinging clean round the wheel of the game in the one engagement of the rubber won by Australia. This innings, maybe, marked the turn of his career.

I have gone into these statistics of Benaud's cricket to show how little indeed 'luck' has had to do with his development and progress. He, like any other man ever to do anything really well, had tested, not only in skill but in patience, philosophy and persistence. The only unmistakable good stroke from fortune to bless his onward course was at poor Ian Craig's expense, when this cricketer and captain of bright promise fell ill, and the Australian leadership passed from him to Benaud. With the swift resolution of something approaching genius, Richie grasped the chance. He directed Australia to victory in the rubber of 1958–59, in Australia. Seldom since then has he looked back. The entire world of cricket knows how he and Frank Worrell, by joint and imaginative agreement, saw to it that the Tests between Australia and the West Indies in 1960-61 produced some of the greatest and most thrilling and memorable cricket of our or any other time.

Richie, as befits an Australian and Sydney-sider, understands the value of realism. This good-looking captain of Australian cricket, with his frank eyes, and pleasant smile, scarcely fits at first sight into the general picture of an Australian skipper – think of dour immovable Armstrong, the lynx-eyed Herbert Collins, the shrewd, watchful Sir Donald. But Benaud is not wholly the cavalier batsman and the speculative leg-spinner (all leg-spinners must necessarily be speculative!). He knows that the time to be there is 'when the chips are down'.

His precious contribution to the game has been, of course, not his flair as a cricket captain; not even his ability to steer an XI to victory in a rubber in England, with a bowling team fairly to be called one of the weakest ever, Benaud himself an incapacitated member of it for weeks. No: Benaud has so far enriched cricket best by his leg-spin. This beautiful and difficult art, and any kind of spin if it comes to that, has been discouraged by legislation which has aided and abetted seam bowling. Any healthy, bodily fit, even brainless, young man can readily learn to swing his arm holding the ball's seam in his fingers the right way up. To master spin from the back of the hand, spin involving turn of the wrist and flick of fingers right to left – here is an art or craft calling for years of practice, and beautiful is it to watch a great leg-spinner, to follow the ball's seductive flight (or it might easily pitch halfway!) as it lures the batsmen forward, then drops on the earth; and it whips away or, the 'googly', comes back! Nothing mechanical here. Leg-spin insists on constant careful manipulation from its exponents – and constant concentration of mind.

So you see, this 'lucky' Benaud has not only fought through preliminary setbacks of form. While opposing them he also learned and mastered one of cricket's most skilful and enchanting arts, leg-spin with changeful flight that asks questions in the air.

Len Hutton

Len Hutton was the only batsman of his period to whom we could apply the term 'Old Master', referring in his case not to his number of years but to the style and vintage of his cricket. He followed in the succession of the classic professional batsmen who each went in first for his county and for England: Shrewsbury, Hayward, Hobbs and Sutcliffe – though Sutcliffe wore his classicism with a subtly Sutcliffian difference.

As Old Masters go, Hutton was young enough; the sadness is that physical disability put an end to his career in its prime. He had all the classic points of style when, not much more than 19, he came to Lord's in 1936 and scored 55. I then wrote of him in this strain of Cassandrian prophecy: 'Here is a young cricketer who is already old in the head and destined to enliven many a Lancashire and Yorkshire match of the future.'

If by means of some Time-machine capable of television

we could today see a picture of Hutton batting twenty years ago, and one taken of him during his maturity, we would notice no fundamental difference in technique. We would see that his cricket had grown in experience and finish, that is all. Like the music of Bach, Hutton's batsmanship in its evolution from an early to a late period presented no marked divisions; it was never raw, unprincipled or embryonic. He batted grammatically from the start, choosing his strokes as carefully as a professor of logic his words.

Even when he first played for Yorkshire, beginning with o, he seemed to begin an innings to a plan, building the shape and the duration of it to a blue-print in his mind, and to a time-table. But once in the greenest of his salad days he fell into error. He opened a Yorkshire innings on Saturday at Bradford with Arthur Mitchell, dourest and most unsmiling of the clan. After a characteristically Yorkshire investigation of the state of the wicket, the state of the opposition bowling, the state of mind the umpires were in, the state of the weather and barometer, and probably the state of the Bank of England itself, Mitchell and Hutton began to score now and then.

Young Hutton was feeling in form, so after he had played himself in he decided to cut a rising ball outside the off-stump. Remember that he was fresh to the Yorkshire scene and policies. He actually lay back and cut hard and swiftly, with cavalier flourish. He cut under the ball by an inch, and it sped bang into the wicket-keeper's gloves. And Mitchell, from the other end of the pitch, looked hard at Hutton and said, 'That's no——— use!' This was probably Hutton's true baptism, cleansing him of all vanity and lusts for insubstantial pageantry and temporal glory.

He observed the classical unities: that is to say, he did not venture beyond reliable and established limitations of batsmanship learned in the traditional school. Geometrical precision in the application of bat to ball, each movement of the feet considered until the right position was found almost instinctively, not bringing him merely to the ball and, as far as possible and if necessary over it, but also with body at the proper balance.

Never, or hardly ever, did Hutton play a thoughtless innings; his mind usually seemed to move a fraction of time in advance of his most rapid footwork and sudden tensions of limb, sinew and nerve. It is, of course, wrong to suppose that Hutton was at any time a batsman slow in his mental and physical reactions at the crease.

The scoreboard may have told us that he was not getting runs feverishly, but the vigilance of Hutton was eternal; the concentration in him was so intense that it frequently exhausted his not robust physique much sooner than did the more obvious toil and burden of the day. In the most austerely defensive Hutton innings we could feel a mental alertness; purpose in him suffered no weariness.

And whether or not he was putting into practice his wide repertoire of strokes, he was the stylist always; rarely was he discovered in an awkward position at the crease, rarely was he bustled or hurried. Once at Kennington Oval, Lindwall knocked Hutton's cap off in a Test match. Such an outrage could be equalled in a cricketer's imagination only by supposing that Alfred Mynn's tall hat was ever likewise rudely removed.

On a bowler's wicket, when the ball's spin was angular and waspish in turn, he could maintain his premeditated technical responses, often using a 'dead' bat, the handle held so loosely that when the ball came into contact with the blade's middle it was as though against a drugged cushion: the spin was anaesthetised into harmlessness.

But Hutton was, when grace descended upon him, a versatile and handsome stroke player. Old Trafford will remember that in 1948 he made a century of a brilliance which, in the circumstances – Bank Holiday and a Lancashire v Yorkshire match – was almost pagan.

He drove Lindwall with Spooneresque charm and panache at Brisbane in December 1950; at Lord's in the Test Match of 1953, he played one of the most regal and most highly pedigreed innings ever seen in an England and Australia Test Match on that hallowed ground. And he has contributed to a festival at Scarborough.

If Hutton had lived and played in the Lord Hawke epoch, when even Test cricketers in England had somehow to adapt themselves and their skill to matches limited to three days, he would have been a different batsman in his tempo and mental approach. But he could not possibly have been greater.

Any artist or master of craft is an organism in an environment; he is very much what circumstances and atmosphere make of him. His very greatness consists in how fully he can sum up the technique of his day as he finds it, and how representative he is of his day's spirit. MacLaren, lordly and opulent at the crease, was a representative man and cricketer in a lordly opulent period; Hutton's cricket has been as true as MacLaren's to the Zeitgeist, to the feeling, temper and even to the economy of the age which shaped his character and his skill, both conceived as much as in integrity as in joy.

As a captain he was shrewd but courteous; he knew the game's finest points and, though never likely to give anything away, was too proud to take anything not his due. Sometimes he may have allowed thoughtfulness to turn to worry; but this is a natural habit in the part of the world which Hutton comes from.

Hutton certainly showed that a professional cricketer can wear the robes of leadership in the field of play with dignity. At first, no doubt, he appeared at the head of his troops not wearing anything like a Caesarian toga, but rather the uniform of a sergeant-major. But he moved up in rank and prestige until he became worthy of his command and defeated Australia twice in successive rubbers, wresting one from the enemy at the pinch and looting the other after a series of Tests which were, if I may be free with my allusions and metaphors, the Australians' Austerlitz.

One of Hutton's most winning characteristics – and

his personality is extremely attractive — is his smile, a smile with a twinkle in it. He had many occasions in his distinguished career on which to indulge this smile, many provocations to it, and he never missed the joke. A Yorkshireman has his own idea of humour, and Hutton, as great or famous as any Yorkshireman contemporary with him, relished his laugh all the more because very often it came last.

Keith Miller

Keith Miller, an Australian through and through, is obviously an Australian at first sight, though not at the first sound of his voice, for he speaks English as it is pronounced, say, in Streatham. His appearance, the physical shape of him, is pervasive presence – he is pure eternal Australian, sun-saturated, absolutely 'dinkum'. See him in flannels, his wrinkled brow glistening with sweat, and surely you'll agree that he should inspire a sculptor to make an image of him to be erected in some public square in Canberra, there to stand down the ages as *Australia in excelsis*'. I commend the idea to Prime Minister 'Bob' Menzies.

I could have sworn that he was a 'Sydney-sider', born near Randwick's racecourse. As a fact, he first saw the light of day in Melbourne, and so I suppose we must call him a Victorian. I came in good time to live in Sydney, where Bondi beach, Dee Why, Elizabeth Street and – of course – Randwick, acclimatised him, expelled all decorum and released any inhibitions acquired while dwelling in the elegant city of the Yarra. I have said always that Melbourne is Australia in a top hat and a starched wing-collar. Sydney is inclined to be raffish, uncollared, racy, even indifferent to manners that get in the way of natural impulse. The solidity of Melbourne, social and economic, has somehow been hinted at by most of her greatest cricketers – the sane, down-to-earth Armstrong, Woodfull, Ponsford, Hassett, McDonald, Ian Johnston, to name a few. Neil Harvey, a brilliant deviation from type, gravitated, like Miller, and as inevitably as needle to pole, to Sydney.

If we come to reflect on the matter, most of Australia's spectacular cricketers have been nurtured in New South Wales and tanned by the Sydney heat and the Sydney 'Southerly buster' – Trumper, Macartney, Bradman, Kippax, Andrews, Mailey, Jack Gregory, Archie Jackson, Johnny Taylor, Bertie Oldfield, McCabe, O'Reilly, O'Neill... Miller fits into the Sydney scene every inch of him. Merely to get a glimpse of him prompts me to see, with my mind's eye, Randwick, Castlereagh Street, 'Ushers' and the Domain and the long bar in the Australian hotel and the lovely sweep of the green oval of the Sydney cricket ground. "Ow yer gow-in', Keith?' they hail him; "E's dinkum, too right, 'e is.' In our time no Australian has vied with Miller for first place as a national hero and symbol.

Miller, nearly six foot tall, knows the almost forgotten secret these days of *panache*. Loose of limb with good shoulders, he is alluring in the eyes of the ladies who sit in the Sheridan stand at Sydney. In the Test match v England at Sydney in January 1951, Hutton and Simpson were well-rooted and the score 128 for 1. England had lost at Brisbane and Melbourne; the rubber was now at stake. Before this third Test, England had prayed to win the toss. 'Let us only bat first on a good wicket,' they had said. Well, England was, on this hot scorching afternoon at Sydney, batting first. And Hutton and Simpson seemed impregnable. The Australians were waiting without much hope for the new ball.

Ten minutes from tea, Miller had strayed from the slips to the outfield. He stood in front of the Sheridan stand. He was communing between one ball and the next with the ladies. Then Hassett, Australia's captain, called on him to send down a few overs, merely to mark time, till the interval and to give the other perspiring bowlers a rest. Miller reluctantly took the old ball, and at a deceptive medium pace relaxed like a fast bowler formally swinging his arm in the nets, he got rid of Hutton and Compton in an over, suddenly, from a short run, delivering streaked lightning. Immediately after tea he had Simpson caught at short leg. In 28 balls he took 3 for 5, and by sheer improvisation he won the rubber for Australia.

He was, in fact, a great artist in improvisation. When he bowled, he often ran to the crease from different places and always did he attack along a shortish distance. He couldn't bear to waste time. If a ball was played defensively from him he would clap his hands at the fielder retrieving the stroke, eager to 'get on with it'. At an inning's beginning his pace and bounce from the pitch were terrific and as though combustible. Certain England batsmen feared him even more palpitatingly than they feared Lindwall. He was 'at them' so abruptly, swinging round after his few impatient paces, his shoulders generating a last-second propulsive energy. 'If Keith had never gone in for batting', Cyril Washbrook one day told me, 'he would have been the most dangerous fast bowler ever.' He was quite dangerous enough. At Melbourne, he came close to equalling S. F. Barnes's wonder-bowling there, in December, 1911, when the Master took four wickets before lunch for one run, in five overs. Miller, at Melbourne in December, 1954, bowled throughout the 90 minutes before lunch, and took 3 wickets for 5 runs in 9 overs, despite a suspect knee. But when the mood to action visited Keith he was not conscious of physical impediments.

He was incalculable. Only mediocrity is always at its best. One day we would see Miller's bat trenchant and powerful, driving with a conquering swing, upright and free. Next day he might dismay us by pushing forward full stretch, groping at a good length ball, apprehensively groping. In 1945 he was the living embodiment of the game's and of London's resurrection from the ruin and the graveyard of the war. He came to Lord's, fresh from intrepid feats of battle in the air, and playing for the Dominions against England, enchanted the watching rationed English crowd by batsmanship glorious and visionary. He hit seven sixes and added 124 to a night before's score of 61 – in 90 minutes. An imperious drive off Eric Hollies landed on the roof of the broadcaster's box, but for which obstacle the ball would have cleared the pavilion, even as Albert Trott's gigantic hit had cleared it years previously.

Incalculable and unpredictable. One day he is in the slips interrupting conversation by a sudden leap or thrilling dive to take a sinful catch. Next day he is at cover, his mind wandering or pondering the 'odds' or the 'weights' and an easy chance, possibly from Washbrook in a Test, goes almost unnoticed by Keith, who hardly unfolds his arms. He is a law and lawless to himself. In fighting mood he could hurl a 'bumper' with the jubilant ferocity of a 'Digger' at Gallipoli throwing a hand grenade. In some other mood of his own fancy, he might go on to bowl like a middle-aged gentleman playing with young folk on the sands, rolling along donkey drops square-arm. During the course of F. R. Brown's England team's campaign in Australia in 1950-51 Miller promised on the eve of the third Test match at Sydney to play for me a dazzling innings tomorrow – 'if we win the toss. And if we lose it, when we bat I'll give you something to write about.' Then, against an England XI with an attack reduced by injuries to Bedser, Brown and Warr, he batted five hours for 99 in scourging sun.

In this same Australian summer of 1950-51 Victoria's spinner, Iverson, was a sore thorn in the sides of England's batsmen. On Sunday night as I was dining in Usher's Hotel, Keith dropped in and while we talked he asked, 'Why don't your chaps get into Jack Iverson and beat the hell out of him?'

I replied that it was easy for him to talk but it was 'our chaps', not Miller, who had to cope with Iverson.

'But New South Wales are playing Victoria next week,' responded Keith, 'come along and I'll show you.'

Show me he did: he flayed Iverson's attack, went down on the left knee and pulled off-breaks out of sight. Miller was not boasting as he spoke of Iverson's bowling and what should be done with it. In fact he was a great admirer of Iverson. But it is not in his mind or nature to understand submission to any obstacle or any antagonism. The stronger the odds in front of him the greater his relish of the game – game of cricket or game of life.

His technique as bowler or batsman could not be described as classic. The energy in him galvanised him to action which could not take the form of Lindwall's smooth poise and balance. Miller was the romantic, sometimes even the eccentric. With the new ball he could rap the batsman's gloves, even threaten the breastbone, from a good length. He could swing away very late at a pace which seemed to accelerate cruelly after the ball had pitched. I fancy his fastest ball was one of the fastest in all cricket's history. As a batsman he delighted the most critical eye whenever he was on the attack. Defensively, he prodded most gingerly. A certain great Australian batsman, now dead, once startled me by saying of Keith as a batsman – 'He knows nothing about it really.' In other words, Miller plays by intuition, making up all his strokes as he goes along.

Certainly he never played as though cricket were a problem for mathematicians or a duty for the consideration of moralists. If he lost his wicket to an absolutely crude stroke, he would just shrug his shoulders, but without contrition. In his Test match career, short and sweet, he scored for Australia 2,958 runs, average 36.97, and took 170 wickets, average 22.97, proof of rare all-round powers, seldom surpassed. Yet when we think of Miller now, we don't dwell too much on his skill or on his performances. It is the man, the Australian, the personality of him, that we remember. This summing-up may seem trite enough, but it's true. He was a virtuoso.

Possibly he didn't consciously *present* himself. He was natural Keith when he tossed back his mane of hair, or when, if a bowler stopped a return from him and made aim as though to run him out, he would put forth an admonitory hand at the aforesaid bowler. He was himself one morning in a Test match at Sydney – he had just passed through the gates on his way to the wicket to bat v England when a small schoolboy ran after him, for his autograph. The gatekeeper, scandalised, went immediately in pursuit of the schoolboy. Miller waved the gatekeeper away, handed his bat to the schoolboy to hold while he signed the autograph book. Meanwhile sixty thousand people waited. Imagine the

small boy's ecstasy. Not only was he getting Keith's autograph: he was holding his bat while, in his eyes, all Sydney
looked on. Keith was simply doing the natural thing: he
could no more act unkindly to a schoolboy than he could be
discourteous enough not to admire a pretty girl. At Lord's,
on the Saturday evening of June 23rd, he had scored 30 and
looked good for a century when he was caught at the wicket
off a truly grand ball from Trueman. He at once raised his
bat as a salute to Trueman. Another quite natural gesture
of a cricketer who, with all his recurrent tantrums, was
chivalrous opponent.

When I was a resident in Sydney, Keith for a while lived
in the same block of flats as myself – in Crick Avenue,
King's Cross, Montmartre – or shall we say the Soho – of
Sydney. He would come up to my room and ask if I would
play the gramophone for him.

'What record, Keith?'

Always he would ask for a piano concerto. Sometimes I
would say, 'Why not a symphony this time?'

No: it had to be a piano concerto.

I imagine that he has scored hundreds of his runs and
taken many, many wickets to the accompaniment, supplied
mentally by himself, of the 'Emperor' concerto. The right
music to go with his cricket at its greatest! Or perhaps
something 'hotter' – say, Johnny and the Hurricanes.

Fact and Fiction in
the Search for Truth

Of the making of books about cricket there is no foreseeable end. Players compete with professional writers; players not accustomed to an intensive reading of books apparently find no difficulty about writing them. As far as I can gather, I am probably the only man in the profession who can't sit down at will and write a cricket book.

But an addition to the library, well worth while, has just come my way: *Sing all the Green Willow*, published by the Epworth Press at 25s. Don't let the title put you off, as easily it might. The book has truly been written by the author himself – Ronald Mason who, a year or two ago, produced a classic biography of the incomparable Walter Hammond. Ronald Mason, in this engaging book, writes on a variety of things, from Hornby and Barlow to P. G. Wodehouse and cricket. For purely personal reasons I was especially interested in the introductory chapter called 'The Truth about Cricket', because in it Mr Mason brings forward evidence that, long ago, while reporting a Lancashire v Oxford University match for this newspaper, I wandered or floated from actual fact to the higher Truth.

I described how Lancashire batted throughout a bitterly cold May day at the Parks. The day was so cold that Parkin, Dick Tyldesley, and the other tail-enders never left the warmth of a fire, never saw an Oxford bowler, until Dick went to the wicket half an hour before close of play, by which time Oxford's two really fast bowlers, Hewetson and Holmes, had spent their forces, so that Dick could lambast twenty or thirty runs off slow stuff. So much did Dick enjoy himself that, back to the warmth of the pavilion, not out, he said to me: 'Coom to ground early tomorrow, and Ah'll give thi summat to write about.'

Next morning, Hewetson, fresh and erratic, let fly at a terrific velocity, bang into Dick's bread basket, then whizzing past his head. Dick, next ball, retreated to the square-leg umpire and watched the total wreckage of his stumps. When I asked him what about the grand strokes he had promised, he honestly replied: 'Eh, Mr Cardus, Ah didn't know them two young buggers was playin'.'

Mr Mason has taken the trouble to investigate, and has discovered that Holmes and Hewetson played together only once against Lancashire in the Parks, and that on that occasion Dick Tyldesley went in late on the second morning and was caught off J. L. Guise. Moreover, Holmes did not bowl at all! Mr Mason is charitable; he notes the distinction between 'science' and 'Art'. The astronomer, he points out, can tell us all about a sunset but only a painter can tell us what it looks like. All very well; but in my mind's eye I can still, to this day, see Dick Tyldesley assaulted by Hewetson, see his vast rotundity shaken and toppled. And Mr Mason goes on to ask: 'Likewise with a number of other stories that, with the aid of this author's native genius' (meaning me) 'have passed into the language, about Barnes, or Brearley, or MacLaren ... Can we trust them, or him, at all?'

Before I plead guilty, m'lud, I'd like to point out that I have always tried to observe truth to character. And I was lucky, in my epoch, to have before me, every day, material for my work, a column every morning, wet or fine. One August holiday, completely wet and washed out at Old Trafford, I was welcomed by huge smiles by the Manchester *Guardian*'s chief sub-editor. 'Thank God,' he said, 'there's been no play – perhaps we can find some space for other events today.' But I had written an even longer piece than usual on what might have happened that day at Old Trafford had the weather kept fine for it.

Such cricketers as Parkin, Dick Tyldesley, Herbert Sutcliffe, Maurice Leyland, simply set the humorous or picturesque imagination free to go its way. Once, at Sheffield, Herbert Sutcliffe, glossy and immaculate, was fielding close to the bat. A terrific leg-hit struck him on the knee. Momentarily he winced, and bent down to rub the bruise. One or two of his Yorkshire colleagues solicitously approached him; but Sutcliffe waved them comprehensively away; as though saying 'I am all right. We Sutcliffes do not suffer pain.' True? How could I have invented something so penetrating to the quiddity, the essence, of the Sutcliffe presence and temperament? These 'natural' cricketers, pre-television and computer age, not yet standardised, simply prompted the reporter's sense of character.

It was, in respect of the inner and only truth, necessary for the writer to go beyond the potential, to complete the ripe human implications. For example: in a match at Old Trafford, Dick Tyldesley apparently brought off a marvellous catch in the leg trap. (With all his assemblable bulk, he had alacrity.) But, as the batsman was departing pavilionwards, Dick called him back; the ball had just touched the grass. I congratulated Dick, in print, on this act of sportsmanship. Also, next morning I congratulated him by word of mouth.

'Thanks, Mr Cardus,' he said: 'Westhoughton Sunday School, tha knows.'

Did he really say it? To fulfil and complete him, to realise the truth of his Lancashire nature and being, it simply *had* to be said. Whether he himself said it, or whether I put the words into his mouth for him, matters nothing as far as truth, as God knows it, is concerned.

I am myself often at a loss to remember if I am accurately reporting an event or a saying. My hand on my heart, I cannot be sure if Ted Wainwright, at Shrewsbury School, once said to me, after I had asked him how did Ranjitsinhji

really bat – "'E never made a Christian stroke in his life.'
But I am able, on oath, to affirm that Wainwright's own
words remain vivid in my memory, the identical words he
used to describe an event at Lord's: 'Year before, Albert
Trott hit ball reight over pavilion. Next year he set 'isself
to 'it ball reight out of ground t'other end, into Nursrey. Ah
were fieldin' near Nursrey sight-screen. Suddenly Albert
lets fly, and oop ball goes, 'igh as Blackpool Tower . . . Ah
loses sight of 'er 'genst black pavilion – then Ah see 'er
agen, high as Blackpool Tower, mind you. An' Ah sez to
myself, "Tha can catch it, Ted, tha can catch it.' Then Ah
'ad another look at 'er, and Ah said, "Oh bugger 'er," and
lets 'er go. And Lord Hawke 'e cooms racin' over field, and
sez, "Ted, why didn't you try to catch it?" and Ah sez, "Well,
your Lordship, it were a bit 'igh, weren't it?"

I vouch also for the factual accuracy of the remark made
to me in the press box at Brisbane at the beginning of a Test
match between Australia and England. Sydney Barnes,
the superb Australian batsman, and a true Sydney-sider,
had retired from actual playing, and was now reporting.
He sat behind me in the press box, and, before a ball was
bowled, moved over my shoulder, saying, 'This is going to
be an exciting rubber; and you and me, Neville, will have
plenty to do – never mind these other blokes and their
typewriters. Now, when you are hard-pressed, I'll take on
from you. And when I am hard-pressed, you can take on
from me. Similar styles, you know . . .'

A year ago Mr P. G. H. Fender expressed the opinion that

the public is discouraged from attending county matches by the press. Reporters, he argued, concentrated overmuch on statistics and technical fault-finding, and didn't write enough about the personality of the players, the scene and the atmosphere. By all means, a cricket writer should keep his eye on the ball, and give his readers the technical clues and explanations. But while he is describing how the ball 'moved off the seam', he should try to tell us what the bowler is thinking and saying, or what he is very likely to be thinking and saying, as he delivers the ball – especially if a catch is missed off it . . .

Walking Out of Lord's, 1969

ENGLAND V NEW ZEALAND, FIRST TEST, 1969

I could not have believed, a few summers ago, that the day was at hand on which I'd be leaving Lord's on a sunny day, after watching a Test match there for only an hour or so. I departed from Lord's last Saturday, bored to limpness, because I had seen Boycott and Edrich compile, or secrete, 100 runs from 56 overs, bowled by game, enthusiastic, inexperienced New Zealand cricketers. What would Boycott and Edrich have done confronted by Lindwall and Miller, Ramadhin and Valentine, Hall and Griffith?

In a full day, England, in a winning position versus a team not stronger all round than, say, Leicestershire, produced fewer than 300. Yet, on television, someone described the innings of Edrich as 'brilliant'. Had he, as he made this public pronouncement, forgotten Bill Edrich, who one day, on a spiteful 'green' pitch, flayed his spin within an inch of its life?

The poor, hard-worked TV commentators, those of them once upon a time Test match cricketers, did their best to gloss over the England batsmen's terribly tedius anonymity. Trevor Bailey referred to New Zealand's left-arm bowler, Howarth – he said he was 'operating' – as if he were a Verity come back to revisit the glimpses of the moon. (Mr Bailey usually refers to a bowler as 'operating' – probably, I am inclined to suggest, armed with an anaesthetic.)

All sorts of excuses for the England batsmen's sterility are put forward by the television commentators. Mr Laker informs us periodically that the ball is turning 'appreciably'. The commentaries go on like a chanted rubric. Motz is 'coming up' to bowl; Edrich 'plays him hard to mid-off, where so-and-so picks up – no run.' Hardly a hint of humour or irony on television: the radio chatterers are much brighter; they are free to take their eyes from the static, somnambulistic scene, and talk of irrelevant, and refreshingly irrelevant, things.

The prodding and 'tickling round the corner' persists every day on most first-class cricket fields in this country. And every day we hear the same justification for strokelessness: the ball is 'doing something off the seam', the wicket is 'green', or 'the ball is not coming off the bat'. I was brought up to believe that some physical propulsion, on the batsman's part, is needed to project a ball from the bat. The bowling, so we are told *ad nauseam*, is just short of a length; Bradman himself would, at his best, be 'kept quiet'. If you can believe all these 'scientific arrogances' you can believe anything.

Do the seam-short-of-a-length-devices check or 'keep quiet' the scoring strokes of overseas batsmen such as Goldstein, Richards, Ackerman, Pollock or Younis Ahmed? Does it paralyse Marner? None of these stroke players are half the equals of Bradman, Hammond, Compton, McCabe, each of whom would have watered at the mouth at the sight last Saturday of the attack (a technical term) of New Zealand's Taylor, Hadlee, Motz and Pollard. Howarth is undoubtedly a promising slowish left-arm bowler but, bless us, he was free to toss them up with no fieldsman behind his arm in the deep.

I remember a description of Charles Parker's spin on a dusty Cheltenham pitch, given to me by 'young' Joe Hardstaff, whose very presence at the wicket at Lord's on Saturday would have seemed to bring Derby breeding to a company of carthorses. He was then young, and he went in to bat for Nottinghamshire number six or so 'in the order'. He received the last ball of an over from Parker, which pitched on his leg stump then fizzed viciously across, just missing the off stump. So Hardstaff walked down the pitch to talk to George Gunn. 'I can't play this kind of bowling, Mr. Gunn,' he said, whereat George said: 'That's all right, son, just watch me for a little while.' And for half an hour Hardstaff had not to cope with another ball spun by Parker. Gunn kept him away from Parker.

Compensations of Viewing

The other morning, John Arlott came out with a most pregnant remark, more pregnant perhaps than intended: 'It has been suggested that the fact that only the last two days of the Lord's Test, and nothing at all of those at Trent Bridge or Edgbaston, was shown on television gave the impression that the cricket (in the England v Rest of the World series) was not worthwhile.'

I am reminded here of something said to me years ago by J. B. Priestley: 'If you are not on television, you don't count nowadays.' I have myself been on television – and have not received a single fan letter. Yet whenever I write, letters come to me abounding. Television appeals mainly to what George Meredith called 'the impressionable senses'; and *he* was known before the advent of television, and today reposes in the limbo.

Nonetheless, television has its uses for the lover of cricket unable, or disinclined, to go to watch an actual match. On the screen he misses the living panorama, but he can see what the ball is doing after it has left he bowler's hand and has pitched; he can see the turn or swing to an inch.

At Headingley last week the television commentators unanimously agreed that Sobers was bowling 'magnificently', with 'no luck': 20 overs, 11 maidens, 24 runs, no wickets — nary a wicket in nearly two hours' individual work. As a once-in-a-time bowler myself, I do not believe that anybody can bowl 'magnificently' for 20 overs without taking a wicket. I happened to scrutinise the bowling of Sobers on television during his delivery of these 20 overs. Time after time he swung the ball outside the batsman's danger-zone; he could often be 'left alone'.

I recall a stern observation of the incomparable Sydney Barnes as he looked at a bowler 'moving' the ball a foot or so away from middle stump past the off stump, from middle past the leg stump. 'Why', queried the Master, 'does he not keep the batsman playing? I never give 'em a moment's piece.' Barlow got his wickets at Leeds by a threatening line of flight, with not too much swing. The new-ball obsession has reduced the efficiency of more than one top-class bowler I could name.

I wish we could go back to the old-time rule which allowed the use of one and the same ball throughout a team's longest innings. As Jack Gunn said, with rueful ripe flavour, 'Aye, we 'ad to mek do with same ball unless it come in two.' With an old ball shineless, almost seamless, Tom Richardson took 1,000 wickets in four consecutive seasons, bowling fast on the flawless Oval wickets of 1894–1897.

The television and radio commentators wax warmly and sympathetically about some bowler's endurance: 'This is his twenty-fifth over, and he must be tiring.' At Old Trafford in July 1896, Richardson bowled without rest for three hours for England v Australia. In his thirty-fourth year E. A. Macdonald took 205 wickets for Lancashire, in 1,249 overs. For all the talk about over-worked first-class cricketers, no bowler gets through 1,000 overs in a summer. But no bowler of 1970 has the perfect action of a Macdonald or Richardson, though Snow is an example of finely accumulating rhythmic movement. And there are possibilities of a Trueman sort of dynamic onrush in the action of Ward of Derbyshire.

The fact about these England and the Rest of the World matches is the players in them include some of the most gifted, the most fascinating to watch, ever to be seen in all my long experience of cricket. Jessop himself was not more exciting, more creative, at the crease or in the field than Clive Lloyd. I have seen him make strokes which have caused me to catch breath – a pull square for six from a ball rising awkwardly on his off side. He is violent, Wagnerian, with the wonderful relaxations of Wagner.

Sobers, as batsman, is entirely and easefully musical. He performs his wonders without rhetoric, without strain. He puts the bloom on the orthodox. There is an impersonal air about his batsmanship, a certain self-detachment, as though he were spreading his genius over the field like a disinterested spectator.

Frank Woolley had the same kind of aloofness. It is as though Sobers, as Woolley did, takes his gifts for granted and thinks no more of them, phenomenally, than of the continuous motions and functionings of his respiratory organs. The art that conceals art. But I am often at a loss why, when a tail-end batsman confronts Sobers as a bowler, he sends down to him balls which the said tail-ender is not clever enough to play.

Then there is the magic of Kanhai, the configurations of Intikhab, alluring to the spectator whether he is getting wickets or not. There is the gusto of Barlow, hugging himself whenever he breaks a partnership. And there are Mushtaq, Richards, Procter, all endowed with personal identity, ready to give rein to inborn talents. Never was cricket more generously dowered by inimitable skill and personal presence than in this Rest of the World XI.

And what of the England team for the personal play which goes beyond, and cannot be reflected in the scoreboard? Boycott has class, so has Cowdrey – in form or not. Knott, behind the stumps, is unmistakably himself, alert, ever exercising, ravenous of appetite. The other England cricketers of the moment are admirable craftsmen, good batsmen, bowlers and fieldsmen. Do they hold me, so that I cannot take my eyes from them, on television or on the field of play, for a moment? Frankly, no. The reason for this finely competent anonymity? I don't know.

Cricket's Transmogrification

Cricket has been obliged to change over the decades in technique and manner, obliged to alter as it alteration found – if I may be Shakespearian and platitudinous at the same time. But in the main, the game, in its broad outlines, has remained recognisable at first sight: batsmen have gone through traditional motions, bowlers and fieldsmen too; and umpires have administered law in much the same way, though the old long stately coast has gone, more or less, causing the Dogberrys of cricket to assume the clinical aspect of dental surgeons, in wear of shorter, severer cut.

If Frank Woolley had been present at Kennington Oval the other week, watching Sobers, he could well have felt time had turned in its tracks and he himself was in full play again, at the turn of the century. And if, also at Kennington Oval last week, Cyril Washbrook had been present, as spectator, he could justly have exclaimed, witnessing a square cut by Intikhab, 'There by the Grace of God go I!' It was probably the first great square cut executed by any cricketer since Washbrook and the Australian Sydney Barnes.

It is not in the field of play, so much as in the Press Box, that cricket's aspect and procedure have been, as the man in Dickens says, transmogrified. The Press Box today is a populous, efficiently statistical concourse of accountancy and sleepless vigilance, typewriters in perpetual motion, some of them tapping away as though on the padded surfaces of half-cooked steak puddings.

When I myself first ventured into a Press Box, told to occupy the back seat to begin with, not more than five or six scribes were in it to report an everyday county match. No television and, for radio, only the resonant Gobbi-toned voice of Howard Marshall to speak from time to time. Silence reigned supreme. There was no specialist statistician to inform us that so-and-so had bowled so many overs, or that so-and-so had completed his 50 in two and a half hours. We had to make our *own* statistical recordings. Jimmy Catton, of the now defunct *Manchester Evening Chronicle*, himself wrote down a ball-by-ball analysis of each bowler, also detailing the value and direction of every stroke. So did all the other cricket reporters.

Also, they wrote in a traditional prose, employing sentences to fit certain occasions, with the reverence and repetitiveness of *rubric*. For example, the last batsman of a team always 'whipped in'. I particularly loved the phrase,

'Tyldesley, having driven Hirst for four, turned his attention to Rhodes.' 'Turned his attention to' – why, the echo of this language brings back, ages after, the vision of J. T. Tyldesley on the attack.

Other conventional phrases handed down in the old Press Boxes, father to son, included, 'Hobbs was guilty of obstruction.' Dear Jimmy Catton, small, rubicund and rotund, was the first of the old school to experiment with venerable clichés. He once wrote, 'Maclaren drove Noble for the full complement,' which, of course, appeared in print, 'for the full compliment'. Ronnie Simmons, a reporter daringly *avant garde*, one day at Lord's risked airing his knowledge of German in his report. 'Jim Smith', he wrote, 'drove a ball from Fender into the *Ewigkeit*'; meaning that the ball had been dispatched into the blue of eternity. He was naturally frustrated to read, next day, that Jim Smith had driven a ball from Fender 'into his wicket'.

I also began studiously to take these notes of accountancy on my first appearances in the Press Box. At Lord's, I dared not for a summer to venture into the Press Box *at all*. I felt I had not yet graduated, was not ready to go into the presence of Sydney Pardon, All-Father of *Wisden*, who watched cricket through tiny ivory-covered opera glasses, which he used night after night at Covent Garden Opera to look at Frida Leider and Tetrazzini. I used to write my reports sitting on the Green Bank at Lord's at the base of the Old Press Box next to the Pavilion. Pardon saw me at work there one afternoon, and insisted in taking me up to the Press Box and introducing me to the members – I mean the Life members – Hubert Preston, Stewart Caine, Harry Carson. They bowed to me: it was like a levee.

I adored Pullen ('Old Ebor') of the *Yorkshire Post*, once described by Lord Hawke as Yorkshire's Twelfth Man. Pullen never saw Peel and Wainwright, and never really accepted 'modern' methods. Whenever George Macauley, superb off-spinner, went on to bowl over the wicket, then, seeing the ball nip back inches, went round the wicket, Pullen would invariably report that Macauley, 'obviously having difficulty in maintaining a foothold, was obliged to bowl round the wicket'. I would spoil this gorgeous story if I were to give away the technical clue.

All the reporters of my early salad days travelled up and down the land with our respective cricket teams – by train, not individually and alone by car. So we became a community, the players knew us, and we knew them. None the less, our cricketers retained independence, which we, the reporters, shared. One Saturday evening, in a Lancashire and Yorkshire match, at Old Trafford, Richard Tyldesley suddenly lost his length and 'sent down' some dreadful and expensive overs, at a critical point of the proceedings. I dealt with this lapse rather severely in my *Manchester Guardian* notice (1,500 words at least). I saw Harry Makepeace on the Monday morning, and he said to me, 'We've just shown your article to Dick. He read it, then threw the paper down on the table and said, "Ah'd like to bowl at bugger."' The right and proper professional retort.

There was also, in the old Press Box at Old Trafford, Johnny Clegg, of the *Manchester Evening News*. One of his phrases comes back to my mind with eternal freshness: 'The game was held up by a shower of rain; and on resumption, Parkin had recourse to the sawdust.'

During this period of cricket's history, the players were known as Amateurs or Professionals, even as Gentlemen and Players. The poet Craig, at Kennington Oval, would go about the crowd selling his broadsheets, assuring us, in deliciously Cockney sententiousness, 'all the Gentlemen are players, and all the players are Gentlemen.' In the reports of *The Times*, of the period, an amateur player was always named with the affix 'Mr'. Thus: 'Mr Warner drove Hirst for four.' All an Australian XI were addressed, in a *Times* report, as 'Mr —'. 'Mr Jones bowled at a great pace.' Jones was a typical Aussie, dinkum as Melbourne ale.

Into the Press Boxes of the ancient years – circa 1920– 1930 – tea was actually served at 4.15, by a white-ribboned waitress, at sixpence a head. As I say, on quiet sunny afternoons silence would reign supreme in the Press Boxes, as we wrote out our reports, on telegraph forms (80 words to the page, each in a framed space). It was my practice to dispatch 800 words at the tea interval, and another 500 or so at close of play.

There was a lot to write about then, from Old Trafford to Dover, but not much more, either in number of words or in adjectival power of words, than could today be written about the cricket of Marshall, Intikhab, Clive Lloyd, Lancashire's Pilling, and Lancashire's (and/or Yorkshire's) Wood, and Kent's Denness, and Surrey's Edwards, and Snow of Sussex. The game was always as good as it used to be.